DON NOEL

# Near A Far Sea

## A Jamaican Odyssey

Bloomington, IN  Milton Keynes, UK

authorHOUSE™

AuthorHouse™
1663 Liberty Drive, Suite 200
Bloomington, IN 47403
www.authorhouse.com
Phone: 1-800-839-8640

AuthorHouse™ UK Ltd.
500 Avebury Boulevard
Central Milton Keynes, MK9 2BE
www.authorhouse.co.uk
Phone: 08001974150

First published by AuthorHouse 3/21/2006

ISBN: 1-4259-0892-6 (sc)

Library of Congress Control Number: 2005911338

Printed in the United States of America
Bloomington, Indiana

This book is printed on acid-free paper.

To my wife Brad, who inspired me to write this book; to the brave
fishermen who go to Far Sea; and to the many Jamaican neighbors
and friends who have generously let our lives touch theirs.

# 1

## Reminiscing

**"I** tell you, Mist' Don, blowing that reef was the finest thing anybod' ever did for this village!"

Mister Arthur -- in 28 years of friendship and collaboration I've never called him anything but that; it is a custom of polite address here -- has walked over for a late-afternoon visit, and is trapped on our sheltered patio by a pelting tropical rainshower. It is a gift: We have time to share memories.

Arthur James will be 75 years old in a few months, a ripe old age in Jamaica. He remembers when men went to sea in their oversized dugout canoes – 100-mile round trips -- by sail, before the Second World War. He learned from his father to hew those boats from giant trees; he has made and repaired them all his life. His neighbors have hired him and respected him for those skills. But even more they honor his fairness, even temper and quiet way of mediating disputes.

He is a church-going man. Many a Sunday morning I've seen him in a dark suit and tie, walking two miles up the sun-broiled, dusty road with his wife -- she in a bright-flowered frock -- and children or grandchildren in shirts-and-ties or neat dresses. Tens of thousands of Jamaicans make such pilgrimages; main roads and side roads are lined Sundays with pedestrians on the way to or from church. The women wear light colors and sometimes deploy parasols, but the men are always in black or dark grey suits with at best a straw hat.

White suits would make the walk more pleasant. No Englishman would have gone out even mornings, let alone in the noonday sun, in a dark suit. But the colonials' white suits never caught on. One suspects a belief in a stern deity; surely no merciful God would condemn his faithful to bake in black once a week.

Mister Arthur has always been lankier than I and almost as tall; the dark Sabbath suit only accentuated his gauntness. Like most in the village, he is hardly more brown than a sun-tanned tourist, and his features are aquiline, craggily handsome. There is a legend of seamen shipwrecked here -- British, German, Irish, the story varies -- who stayed and raised families. The real forebears may have been early-1800s indentured servants from the British Isles who earned their freedom and a grant of land -- although there's no explanation why they might have clustered here. I prefer the more romantic shipwreck version. In any case, most folks on this five-mile stretch of coast called Treasure Beach are markedly lighter-skinned than most of their countrymen.

This evening he seems thinner than I'd remembered from our last visit, but apart from a few aches and pains he is in fine health. "Too fine," he says; he's not sure what he's still living for. The wild ways of the younger generation don't suit.

"Don't suit." I'll not often try to replicate the Jamaican patois, and certainly not Mister Arthur's, which is so rapid and thick that after all these years I still strain to follow him. But perhaps I can occasionally catch the timbre and cadence: Not "it doesn't suit me," but "it don't suit."

I demur about the reef; he insists on more praise than I deserve. "Before that, men had to come from far sea before dark, so the boats wouldn't be mashed up ('mahshed up'). After you he'ped us blow the reef, we could build bigger boats. The men could stay out longer if the weather was hard and the work was slow. So they could put out more pots and make more money."

We pause; I savor a whiff of that harvested sea. At home in New England, ocean air is as much fish and seaweed as salt; here it seems pure salt. A few dead fish wash ashore, mostly bony trunkfish tossed overboard as the men sort the catch on the way home, but in this arid, sun-drenched climate they are desiccated before they begin to stink.

Or the turkey vultures scavenge them. We rarely see noisome seagulls; too far south, perhaps. Vultures are ugly, but I admire them. Mornings they perch in our tall casuarinas trees or on the water tank, wings akimbo like the eagle on our 25-cent piece, facing the morning sun to dry the night dampness. As the day warms, thermal updrafts form; they flap away, clumsily at first. Once aloft, they soar effortlessly; often a dozen circle high above us.

Our friend Bill, a frequent guest, used to tease our daughter when she sunbathed. "Move an arm, Emily, so they'll know you're not dead yet." In fact, they're waiting for a whiff; amazingly, they rely on olfactory senses rather than sight to find their next meal.

In late afternoons, they sometimes surf the onshore breeze at treetop level in front of the house; we're high enough to look down to see them trim their flight with subtle shifts of shiny black wingtips. They bring to mind a line from Gerard Manley Hopkins' *The Windhover*: "striding high there. . . upon the rein of a wimpling wing."

There are no vultures now. The sea, less than a hundred yards away, is hardly visible in the gathering dusk.

Earlier, we watched the rain come ashore, a short-lived cell energized by sunlight on a still ocean. It roughened the glassy sea, then made a hissing, washing noise in the lignum vitae trees below the terrace, and finally beat on our aluminum roof like a snare drum. Real storms, with strong winds, can trick me into feeling chilled, although we've never had a temperature below 72° Fahrenheit. This evening's shower is just a cool respite from the afternoon heat.

But it hastens the dark. I turn on the floodlights at the edge of the patio, aimed at the terrace below. In the sudden glare we see the rain falling as straight and hard as lead shot. I can just glimpse white water, caught in the light, where waves break over the reef.

My wife brings us another Red Stripe beer, and Mister Arthur another glass of cola; he is a teetotaler. "Thank you, Miss Brad." His wide smile is luminous, even teeth that I suspect are choppers; he's one of the few in the village who could afford false teeth. In the gloom, he takes off the cloth-and-straw porkpie hat that is part of his persona, uncovering a balding pate that seems further reminder of Caucasian genes.

●

"Far sea," where many of our neighbors fish, is the Pedro Banks, an undersea coral and limestone formation 50 miles offshore, as big as Jamaica itself, with occasional small islands, written cays but said "keys."

Far-sea fishermen make the trip more or less once a week. They wait for calm weather, relying on radio or satellite TV forecasts from Miami, whose meteorologists have more information and seem more reliable than those in Kingston. Each captain has an unwritten contract with a man with a pickup truck who will buy the catch, and who brings ice in late afternoon before a voyage. The hundred-pound blocks are loaded into wooden chests amidships, covered with gunnysacks to slow the melting.

They push off about midnight. Flashlight beams seek out the white foam where waves break over the reef that protects the Billy's Bay cove; they aim for the dark water that marks the narrow opening. We've occasionally gone down to watch them leave, but they don't welcome Brad or other women then, because to load the boat and get it into deeper water, they strip down to skivvy shorts. Or less. They want dry clothes when they climb aboard, against the wind-chill of the open boat in an inky-black night.

We hear them from the house: the cough of outboards at the pull of starter cords, sputtering and dying, settling into a dark staccato, then gunning as each captain darts through the reef opening and throttles back. From the patio we see the wink of flashlights; the first boats wait until the little flotilla of a half-dozen assembles. They stay together the first part of the trip, for safety's sake.

As dawn nears, they will go separate ways to the place in the rolling, trackless ocean where each thinks he has found a productive spot. Ernie James, Mister Arthur's son, once told me he could put his face into the sea and read the bottom 50 fathoms down -- 100 yards! -- to lower his traps into a sheltered mini-canyon in the reef where fish eddy to and fro.

Those traps are like Yankee lobster pots, but made of chicken-wire on a frame of one-inch poles; at first glance they look like poultry cages; fish and lobster swim or crawl in easily through mesh funnels in the upper part of the trap. Fish look down, a pot-making neighbor tells me, so they can't find their way out easily; the narrowing funnel makes escape even less likely.

Modern technology is just beginning to be affordable: Some men nowadays have sonar "fish finders" to read the sea below them. A few even have global-positioning-satellite devices to pinpoint their locations far out of sight of land.

Most, however, still go to sea as they have since sails were replaced by outboards a decade or more after the war. The captain sits sidewise in the narrow stern of the 40-foot boat, a firm grip on the handle to steer. A binnacle, for years his most sophisticated piece of equipment, is mounted on the plank seat in front of him; he will for the most part steer a compass course. Gasoline is in 10-gallon plastic tanks that he changes as they are used up. He gauges his course by direction and time, wind and wave -- and tank changes.

The first mate and bowman are supposed to take turns staying awake to watch for freighters that might run over the little boat, which carries no running lights in the dark ocean. The crewmen, however, often steel themselves for the trip by toking hand-rolled marijuana cigarettes -- ganja, we call it -- and so make unreliable watchmen.

●

I've never found the courage (or connubial assent) to go to far sea. But I've joined Mister Arthur and some of the older men who go at dawn to "near sea," an underwater coral ridge three or four miles out.

Near-sea fishermen find their pots by reference to land -- our house, prominent on its sandy knoll, washed white in early-morning sunlight against green hills, is a landmark -- but even so, it takes time to find the first one. When he thinks he's close, Mister Arthur throttles back and begins an ever-widening spiral. I stand with his two crewmen at the gunwales, squinting out at the blue, glistening water, watching for a white Styrofoam float. If there is a heavy swell, floats are tugged below the surface on taut lines, and we must watch for them in the troughs of waves.

We find one, and trace back the string of floats to the start of the pot-set. The crewmen reach over for the line and haul a pot up hand-over-hand while Mister Arthur steadies the boat with the engine. The trap breaks the surface; they muscle it aboard and lay it athwart the gunwales.

There are usually only a few fish in each – fat grouper, turbot, blushing snapper, the little rosy-red goatfish, the blue-and-white parrotfish -- and sometimes a lobster. At near sea, a pot with a dozen fish and a lobster is a lucky catch these days. Old-timers remember better catches when there were fewer fishermen.

The crewmen untie a bit of the "lacing wire" that holds the chicken-wire on the frame, and spill the fish into the boat. They know from markings which pot is whose. The captain's fish are spilled astern, at his feet; the first mate's, amidships; the bowman's, up forward; then the wire mesh is laced back again. Elsewhere on the South Coast, fishermen bait their traps with stale bread. Our men use no bait, unless they happen to catch a crab, which (unless a visitor has said "bring me some crabs") they dispatch with a slap on the side of the boat and toss back into the trap.

The crewmen stand the pot upright on a gunwale, then tip it over; it lands flat on the water and sinks out of sight. The frame has stubby two-inch legs so it will stay put in the sandy patches between reef outcrops.

We work our way to the last float, empty the pot, and head back to the harbor -- 50 yards of open water, no more than five feet deep -- inside the barrier reef. Although we are home by late morning, the onshore breeze is already up; there is a chop on the water, even a few whitecaps.

The reef opening, when we came in 1972, narrowed to less than eight feet at its throat. The largest boats -- Mister Arthur carved them from giant *ceiba* trees, which we call here the cottonwood -- were six feet wide amidships. Even in daylight with a mild swell, he circles several times, feinting like a sparring boxer, to line up on the opening and gauge the sideways drift. Then he guns the outboard as a swell gathers behind him, riding the wave through the reef.

Coral is sharp and unforgiving; the cottonwood, a cousin of balsa, prized for its bouyancy, is fragile. The least miscalculation rakes the bottom or sides on abrasive outcrops. Mister Arthur spent half his time at the beach making repairs. Every patch made a boat less seaworthy for the trip to the Pedro Banks.

At near sea, the winds are light and local; we are in the lee of the island of Jamaica itself. A few miles farther south into the open

Caribbean, the northeast trade winds resume; waves grow larger. The wind can turn hard during the 18-hour trip, making slower work to find and draw the traps, and assuring a hull-slapping, slower homeward ride.

If far-sea men got back after dark, the reef passage was downright dangerous. I have seen our next-door neighbor Philip Gordon, one of the ablest captains, a big man and strong, come through first, then jump out and wade back chest-deep into the narrow channel with a flashlight to help others find their way in.

# 2

# Blasting the Reef

**B**lasting a wider reef opening was Mister Arthur's idea.  He talked about it with me, but more important, with our friend Bob Satter, one of the first to vacation at our house.  Bob, a trustee of a small foundation -- by a charming coincidence, the Cottonwood Foundation -- arranged a $500 gift.

I brought the money in February 1973, and deposited it -- lodged it, we say -- in the Black River bank account of the Calabash Bay Fishermen's Co-op.  It was a suitable non-profit recipient, and we hoped to encourage more Billy's Bay men to join.

Five hundred dollars wasn't enough to do the job.  Mister Arthur and I agreed that a project vital to everyone's livelihood shouldn't depend on American beneficence; he soon matched the Cottonwood grant, setting a "suggested contribution" for every captain, crew member and fish buyer.  A persuasive man, he got close to 100 percent participation, and even cudgeled some out of a hardware store owner with whom some captains traded.

As we left after our ten-day vacation, we could hard wait to see the changes that would greet us on our next visit.

Six months later, we arrived to find . . . no progress!

Jamaica's coastal-protection agency had to approve any change in the reef -- admirable environmentalism in a developing country, but prey to "soon come" bureaucratic lethargy.  The men had become impatient and insisted that Mister Arthur give back their money. Little wonder: Many had put up half a week's catch. This is not a society with money to spare for distant goals.

Sunday I drove to see Ted Tatham, a great bear of a man, British-born, now a Jamaican citizen, whom we'd first met through my father's connection to Alcan Aluminium. Alcan had loaned Ted to the government to run a farm development project; he had *connections*, Mister Arthur said. Ted was weekending at his Great Bay house two miles from us. Come up to Mandeville, he said.

Monday I set out for his office, an hour's drive into the mountains, leaving the dauntless Mister Arthur the task of re-collecting money.

Ted put in a call to Kingston, to the man who oversaw the coastal-protection agency, pleading urgency. He covered the mouthpiece: "He wants to know who the blaster is."

I had no idea; Mister Arthur had arranged that through Bunny Delapenha, another Mandeville man with a weekend place.

Telephones were scarce; it would be 20 years before we had one at Treasure Beach. Ted, heading a government project, had not one, but two. "Call Bunny," he said, covering the mouthpiece. He thumbed the all-Jamaica phone book – less than a quarter as thick as ours at home in Hartford -- found the number, and went back to prolong his conversation with the agency head while I reached Bunny. Blessedly, he was "in office," as Jamaicans say.

"Ashmead," Bunny said, a man who'd dynamited a commercial-building foundation for him. I whispered the name to Ted.

"Has he dynamited a reef before?" I relayed the question. "Oh yes," said Bunny, "he's an experienced sea-blaster." He said it "sea-blahster". Kingston seemed satisfied. A man would be down in a day or two to inspect the project and sign off. Bunny would send Ashmead down to start the job while I was still there. I thanked Ted and drove back to Billy's Bay in time for a quick dip -- a sea-bath, we call it, said "sea-bahth".

The agency man came as promised; Mister Arthur took him to inspect the harbor reef. He pronounced the project acceptable so long as we enlarged the opening not more than another six feet, lest a wider opening suck the sandy bottom out of the cove. We readily agreed; that would be plenty of leeway for captains to get through without mashing up their boats. We could start work; the paperwork could follow.

Ashmead arrived the next Monday in late morning, a dark, pleasant, paunchy man. Ernie James took him to see the reef. They were back in a half-hour, Ashmead shaking his head. It can't be done, he said; too much water over the reef.

"Well of course," I said. "It's high tide."

The experienced sea-blaster looked blank.

"Besides," I added, "it's just past full moon. Tides are always higher at full moon. If we get an early start in the morning, it will be neap tide."

I might as well have been Cyrano explaining how a man lying on a wet beach could be drawn aloft by the gravitational pull of the moon. Ashmead looked at me as though I were daft.

Ernie rescued me: "It's in the Gleaner," he said. I fetched a copy of yesterday's *Daily Gleaner* to where we stood in the sunshine, and Ernie leafed through to the tide tables. There was none for Treasure Beach, of course, but those for Kingston and Montego Bay confirmed that it was now high tide.

Accepting the authority of the printed word, the experienced sea-blaster relented. He would be down Wednesday morning -- early, at low tide.

●

After an early breakfast, I was waiting with Mister Arthur, Ernie and half the village when he arrived at the fishing cove, towing a compressor behind his Land Rover. The sea was calmer. Our tidefall is no more than a foot; a stiff onshore breeze can make more difference than the tide stage. We had both a low tide and no breeze; waves barely sloshed over the reef.

Ashmead, in bathing trunks and battered sneakers with a faded red tank top over his belly, surveyed the beach. The sand was soft, he complained: the compressor and Land Rover might get stuck. He didn't want to take his air hammer out to the reef to drill holes for the dynamite – if in fact he had ever done that. He would use satchel charges.

We protested. We had enough manpower to pick the damned compressor up and carry it back to firm ground if need be. He was adamant: He would take the dynamite out to the reef and cover it with gunnysacks -- we call them crocus sacks -- full of sand. Ashmead began stringing detonator cord out to the reef, leaving Mister Arthur to have villagers fill crocus sacks he'd brought. He waded back out with the dynamite, attaching it to the lines. Men brought him heavy sacks of sand to place on top. He waded back and attached the lines to the detonator.

The equipment he was proudest of, it seemed, was a siren on the Land Rover. He sternly instructed everyone to take cover, and set it to wailing. Few if any had ever seen a dynamite blast; the siren added to their intimidation: Everyone cowered behind sand hillocks or boats. Every eye was on Ashmead as he turned off the siren and, with a sure sense of theater, poised over the plunger.

A dynamite stick tamped into a drilled hole is a surgical instrument. A satchel charge is a blunt weapon. Ashmead depressed the plunger, and the clear blue sky over the reef was filled with geysers that rivaled Old Faithful. I snapped photos; then as the plumes fell back to the sea the onlookers rose from their bunkers – some cheered -- and we all waded out to inspect.

Despite the energy sent skyward, the charges had done some good: Huge chunks of coral that we could scarcely wrap our arms around lay in the clouded water. Mister Arthur gathered his troops; we all dove down to roll the jagged chunks ashore lest they fill up the reef passageway and defeat our purpose. An impressive pile of coral began to rise onshore.

Ashmead began laying a second charge. But he'd blown up all his sandbags. "Crocus sacks!" he called. "Come, mon, I need crocus sacks!"

Every captain had a few tattered sacks to insulate his ice-chest, and an intact sack as a seagoing toolbox. Sacks were scarce; no one wanted to sacrifice one.

Happily, I'd brought a supply of large plastic garbage-barrel liners for the house. I ran back for a dozen; Mister Arthur directed our volunteer crew to fill them and carry them out to the reef. We repeated the drama of the first blast: the siren, the dark pot-bellied man taking the handles while everyone took cover (although most peeked this time). Ashmead thrust the plunger home again; there were again geysers over the reef.

Mister Arthur led men and boys into the breach to roll out fresh chunks of coral, and consulted with Ashmead about strategy. A coral head poked up beyond the barrier reef, impeding the passageway. We launched a boat, and one of the few men who could swim dove to tie a charge at its base to topple it. At the main reef, we were shearing off the top, but had to blast all the way down so that boats' keels would clear. I went back for more plastic bags.

At noon, after the fourth charge, Ashmead announced that he was out of dynamite. He had nibbled at the reef, but the job was clearly not done. He would be back next week.

The hell he would, I said; he'd better be back tomorrow. I wanted to see this job done before I left. If he'd brought his damned compressor down to the water's edge and drilled holes, the work might be done by now. I would tell Bunny Delapenha, who would tell other contractors.

Mister Arthur let me rage, then whispered to me to lay off and go home. I understood: tough cop, nice cop. He invited Ashmead up to Moxam's bar. After a few drinks, Ashmead drove off, promising to be back next morning.

The next day was a carbon copy of the first. We importuned Ashmead to use his drill -- he had again towed the compressor down -- but in vain. He laid satchel charges and showed off his siren, blowing up more of my garbage bags and more of the reef. Mister Arthur directed the villagers at rolling out the debris.

Ashmead again ran out of dynamite at mid-day, and said he'd return the next week. I raged again; the men took him up to Moxam's. He agreed to be back next day.

It took four days. The sea remained calm, but was so dynamite-roiled that by Saturday the satchel charges had to be placed mostly by feel and by Mister Arthur's intimate sense of the reef structure. I ran out of plastic bags about the time Ashmead ran out of dynamite again.

We had the fisherman's co-op pay him most of the agreed price; I insisted on withholding the balance until the water cleared. Mister

Arthur would assess the work, write me, and complete payment if the reef opening proved satisfactory.  We left for home Sunday morning.

A week later, Mister Arthur wrote to declare the reef well-blown. The reef and the hammock -- more of the hammock later -- made our reputation.  Bob and Mister Arthur found the money, but I got the credit.

# 3

## The boat-builder

There was always a boat being built in Arthur James' yard. Without blueprints or plans, but with the eye of a sculptor, he transformed huge logs into sturdy craft perfectly suited to this sea and the way men fished here. He'd learned the art from his father.

He and his wife Idova lived just behind us. They had several sons – some became fishermen, although none took up their father's craft -- and daughters. They shared their little home with his sister Mary, a slight, graying woman who was retired from the housekeeping staff of a Washington, D.C. hotel; her monthly American Social Security checks made her a welcome guest. Suffering mild dementia – "Crazy Mary," some called her – she walked down the road every day to smoke cigarettes at a leisurely pace in the shade of a favorite tree.

On one side of their yard, in a tiny shack on a small lot, was another sister, Miss Lou; on the other side, his brother Mister Elbert, who would become our gardener and trusted factotum.

A decade earlier, their father had sold the beachfront land on which our house now stood to Major Charles Moody, a director of the power company. Hardly coincidentally, the power line soon was soon extended this far, but no farther. Moody bought several parcels in Billy's Bay, and built a weekend retreat on the far side of the fishing cove.

The first land sold by a Treasure Beach family, some years earlier, we were told, went for enough to buy the fisherman's wife an electric sewing machine. Perhaps apocryphal, but a measure of land prices soon after World War II. Moody sold his land after seven years, making more profit than the James family had after generations of ownership.

None of the yards had a blade of grass. Scant rainfall here is a blessing for visiting sun-worshippers, but a hardship for residents. Lawns would have withered without constant watering; no one had piped water. Besides, every household had a few goats and chickens that foraged freely; to establish plantings, one fenced the goats out. A few folks bought a piglet in summer to be slaughtered at Christmas. Everyone had dogs that barked -- a lot.

Houses were concrete block with corrugated-zinc roofs; a few had glass-jalousies to catch whatever sea-breeze came inland. Cooking was done outdoors, usually on raised hearths; a few had a half-open cookshed. Mister Arthur had a front porch, big enough for three chairs, where the family sat evenings, neighboring with passersby. The unpaved road was ten yards from the porch; a car or truck every 15 minutes was a lot of traffic.

When a son married, or an aging parent came to live, another concrete box was built a few yards away. Most of the three dozen families' yards in Billy's Bay had several such dwellings, and of course an outhouse. Indoor plumbing is even today a luxury not all can afford.

Mister Arthur was among the few who had electricity. The major entertainment (which television would soon replace) was a movie brought in every few months and shown in a zinc-fenced open-air theater —an American drive-in without the cars.

The local government, the Parish Council, maintained thousand-gallon water tanks in every village like ours, perched on low cradles with spigots at bucket height. A battered tanker truck replenished them weekly, usually -- but not always -- before they ran dry. If one put out a 50-gallon steel drum by the roadside, the truckers filled it, too.

Trees prospered on the 40 yards of sandy hillside to the rear of our house, buffering us visually if not audibly from the village. A fence at the bottom of the swale marked not only our line, but the end of the sand; Moody had bought shrewdly. On Mister Arthur's side, baked hardpan supported little vegetation save the omnipresent lignum vitae tree, which puts down a prodigious root system and stays green through the worst drought.

Near the fence, the hardpan was littered with rusting cans. With no garbage pickup, people fed food scraps to the livestock and piled the rest of the trash in the back yard. We buried our garbage in a pit where it slowly composted, and dug a new pit when one filled up; but that was easier to do in sand. We tactfully ignored the dump adjoining our back yard – the goats and chickens at least kept it odor-free -- and were grateful for our thick greenery.

A dozen yards up Mister Arthur's side of the swale, the rust-heap gave way to bare ground, and then to a carpet of wood chips -- some as big as fists, some mere shavings – that led into the afternoon shade of his largest lignum vitae. This was where he built boats.

●

He would borrow a motor scooter to go inland to forested areas, looking for cottonwood trees. A mature *ceiba* is five or six feet in diameter at the ground. Even when we first knew him, in the early '70s, good trees – shaded as saplings, so low branches wouldn't leave knots that would weaken a boat -- were becoming scarce. Because the low trailer he hired could haul two logs as easily as one, he'd scout out two each time he went searching, dickering with the landowners to buy them as they stood.

It took several days to fell them. He'd set out at dawn with Goof on the rear saddle, with two axes. Goof, the mildly retarded man who also went to near sea with him, was shorter and no stouter than Mister Arthur; I marveled at the strength in those wiry frames. They'd return at dusk, sweat-rimed. I would have downed several Red Stripes, and so would most of the village men. Mister Arthur would go down to the sea to bathe, have a soft drink and supper, get a good night's sleep, and set out again next morning.

Felling a tree with axes eats up wood; a 32-foot boat was the typical outcome. A few years later, with a long-bladed, borrowed chain saw, he could fell a tree at ground level, saving the strongest and best wood at the base. Boats six feet longer became the norm.

One day a truck would arrive, its deep-throated Diesel *blat-blat-blat* heralding it from a half-mile away. Mister Arthur would take down his barbed-wire roadside fence, and the driver would back the trailer skillfully to that spot by the lignum vitae. Although the truck had a derrick arm to help hoist the logs out of the cradle, it took a lot of just plain muscle.

Then the real work began. I'd often spend a few minutes each morning I was there, watching from the shade. It wasn't a conversational time; Mister Arthur was seldom loquacious, and he didn't have the knack of talking while he worked.

While he had the truck's derrick, he'd had each log set so the best side for a straight keel was on top. He'd begin chopping with a hatchet, what seemed a toy against that massive tree. Then one morning the log began to look like an upside-down boat. A few weeks later, it was unmistakably a boat, its stubby keel straight, the prow and blunt stern easily discerned.

This was not only hard work, but hard on hatchets. He complained about those available in Jamaica: "De steel too soft, sah; it don't hold an edge." I sent him, by way of guests, a better hatchet, and he got a few boats out of it before he'd sharpened it to the nub. Over the years, I must have brought or sent him a half-dozen hatchets.

The exterior once shaped, he rolled the log over to rest on its new keel, propped it up and began hollowing it out, often starting with fire. Then he'd go back at it with the hatchet until it began to look like a finished boat.

How did he know when to stop hollowing? I asked one day. He grinned that wide smile, and showed me: Before rolling the log over, he used a bit and brace to drill a series of holes into the bottom and sides. Then he drove in home-made dowels, each cut to a length that matched the desired thickness of the hull at that point.

"So you see, Mist' Don, I'm gettin' close when I come to the hole; then I chop more keerful until I come to the plug." His boats were of varied thickness, calibrated to the stress they would encounter at each point.

After perhaps four months he'd have a dugout no wider than the original log. The wood was still green and pliant, however. He'd cut stout braces (usually of lignum vitae, so hard that colonials had used it for mill-wheel bearings) and wedge them inside, forcing the log to belly out, hammering in new braces every week until a five-foot dugout measured six feet at its widest. He then cut and nailed in thwarts, seats and permanent braces.

A boat at this stage would suit for near-sea trips, but needed more leeboard for far sea, where it would encounter larger waves. He'd buy and fit boards to make the sides higher, nailing them in and caulking the seams. After six months' work, a boat sold for Ja$2,000 to Ja$2,500, about US$1,500 at that time. His costs of buying and trucking the tree left him a profit of at best Ja$1,500 – not much by U.S. standards, but enough that he was the most prosperous man in the village, even without Miss Mary's checks.

In the next few years, Jamaica would discover fiberglass. A few captains tried plastering mesh onto the exterior, making boats less susceptible to damage if they scraped the reef. Some of the early efforts blistered off, but by 1980 everyone had the hang of it: Fiberglass-sheathed cottonwood boats became standard. It was no longer necessary to drag boats onto the beach after each trip to keep the wood dry and buoyant; they could be anchored in the shallows.

That was a loss, in a way. It took eight or ten men to get a boat ashore; neighbors helped neighbors. The first few men with fiberglassed boats found it inconvenient to bear a hand with those that still needed to be dry-docked; men slow to adapt had to plead for enough manpower.

Nowadays, a Kingston factory makes all-fiber boats; there are no longer even boats whose core is a hand-hewn shell.

The original cottonwood boats might last five to seven years before succumbing to dry rot or reef damage. Fiberglass lasts several years longer, but there are tradeoffs: They're heavier, and need bigger engines; swamped, even flotation chambers may not keep them up. The unsinkable buoyancy of Mister Arthur's dugouts is history.

●

I am far ahead of myself. Before we got to know Arthur James and blew the reef, we found this village and bought the land; before that, we found Jamaica -- 200 miles from the United States' doorstep, but far more distant in history and tradition and economic development.

We hadn't meant to make Jamaica part of our lives. We just went for a vacation, and kept coming back. Our first visit, in 1966 -- Jamaica's fourth year of independence -- gave us a perspective from which to gauge the new nation's growing political and economic democracy, as well as a lens through which we saw our Jamaican neighbors at home in Hartford more clearly.

We would also experience the shortcomings of Third World nations. Shortages were chronic; transactions that would be routine at home proved bureaucratic nightmares.

The winter of 1965-66 was snowier than usual. Brad, afflicted with cabin fever, had come into a small inheritance; for the first time in our dozen years we considered a vacation in the sun. We would leave our daughter and son, 7 and 5, with friends.

A friend who annually sojourned with a Jamaican Quaker family advised that Florida can be cold, but "it's never cold in Jamaica." I got literature from resort areas. Too pricey, I told him at Quaker Meeting. "Try the Treasure Beach Hotel," he suggested. Touring the South Coast, he'd lunched there. He thought a letter addressed to Treasure Beach, Jamaica would get there.

It did. The proprietor, Mr. Muirhead, wrote that he could accommodate us in February for $9 each per night, including breakfast and dinner; did we want someone to meet us? Our kind of price! We sent a deposit. We had PanAm reservations arriving in early afternoon, but were standby on an earlier Lufthansa flight, so we wrote him no thanks, we'd manage on our own rather than make someone wait for us.

What naifs! Our education was about to begin. *Lesson No. 1*: Waiting is part of life in Jamaica. "Soon come" is not merely a common figure of speech, but a mantra. Only novices would hesitate to have a driver meet the first flight, and if necessary sit around for the second. It wouldn't have occurred to Muirhead's man to complain.

*Lesson No. 2*: You can get to Treasure Beach by public transport, but not easily. It was like taking a steamer -- "Getting there is half the fun," the Cunard Lines used to advertise – instead of an airplane. Although our bus trip was fun, a not-to-be-missed introduction to the country, we've never been tempted to try it again.

Lufthansa deposited us in late morning at Montego Bay airport, a sleepy place with a half-dozen arrivals a day. A taxi driver took us through Doctor's Cave, a short string of hotels and shops in the historic tourist area, to the bus depot in the city.

City? It was hardly busier than its airport: a few dozen blocks of two-story commercial buildings, shops at street level, offices or apartments above, many of sun-faded wood. A few bank or insurance buildings shouldered above them. The narrow streets were crowded more with pedestrians than cars. Policemen in shorts with white chest straps stood on boxes in the intersections to direct traffic and discourage pedestrians from becoming accident statistics.

A dozen buses were lined up at the depot, a patch of bare ground; our taxi man found the one bound for Black River. Barely recognizable as American-built school buses, the buses had sturdy roof racks, and instead of our familiar yellow paint were gaudily decorated in red, blue and green, most with a religious motto -- a kind of prayer for the road -- on the front and back.

*Lesson No. 3*: A prayer before embarking on Jamaican roads is well-advised.

"Soon come," the bus driver told us. Pressed, he said we had a half-hour, long enough for an introduction to Jamaica's equivalent of a Big Mac: the ubiquitous meat patty, peppery ground beef in a golden-brown pastry turnover. It's often eaten with a coco-bread bun: wheat flour flavored with a tropical tuber, the coco, no kin to either the coconut or the chocolate cocoa. The patty is crammed into the bun, making a sandwich of Dagwoodian proportion.

Jamaica still used pounds, shillings and pence. We bought patties and coco bread from one stall, and from another squat bottles of Red Stripe, the Jamaican beer. Fortified, we took the front seat behind the driver.

We were no strangers to such transport. We'd met and married at Cornell in 1953. A year later we'd set out for a two-year stint -- my alternative service as a conscientious objector -- with the American Friends Service Committee in Japan. We'd then spent a year wandering home through Asia, shouldering a backpack apiece, often using village buses like these.

Nor were we taken aback that ours were the only white faces; that was familiar, too. Brad (Elizabeth, but she took a nickname while at Oberlin, before we met) is pretty, vivacious and outgoing. I'm tall and lanky. We make friends easily. We were in our mid-30s, still young enough that hard bench seats with too little legroom didn't dismay us.

We left the depot with only a few passengers, but the bus filled up a few blocks away at the farmer's market. In every big town, the government builds a huge shed, and leases stalls to farmers who bring their vegetables, fruit, dried beans, fish, chickens, hog-meat and beef at dawn. Although we didn't go in, we could smell it amply. In Black River, where we now shop, only Fridays and Saturdays are market days; the sun sterilizes everything in between. Montego Bay market, open six days a week, was pungent of ripe fruit, vegetables, fish and people.

We stayed close to the bus, lest we lose our front seats as new passengers boarded: farm folk with unsold produce, housewives with their groceries. The agile driver's assistant strapped straw baskets, crocus sacks and a cage of chickens to the roof. We chatted with people about what they'd bought and sold.

If you could squeeze Connecticut between your hands to make it longer and skinnier, you'd have Jamaica: 145 miles east-to-west; almost the same land area as our home state, with a bit less than Connecticut's three million population. In squeezing, you'd have made a mountain spine down the middle -- 7,400 feet at Blue Mountain to the east, less than 2,000 feet just west of mid-island where we would cross.

Within a mile of the bustling market, all hints of an urban center disappeared. The two-lane road passed through sugar fields, the nearly mature cane as high as an elephant's eye or an Oklahoma cornfield. In another mile we turned away from the coast and up a hill.

"Hill" doesn't describe it. The road wound up a steep ravine flanked by tall, light-green, feathery bamboo, thicker than a strong man's forearm. On the inside of the pavement were limestone and coral banks into which the road had been carved, darkened by decades of sunlight. On the outside were low walls of cut stone, beyond which one glimpsed the creek bottom below, some of it scoured bare by occasional cloudbursts.

Our bus groaned up the hill, spewing exhaust that blended with the fumes of trucks and vans laboring up with us. Occasional sedans, their drivers imagining they could see ahead safely, seized tiny stretches of straightaway to zoom past us. One wondered how strong the roadside walls were.

The road almost leveled -- the driver could finally shift out of low gear -- and led through gentler valleys, passing tiny Anchovy and unnamed hamlets, working upward still. We began to recognize ramshackle bars, identifiable by a kind of legal notice in hand-painted white letters on a black board, the owner's permit. Jamaica must have more bars per capita than Ireland.

Houses had small gardens. We recognized corn, and from our Asian travels, banana, pepper and cassava. Fellow passengers identified papaya, castor-bean, yellow yam, coco and an occasional breadfruit tree. (Captain Bligh brought the breadfruit. It was part of his cargo from Tahiti when mutineers seized his *Bounty*; he eventually went back for more.)

Cows, dogs and goats wandered about. The driver had used his horn incessantly on the way up the ravine; road signs encouraged honking to alert vehicles hidden around a sharp curve. He seemed now to assume that two or four-legged pedestrians would hear or see him coming and scamper out of the way. They did. Animals that survive to adulthood must be those that learn to step nimbly away from oncoming traffic. Perhaps children, too.

We tracked our progress by milestones, knee-high white concrete columns with black letters: *20 miles from Montego Bay* or *42 miles to Black River*. At intersections, wooden posts with wooden wings told the miles to places on side roads. These remnants of the orderly British administration have in the years since faded or rotted or broken off, and haven't been replaced.

Connecticut's population is concentrated in pockets, with long stretches of woodland and fields. Jamaica's population is spread out. If one wants to stop to relieve one's self, I would learn, it's hard to find a spot that is not within sight of someone's house.

We descended into a broad upland pastured valley, through tiny Montpelier and the only gas station we had seen since leaving the coast. At the horizon were craggy mountains, hazy blue-grey under a cerulean blue sky. In between were carpets of fields and forest copses, a palette of every imaginable shade of green.

Much of Jamaica's interior is what geologists call Karst topography. Limestone, formed when the island was undersea, has been dissolved by eons of rain, forming caverns that eventually erode so deeply that their roofs collapse, leaving a deep hole. Tropical vegetation can't mask the abrupt checkerboard of hills and limestone sink-pockets.

*Don Noel*

The first runaway slaves, or maroons (from the Spanish *cimarron*: wild, unruly) fled from plantations to this rugged area, called the Cockpit Country. All but immune from pursuit, they set up mountain redoubts from which an independence movement grew. To this day there is a Maroonland in the interior that claims exemption from some Jamaican law and governance.

Names of towns along our way reflected a British heritage mixed with Jamaica's own history. We turned at Shettlewood to Bethel Town, then wound down through Woodstock and Leamington and Newmarket to the headwaters of the Black River at Middle Quarters.

The bus dropped or took on passengers at one-room grocery-bars with a few canned goods, cornmeal, crackers and candy bars on the shelves; a glass case with patties and coco bread; and a freezer chest behind the counter from which came frosty bottles of Red Stripe or soda. We must have found an outhouse; memory conveniently obliterates the details.

It was dusk as we left Middle Quarters, the road skirting the river's vast marine morass. Full dark had fallen by Black River, the seat of Saint Elizabeth Parish, the biggest town since Montego Bay, with all of four blocks of a now-deserted commercial area. The distance from MoBay could not have been 60 miles, but it had been six hours.

"Where yu goin'?" the driver asked. "Treasure Beach? That's 12 miles; there be no buses now." But he'd find a way. Dropping the few remaining passengers, he drove through a residential area with no street lights to the home of a friend, who agreed to take us the rest of the way in his pickup for $20.

Brad sat in front, and I in back with another man and our suitcases. We'd been up at 4 a.m. in Hartford; I dozed as we drove through the warm night, rousing as we switchbacked down the last coastal hills into Calabash Bay. Winks of lantern-light at houses and bars showed that not everyone was abed yet.

The hotel, however, was dark. We drove up a short, steep driveway; buildings loomed out of the night. Our driver honked insistently until Mr. Muirhead appeared in a nightshirt. He was apologetic: He'd given up on us and turned off the generator. Wait a minute, please; he would fetch a kerosene lantern.

We paid off the driver, who disappeared into the night, and waited. We were at the edge of a steep hillside covered with plantings, exuding a mysterious sweetness. Muirhead reappeared and led us by lantern light to a Spartan concrete cabana. We washed in cold water, blew out the light and slept soundly.

# 4

# Lancelot and Wilton

**K**ipling had it right: The half-light of a tropical dawn lasts only minutes: The tips of a few fleecy clouds fade from deep lavender to rosy-pink; the last morning star fades; and almost like thunder the sun is up, bathing palms, bougainvillea and hibiscus in a soft light, the blossoms lambent pastels. The air is shirt-sleeve warm yet fresh, the sky a robin's-egg light blue that deepens as the day waxes. The sea, taking its color from the sky, assumes deeper shades.

On some seashores, the surf is a regular *ssshhhhh-BOOM! ssshhhhhh-BOOM!* At Treasure Beach a breeze from the southeast usually drives the waves over the barrier reef at an angle, so there is a constant sibilance, punctuated only occasionally by a discernible *boom!*

There were village sounds, too: roosters and the hee-haw of burros that were still common beasts of burden. Here and there wisps of wood smoke revealed where neighbors were brewing morning cups of coffee.

The hotel, built in the 1930s, was a stolid cement structure at the top of the hill, with a few cabanas like ours partway down, and a salt-water swimming pool below, all buried in luxuriant plantings. We went out to the broad beach, swam, then changed and went up to the dining room, its French windows open to the gathering day.

We were the only guests. Later in the week a small United Nations hydrology survey team arrived, but otherwise we had the place to ourselves. A hesitant waitress took our order. She reappeared with platefuls of fruit -- oranges, grapefruit, banana, mango, a cocktail of flavors -- and much later (speedy service is even now not a hallmark) with eggs and bacon, toast and coffee.

We hardly needed lunch, but had a bowl of red pea soup, a spicy, thick concoction made of red beans, which Jamaicans call peas. Dinner each night was a feast of lobster, broiled snapper or jack or turbot, always served with peas-and-rice, those same red beans.

We have over the years marveled at how cultures around the world found proper nourishment without benefit of modern science. Neither rice nor beans have all the amino acids of a complete protein (as an egg does), but together they do the job. The Japanese eat rice with soybean sauce and fermented-bean *miso shiru* soup. Jamaicans and their Caribbean neighbors eat peas-and-rice.

●

We saw little of our host. Mr. Muirhead, a short, light-colored, stocky man, hardly talkative, was not the first proprietor. He was on the verge of bankruptcy, and would soon hand the hotel over to the next in a string of owners who couldn't make money in this out-of-the-way place.

As a sideline, he raised race horses for the track outside Kingston. There were betting parlors in larger towns; races were broadcast on government-run radio. We listened one day as his horse finished out of the money. It seemed he was no more a successful breeder than hotelier.

What the place needed was a chatty, amiable host with better marketing skills. We had a Vermont friend who had hoped to start a ski lodge; we imagined getting him to take over the hotel: With modest advertising (and a shuttle bus to meet people!) it might develop an enthusiastic clientele. Some years later the hotel was bought by a Swiss couple. Good hosts and marvelous chefs, they didn't get the marketing right, either, and soon gave up.

Lancelot Graham, whom we met on our first walk around the village, might have been a marvelous hotel host. A talkative, light-skinned man, as slight and dapper as Gershwin's Sportin' Life, he always wore a short-brimmed straw hat and an engaging smile. He looked after the weekend home of a man of British origin, John Todd, so conversation with visitors came easily. (We met him before we adopted the Jamaican honorific "mister," and so he is to this day, to us, just Lancel, pronounced Lans'l.)

He and his brother Wilton were the fourth and fifth of 13 siblings, ten of whom survived to adulthood. Wilton was as reserved as his younger brother was ebullient; taller, but with the same straw hat. Their father, a fisherman, had died 15 years earlier, but an older sister who'd moved to Kingston sent money to be sure everyone finished high school. Two of the brothers went on to careers in insurance and banking; Lancel and Wilton were content to be fishermen.

Years later, they would recall their earliest "fishenin' ": three reef pots. Youngsters even today make smaller versions of far-sea traps, setting them near enough that they can row or even swim out to retrieve them. Wilton remembers a hollow known as Barracuda Hole (although he recalls no barracuda); they rowed out. All boats carried a sail, and used it when there was a wind, but close inshore there was rarely occasion to raise the sail.

There were plenty of fish then, they said, and a reef pot might have as much as 20 pounds of fish or lobster, enough to feed the family and provide cash income.

Outboard engines had come to Jamaica – that is, to these fishermen – in the decade before our first visit. Lancel and Wilton had an 18-horsepower engine. They went to near sea every Monday, Wednesday, and Friday morning. A man with a motorcycle with deep pannier baskets met them when they came ashore. He bought their fish and went inland to peddle, driving slowly, blowing a horn and calling out "Fish – fresh fish!" Housewives would wave him to a stop and come out to buy.

Larger engines – 40 horse Johnsons and Evinrudes – had arrived within the last year, so there were now more men who went to far sea, a trip that only the hardiest had made in the era of sail. They sold their catch to pickup truck operators, most of whom took the fish to Montego Bay to sell to tourist hotels or to vendors in the market.

Fishing three mornings a week left ample time for conversation; Lancel was a willing guide. He escorted us to the Calabash Bay cove to see the men prepare for a voyage to far sea, whose rigors they gladly described in a patois we could barely understand. He translated, a slight improvement.

We went back with him next evening to watch them return and weigh out the catch on hand-held scales, sorting into baskets. It was dusk; the work was illuminated by rudimentary lanterns: soda-pop bottles with cloth wicks -- like Molotov cocktails, but filled with slow-burning kerosene instead of explosive gasoline.

We knew the clawless lobster; on American menus at the time called South African rock lobster. Lancel named the fish for us: snapper and grouper, "quality fish" that commanded prices almost as high as lobster; turbot, purple with a rounded body and arcing tail, delicious but priced lower; colorful goatfish and parrotfish. The bony, angular trunkfish and some runts of other types might be given to needy older folk.

He also recited the names of men who hadn't made it home, or had been rescued after drifting for days. Our neighbors have an advantage over their inland compatriots: A brave and ambitious man can make a better living here than farming. But the sea is a stern mistress.

Wilton would soon become manager of the Calabash Bay Fishermen's Cooperative, created with the help of an American Peace Corpsman. Selling rope, floats, chicken-wire for traps, and paint for boats or houses, he would run it with punctilious bookkeeping, but little imagination or flair for salesmanship, rarely broadening his stock of goods. He was not a risk-taker; I suppose that's why the brothers went only to near sea.

Their children, the same ages as ours, weren't as tongue-tied and shy as most in the village; their parents urged them to chat with us to learn how Americans spoke English. In the years ahead, they would be good company for our Emily and Ken. Later, they all would study and become citizens in England, Canada and the United States.

●

The gardens below the hotel made Monet's paintings of his Giverny retreat seem parsimonious with color. The thick plantings were the work of many hands: Wandering the village, it seemed everyone had either helped landscape, plant and tend the gardens or had worked as housemaids, waitresses or cooks. Despite its commercial failure, the hotel was an effective school for the business of welcoming tourists.

At the foot of the garden hillside, the pool was drained periodically and re-filled with sea-water drawn through a huge pipe. There were too few guests to warrant a bartender at the gazebo bar, but when I walked up to buy beers, the barman insisted on bringing them down to us rather than let me carry them.

Beyond the pool and plantings was a very wide beach, briefly unimpeded by barrier reefs, with a moderate surf. Once past the waves, there was an undertow, almost the only place at Treasure Beach with a treacherous current. We swam carefully, and sunbathed.

And often, after we finished dinner, the nightingale sang. I don't know what bird entertained the fabled Chinese emperor, but in Jamaica it is the mockingbird that carols into the night; few Jamaicans know it by any name but nightingale.

The mocker is my avian favorite: a saucy bird the size of a robin but not as plump, brown-and-white with white wingbars easily recognized in flight. It likes high perches on treetops or television antennas, from which it sings and often imitates its neighbors. Our Hartford resident can fool me with a "cheer, cheer!" into thinking it's a cardinal, until it segues into more elaborate song. In cities, mockers have been reported to mimic taxicab horns.

Our *Birds of the West Indies* says "the Tropical Mockingbird . . . has a song like that of the Northern Mockingbird, but a little harsher, less melodious." That's a bum rap: The Jamaican mocker often mimics the melodious warblers that are winter visitors. Most important, it occasionally bursts into song during the night. I've never figured out how to predict its nocturnal arias: We've heard it sing in full moon and new moon.

We lucked into several night-time concerts on our first trip, and felt as lucky as a Chinese emperor.

●

On our last night, we went to a party. Windsor and Simone Putnam were the first Americans to build a vacation home here. Their stuccoed, tile-roofed house, on a commanding point, had French doors opening onto a flagstone terrace overlooking the sea. They invited everyone at the hotel: us. We walked 300 yards up the beach and clambered up a sand-and-timber stairway to join them and their house guests.

Windsor, a New York lawyer who specialized in inheritance tax-planning for wealthy clients, came down only periodically. Simone came in fall and stayed into spring. She was a handsome, statuesque blonde of uncertain age, whose French accent did not, we later learned, stem from her New York City origins and upbringing. She alternated between counting the spoons -- fussing over real or imagined thefts -- and giving generously of time and money to village needs.

Rarely without company, she encouraged a coterie of beautiful people, but complained about the cost of feeding them, lamenting that few were thoughtful enough to bring food to replenish her larder. She had an electric deep-freeze, thanks to a Diesel generator far enough from the house that one hardly heard it. Windsor escorted us down to see his greenhouse next to the generator shed, full of orchids and other exotics, his vacation passion.

The Buccaneers played on the terrace. Joel (*Joe-EL*) Elliott, a half-blind albino, picked a mean banjo. Several fishermen strummed along on guitars, only rarely offering melodic riffs of their own. Vincent Smalling sat astride a home-made "rumba box" -- a square wooden drum with a few thin, resonant steel fingers that he reached down to pluck as he slapped and thumped the box, a one-man rhythm section. Endley Parchment sang.

They played some calypso familiar from Harry Belafonte -- *Yellow Bird, Jamaican Farewell* -- and some unfamiliar, of which the most memorable had raunchy lyrics with a refrain, "My donkey wants water." Brad and I, the youngest, danced, joined occasionally by house guests. I sang along with Mister Endley: "Hol' on, Joe; me donkey want wah-tah." A broomstick was produced; we danced the limbo. I surpassed in getting under the bar.

It was hot work. I refreshed myself with a lovely fruit punch whose rum base was not immediately apparent. We chatted with the guests -- I remember only one, a Frenchman, a designer for the newly-ascendant alligator-logo Lacoste line -- and danced some more. And had more punch.

The evening ended; we started home. The rough-hewn stairs were more difficult than I'd remembered, but once down on firm sand washed by retreating waves, I thought I walked confidently. I might have walked miles if Brad hadn't pointed out that we had just passed the hotel gate. I somehow made it into bed, drunker than I'd ever been.

Alvin Senior, the village man who drove us back to the airport next morning, was talkative; I would have preferred silence. He grew peanuts as a sideline, and had a sample for us. Peanuts did nothing for a hangover; the twisting road was pure hell. Mr. Senior was sympathetic, and didn't mind when I had him stop several times while I contributed the previous evening's excess and the morning's peanuts to nourish the wayside soil.

By the time we reached MoBay I was fine. We flew home with nothing but warm memories, sure we would soon come again.

# 5

## Miss Sheila

**W**hat Sheila Hamilton wanted most was to give her children a better schooling than hers, to prepare them for better stations in life.

We first knew her as cook-housekeeper at Folichon, the place we rented in 1968 with another family from Quaker Meeting. (Two years had gone by. While we spent a year living and studying in Cambodia and Romania on a journalistic fellowship, our friends Jim and Cynthia vacationed at the hotel and lined up one of the few beachfront houses for rent at Treasure Beach: Folichon, from the French *folichoner*, to frolic. It was of the same vintage as the hotel.)

A stoutly handsome, light-skinned woman, Miss Sheila was a great cook – her curried lobster was fantastic -- but more than that, was obviously a lady of many talents. Better educated than most in the village, she played the role of servitor without complaint, a gift her generation has not passed on entirely successfully.

If one went to the kitchen to chat, she left no doubt that she was an equal whose forceful views deserved to be heard. She could be politely scolding: "No, mon – hear me now!" I enjoyed the kitchen conversations almost as much as the beach; Miss Sheila was to become a best friend and counselor.

I recall a conversation a few years later, soon after the leftist Michael Manley took office as prime minister. Pushing through a new minimum wage law, .he noted with pride in speeches around the country that the $5.40-a-day minimum for most workers, including domestic servants, replaced a decades-old statute called the "Masters and Servants Law."

Liking the symbolism, we applauded the new law. Miss Sheila worried that Jamaicans who made it to the middle class might be unable to afford domestic help. "But what about the young people, mon?" she parried our applause. "How are they going to afford a nanny or a housekeeper?"

Her sympathies were with the people she hoped her children would become. She spent much of her life working in other people's homes so her children could afford household help.

Her husband Erwin drove an ore truck for an aluminum company (*al-you-MIN-ee-um*, as Jamaicans and the British have it) inland at Maggotty. Such jobs were prized: He made several times what he could earn as a fisherman. He and Miss Sheila planned to send their children to high school, paying stiff tuition even in public schools. Not many from the village could afford to send their children to secondary school.

Bauxite leaches out of soils worldwide, but is concentrated in recoverable amounts in only a few places. Jamaica's deposits are relatively shallow and easily strip-mined; bauxite was Jamaica's top export. Lightweight composites have since reduced demand for aluminum, and recycling has replaced as much as half the United States' need for raw ore. Bauxite and alumina, the semi-refined middle stage, are still among Jamaica's major exports, but contribute less to the economy than three decades ago.

Most Caribbean Basin neighbors had little to sell except sugar and bananas, neither a high-profit export. The region was just beginning to exploit its benign climate to attract vacationers; over the coming decades, tourism would become the major dollar earner. Few tourists reach fishing villages, however; most stay in resort enclaves, so that little of their money trickles past a tiny elite and a small middle class down to farmers and fishermen.

Miss Sheila endeared herself to us by being intelligible. Jamaican patois, an English-based Creole, can be hard to follow even when slowed down to a walk in deference to American listeners. Even after three decades, Jamaicans who want to leave me out of a conversation can slip into a deep patois, like flooring the gas pedal, to leave me in the dust. Miss Sheila never has done that with us, but she has a mind that can out-race her tongue.

A public-spirited woman, she was appalled by the high rate of out-of-wedlock, teen-age pregnancy, and wanted the government to open more family-planning clinics, which existed in larger towns but not in rural areas. She longed to run a clinic at Treasure Beach: She would scold and shame her visitors into using condoms.

She didn't just want a better job: With tips, she made more than a government job would have paid her. She wanted to be of service. In later years she would lead parent-teacher organizations and help create a civic-betterment association.

Miss Sheila was the epitome of the dominant wife. Jamaican men are nominally heads of households, but wives often play the key role -- usually subtly, sometimes overtly.

(Years later, I would watch a neighbor berate her husband for giving their teen-age son the keys to the prized family pickup, which he had driven into a telephone pole. "Wha' fe you gi' him de key? See wha' him done!" It bothered her not a whit that several neighbors and I observed as she stridently denounced her spouse for his stupidity -- nor did he attempt to hush her.)

Miss Sheila's focus on her children's education was single-minded and unstinting. A few years later, Erwin was injured in an uncompensated industrial accident, and had to go back to fishing. It was a hard blow, just as the boys needed tuition for higher education. She invited herself to the United States as nanny for a family that had vacationed in Jamaica, staying several years and sending money back. Erwin got a visa to visit her once or twice during a long American hiatus.

●

Electricity was available only to those like Windsor and Simone, or the hotel's Muirhead, who could afford generators; that didn't include Folichon's owner, who lived in Mandeville. Miss Sheila cooked on a gas stove and kept food in a Servel refrigerator fueled with bottled gas. I'd never heard of a gas fridge. Evenings we played card games and chess with the children by the light of kerosene lanterns in reflective wall sconces. A few adults tried to read, but the light was so dim that game-playing prevailed.

Treasure Beach was re-named by the entrepreneur who built the hotel; it was originally Pedro Beach, a legacy of the century and a half of Spanish rule. (Columbus sailed into St. Ann's Bay on the north coast on his second trip, in 1494, and was marooned there for a year. A decade later, his son was briefly viceroy. In 1534 the colonial capital was moved to the south coast, to what is now Spanishtown. Other nations began poaching; the British took the capital in 1655, fought off Spanish attempts to recover the island, and established a civil government in 1660.) Some early Spanish monarch still gives his name to Great Pedro Point, which juts into the sea, and to a broad littoral, the Pedro Plains.

In much of Jamaica, the mountains tumble down almost to the water's edge; this is the widest coastal plain on the island. Behind it, the Santa Cruz Mountains (another reminder of who got here first) rise some 2,000 feet, abrupt and steep-sided; further inland is the highland spine. As the sun heats the Pedro Plains, rising hot air must be replaced. With the mountain barrier to the north, air must come from the sea. A gentle on-shore movement begins soon after sunrise, so faint one must wet a finger to detect it.

By breakfast, a more persistent breeze ruffles the water a mile offshore; that line of darkened water marches inland until the leaves rustle and one can feel the breeze on one's cheek. By noon there is a steady wind from the southeast, strong enough to produce whitecaps. That mid-day breeze is as constant and predictable as the tides.

We flew kites, tied the lines to the beach fence while we went to lunch, and came back to take them in hand again; they rose to mere specks swept inland. Our son Ken, seven years old, spent so much time kite-flying that his ears sunburned and stuck out like Dumbo's.

Miss Sheila recommended aloe, a cactus-like succulent that grows all over Treasure Beach. It's the same stuff that is put – in tiny amounts – into high-priced soaps and lotions at home. This was the real thing, 100 percent aloe vera.

She showed us how to break off a spear the length and thickness of a celery stalk. Beneath its hard outer skin was a soft, oozing sap, semi-transparent with a yellow-orange tinge. "Mind now, Mist' Ken;

don't you get it on your shirt or your pillow case; it will stain somethin' fierce, and it's me will have to launder it out. Jes' sit still a few and let it dry."

We anointed him again before bedtime, taking care as she advised to let it dry before he lay his head down. Next day the pain and most of the swelling were gone; we slathered suntan lotion on before he sallied forth to fly kites again.

●

Walking the beach, Cynthia stumbled onto something that stung her; her foot swelled and was painful. "Prob'ly jes' an urchin," Miss Sheila said; "we don't have but a few along this beach, and it won't last." Cynthia was frightened, however; Jim drove her to the Black River Hospital twelve miles away.

An Indian doctor was on duty. (Many Jamaican facilities are staffed by interns who come to study at the University of the West Indies. The better Jamaican medical students emigrate to play the same role in more advanced countries.) He reassured her, agreeing that it must have been a sea urchin, a floating hedgehog of sharp spines several times its golf-ball-sized body, which we would learn is common on the North Coast. Its toxin is short-lived, he confirmed, and not life-threatening; aspirin would dull the pain; she would feel better in the morning.

They were glad for the benign diagnosis. The doctor examined her in the sole operating room, whose walls, floor and examining table were of cast concrete struck to an almost-glazed surface so it could be vigorously washed down in lieu of more sophisticated disinfecting. The rest of the hospital was little more than a huge dormitory of cots shrouded in mosquito nets.

There was an ample nursing staff, of limited medical training but sharing a heritage of thoughtful care-giving that makes Jamaicans prized as housekeepers, nannies and companions.

Jim and Cynthia were appalled. We, fresh from my fellowship, were inclined more toward admiration. Black River Hospital was a step up from rural hospitals we had seen in Cambodia, albeit a wide step behind those in Romania, the poor man of Europe.

Back at Folichon, Cynthia's swollen foot did indeed subside. We lucked into a full moon: While the children slept, we walked the beach, etched in a luster exaggerated by the absence of competing electric lights. The sea was calm enough that we dared swim on the hotel beach. We shouted, warning each other to avoid kicking hard lest the splashing attract sharks that might lurk beneath the dark water. Fortunately, our shouts didn't attract them, either.

Walking back to Folichon, hugging our spouses close against the towel-less night chill, we encountered a pair of stone crabs as big as volleyballs, courting tiptoe on long legs stiffened by some marine tumescence, white as ghosts in the moonlight. Back home, smitten by the romance of the moon, still tingling from our swim, we retired to emulate the crabs in tropical courtship.

# 6

# Neil, John Todd, Harvey

**A** young Peace Corpsman, Neil McAuliffe, was one of our new friends on that 1968 vacation; he was helping start the fisherman's cooperative. A stocky, blond, deeply sun-tanned man, he sported a thick moustache. He lived in a beach shack put up by Folichon's owner before the house we were in. Neil was happy to join us for occasional meals while we picked his brains about the village and the fishermen's lives.

Not that Neil was starved for either company or good food. He was an easy-going, sociable man, nothing like the "ugly American" of whom Graham Greene had recently written.

Brad and I knew the Peace Corps: We'd met volunteers around the world, and I had briefly considered directing a program in Asia. Neil was close to our ideal: accepting a living standard not much above the people he worked with; patiently letting good ideas percolate until the fishermen adopted them as their own. He'd made friends with everyone at Calabash Bay, joined the men in the evening bars, and was often invited to dinner.

The first Peace Corpsman here; he left the co-op's operation mostly to Wilton Graham. It was a tiny two-room, concrete-block shed, painted a bilious blue-green, with only two windows, just inside a dirt road on the Calabash Bay fishing beach. The natural reef barrier had been built up a bit, long before Neil's arrival, to make the best-protected cove along Treasure Beach; a dozen dugout boats were drawn up on the beach.

Although the paint Wilton sold was a Jamaican brand, almost everything else was imported: rope from South Korea, wire mesh from Europe. Prices were less than in the commercial hardware stores in Black River, Williamsfield or Southfield, to say nothing of being more convenient.

(A few years later, the imported rope disappeared when Jamaica started its own "rope walk" down toward Kingston. The fishermen grumbled that the new rope was vastly inferior. In several earnest conversations (although avoiding the economic jargon), I argued that import substitution was the only way a developing nation could learn to make new products. We'd lived in Japan when the annual import quota was 1,000 American cars. Japanese cars were shoddy the first few years, but look at their car industry now! In a few years, I predicted, the product of Jamaica's new rope walk would be world-class. And sure enough, by the next time we came, the grumbling had ceased.

Wilton opened the store in mid-morning, did a little business, closed for lunch, and re-opened a few hours in the afternoon. He had plenty of time for bookkeeping.

Neil appeared on first glance to have little to do. He'd helped Wilton get started and register the new venture with the bureaucratic agency overseeing co-operatives; that was all done. But in fact Neil's all-day schmoozing with the fishermen helped build membership; almost all the sea-going men at Calabash Bay belonged. Many shore-bound householders joined, too, when they realized the saving in the commodity everyone used, house paint.

The co-op returned part of the profits to members at the end of each year, a first for its customers and a further boost to participation. We chanced into the annual meeting. Neil helped Wilton round up the membership one afternoon in a classroom at the primary school a half-mile from the beach. Although the meeting was well past the heat of the day, it was still a hot, sweaty room, and we gained an appreciation of the school teachers' jobs.

Neil stayed in the background while Mr. Wilton handed out the mimeographed annual statement, reporting a comfortable profit and cash balance with which to buy more supplies. He detailed the rebate checks that would soon be handed out, and his report was accepted on a voice vote. The board of fisherman directors was re-elected with equal ease, and the annual meeting adjourned to the cooler outdoors.

Neil went off with some of the men to celebrate a successful year, promising to join us for dinner later. We lingered with Wilton, and bought a £5 membership as a gesture of solidarity.

●

Through Lancel we met John Todd, of British ancestry and now Jamaican citizenship, a burly, handsome charmer whose version of a Jamaican accent was almost an Irish brogue; he made our wives' hearts melt. Jim and I were relieved, and suspected they were disappointed, to meet his pretty wife Janet.

They lived in Spur Tree, a mountain suburb of Mandeville, and weekended at Treasure Beach. John was an innovative and hard-working farmer; on one of his plantations, on the North Coast, he was experimenting with using a flaccid river to irrigate rice fields.

A passionate political person who championed the reigning Jamaica Labor Party, John despised the more liberal Jamaica National Party whose Michael Manley would soon become prime minister. (In the year of that election, we arrived to find a water tank boldly spray-painted *Down with the JNP*. Such graffiti were then a New York City art form not yet exported world-wide; we doubted it reflected village passions, and got John to admit he was the author.)

We visited John and Janet. Of Janet's design, their beachfront house was of cut limestone, more handsome to look at than to live in: On its vest-pocket terrace, a small pool barely left room for deck chairs. A bunk-bed room for their children had louvered windows up near the eaves, striking from outside but providing little circulation. I was already studying designs.

Lancel's duties included watering the plantings, being sure the water tank was pumped full when the Todds or their guests arrived, and finding stop-gap fixes to roof-leaks or other problems. Like most who looked after wealthy owners' homes, he earned no regular wage, but was grateful for tips when the master came visiting.

One Christmas, John gave him a small refrigerator. Lancel was overjoyed until the first bill arrived. Electricity in Jamaica was even then twice as expensive as in Connecticut, whose power rates were among the highest in the United States.

●

We'd begun to think about a place of our own. We couldn't rent here whenever we wanted, and concluded there must be a growing tourist traffic ready to defray our costs of owning a beachfront "villa." I was in my second year as editorial page editor of the *Hartford Times;* Brad was head of guidance at Weaver High, a predominantly African- and Caribbean-American school in the neighborhood where we live. Having a Jamaica vacation home seemed a luxury we could now afford, one that might even pay for itself.

Harvey Clarke, an enterprising man who'd made a grubstake as a migrant farm worker (in Connecticut, among other states) was acquiring land to the west, toward Fort Charles. Cynthia labeled him Flem Snopes after William Faulkner's shrewd Yoknapatawpha County character. He showed us a place on a cove protected by a coral point. The dirt road deteriorated along the way; barely wide enough for Harvey's pickup, which he had to put into low gear to creep over raw rock outcrops that were part of the roadway.

The Jamaican owner had built an ugly concrete-block shack and had begun a swimming pool that deserved only to be filled in. It was on a handsome site, though: A hundred-yard-long coral point protected a small, sandy beach in the crook of its arm, and there would be a handsome view of the sunset every evening.

Brad and I swam out from the beach, and worked our way around to the sea side of the rocky point. There was no reef; waves crashed against the rocks. I imagined signs of erosion, and wondered how long the protective barrier would last. (I underestimated the slow pace of geologic change: More than 30 years later, the little peninsula is unchanged; a new owner has built a handsome house facing the sunset, with a gazebo on the point.)

The property was available for Ja£6,500 -- then about $13,000 -- but we blanched at tearing down the shack, worried about erosion, and thought it too far from any village or power line.

Neil urged us to talk with Lancel and Wilton. They and their sisters had inherited a sea-front piece near Harvey's farm. Neil and another Peace Corpsman were buying four acres, half the siblings' inheritance.

We went with our children to look at the other half, a long walk in the hot sun.

A concrete-post geodetic survey marker stood on the lip of the coral cliff, somehow reassuring, evidence that we weren't nowhere. It was one of the few places in Jamaica where I could stop to relieve myself unobserved.

We clambered down a goat-path off the bluff to the beach, a narrow opening between reef brackets reaching into a gentle-looking ocean, and swam out. Unexpectedly, the sea-swell grew; the waves became menacing. Brad had just body-surfed ashore. Ken and Emily and I grabbed at a coral head near the surface and held on, enduring scratches as the waves scoured us against the reef. I left Ken hanging on for dear life, ferried Emily shore, and went back for Ken, frightened but brave. Finally we stood together on the shore, bleeding slightly from reef cuts.

Despite our hard-earned understanding that this wasn't the most hospitable of beaches, we were encouraged by the prospect of having Neil for a neighbor, and decided to buy the land. Perhaps influenced by Folichon's name and Simone's pseudo-French accent -- and my shameless love of puns -- we thought of calling the place *Si Chaud*. Brad liked the play on words, but feared it made the climate sound too hot. We set the question of a name aside.

The Grahams didn't have a title. Five years after their grandfather's death, the will hadn't even been probated. Few could afford lawyers to guide them through the bureaucratic maze. Much of Treasure Beach was still owned by common law. One put a legal ad in *The Gleaner*, claiming ownership of specific metes and bounds; if no objection was raised after a long wait, a title would be registered. We contracted to buy the land when the Grahams could give us a title.

●

I took Brad, Jim and Cynthia and the children to the airport, re-scheduled my own ticket, and drove back to cadge a meal with Windsor and Simone and learn more about land ownership in Jamaica. It proved a happy evening: We discovered that Windsor and I, although more than a generation apart, had studied at a small ranch-college in the California/Nevada desert. They were, as I'd hoped, a goldmine of details about Jamaican law and practice.

Monday I drove to Black River to find Mel Brown, a former schoolteacher who had taken the bar in England, to formalize our bid: Ja£1,200 an acre for a bit more than 3 acres -- about $7,200. I gave Lancel a US dollar check for $240, spent another night with the Putnams, took notes on their layout, picked their brains still more, and flew home the next day.

# 7

# To market, to market

Miss Joy spotted me the minute I walked into the Montego Bay shed; her voice carried over the din: "Come, mon, I owe you a watermelon!"

In 1966, on that initial trip, we'd barely looked inside the market. By December of 1971 we knew it well. It always takes a moment for my eyes to adjust from the bright sunshine. There must be 50 vendors, wares spread out or piled up on ping-pong sized tables; a hundred shoppers crowd the narrow aisles. Save for butchers and fish vendors at one end, the stalls differ only slightly one from the next; collectively they have everything that grows in Jamaica.

Those nearest the doorway are busiest: customers feeling and hefting fruit and vegetables, the proprietress weighing purchases in the shallow pan of a hand-held scale. On our first shopping trip, we'd edged our way farther in, savoring the scene. Miss Joy had beckoned us to her table. "Come, sah, come!"

A tall, dark woman whose buxom figure was not disguised by a baggy dress and cash-pocketed apron, she was younger than most vendors and so was eager to build her clientele, in part by remembering people. On our next trip, six months later, she'd greeted us with sure familiarity: "Glad to see yu'; been a while."

We'd arrived on Saturday and done our shopping before driving over. Now, on Tuesday, I'd returned to meet late-arriving friends, and had a short list to top up the larder from Miss Joy's stall. A watermelon had been on our Saturday list; she'd gotten one from a neighbor's stall, but in packing our overflowing bags it had been overlooked. I'd forgotten; she hadn't. "I give it back to the lady to sell before it spile," she said. "I'll git one for yu' now."

MoBay market had a reputation for being cutthroat: Mind your wallet, our neighbors warned, they're more greedy than we are: "Dey get yu' any way dey can." As I put the new melon into a bag, I made a mental note to tell our Treasure Beach friends that they tarred with too broad a brush.

●

In the United States, life without an electric fridge and freezer is hard to imagine; few of us even remember iceboxes. Having no refrigeration at all changes eating and shopping habits. Most Jamaicans went to market almost daily; many still do.

We stayed at places with a big fridge, and bought for a week: Guests brought the food, except for fish and lobster that came from the beach. We brought from Connecticut a box of things often and unpredictably scarce: flour, cooking oil, rice, soap, mayonnaise, plastic food wrap. (One year we brought sugar, having been warned that Jamaica's harvest had fallen short of its too-ambitious export commitments!) We also brought shopping bags, which food vendors sold rather than gave away.

We'd spend a half hour at Miss Joy's stall, then stop at a supermarket (which didn't deserve the "super") for beer, soft drinks and a few other items – including frozen chicken that often had come from the United States.

We were by now connoisseurs of farmer's markets, having visited Mandeville, Savannah-la-Mar and Black River. Each is a bustling cornucopia of Jamaica's produce that deserves an Impressionist painter; our photographs can't capture the profusion of colors and shapes.

Each proprietress has a government-leased counter, waist-high, divided into shallow bins, laden with produce. In Black River, one can imagine that some things come from the proprietress' own farm. In MoBay we know that stall-keepers like Miss Joy buy from their farm neighbors. The real farmers are more likely to spread their produce on a plastic sheet on a rent-free patch of ground outside the shed. We occasionally buy there, but there's more variety inside.

Outside there also are often tinsmiths, cobblers, sandal-makers, shoe salesmen, tailors, vendors of ready-made clothing from socks to frocks – and more recently, vendors of music on cassettes and CDs. In MoBay, the sidewalk market now stretches several blocks from the main building; even in Black River there's a proliferation of vendors, adding to the hubbub.

We're seldom the only whites, but there aren't many others: Most expatriates as well as affluent Jamaicans send maids. We probably stand out as pale-skinned new arrivals in tourist shorts; or perhaps we're easy to remember because we call the stall-keepers "Miss," adopting the polite formality of Treasure Beach. In any case, we're pleased to be treated as regulars, even though we know that remembering faces is a knack cultivated to keep customers coming back.

●

A few vendors will have Jamaican pumpkin -- like a huge, flattened winter or acorn squash, a remote kin of our Halloween jack-o-lantern. Diced, boiled, and mashed, pumpkin is the base of one of my favorite soups, as thick as a bisque and seasoned peppery-hot.

Some tables have dasheen (taro in the South Pacific), a round tuber whose big leaves join okra, a large onion, a green hot pepper and a chunk of salt meat in a thick soup called callaloo.

Others have coco, yellow yam, sweet potato or "Irish," as white potatoes are called here. Such a variety of tubers is important because they keep without refrigeration. Not surprisingly, soups using these root vegetables are on any list of memorable Caribbean cuisine.

Another mainstay is red pea soup. Our housekeeper boils the red beans "until they burst," she says, then stirs in big chunks of those tubers, along with dumplings. By the time that's all cooked, the soup is thickened. Then she ladles the dumplings and root vegetables into separate serving bowls. (With good reason: On my first encounter, I spooned them into my bowl, then tried to cut them up – ending up with a lapful of hot soup. Now I cut everything to bite-size on a side plate first).

The cassava, a huge tuber, is a worldwide tropical starch. Jamaicans make bammies with it, steamed dumplings a bit denser than cornpone. Bammies once were -- and arguably still ought to be -- the main bread. But cassava is a lot of work: One must grate it, press out its bitter liquid, and wash and press the gratings again – traditionally in a cloth bag wedged between two long boards with a rock atop. It takes several hours, and the resulting coarse farina doesn't keep well. Little wonder Jamaicans have come to prefer wheat breads, even though wheat doesn't grow in this latitude and every loaf contributes to the imbalance of trade.

There are almost always string beans, carrots and cucumbers; sometimes cauliflower; usually a puffy cucumber-like cho-cho (christophene on some other islands; growing on vines on wire arbors, looking from a distance like grapes). There is always cabbage, but rarely lettuce, which easily bolts and turns bitter in the hot sun. There are green and red peppers and red-hot Scotch bonnets; and tomatoes, sweet and juicy, a different creature entirely from the ones we get in winter at home, picked green to endure shipping.

And caliloo, not to be confused with the soup: a leafy green a bit like New Zealand spinach. One plucks the leaves, which add zest to a soup or an omelet or can be a side dish on their own. A breakfast of caliloo with bacon bits is one of my favorites.

Soon after the house was built, we found that Elbert James grew caliloo in our bottom land. We took seeds home, and ate it out of our garden all summer. Brad adapted a recipe for a scrumptious chilled soup, chopping the leaves into a canned mushroom-soup base in the blender.

We forgot fresh seeds on our next trip, and thought we'd have a summer without our Jamaican green. But in late spring it popped up all over our vegetable garden, having self-sown prolifically. We've never since been without volunteer caliloo; we sometimes transplant seedlings from distant flower beds.

Another specialty, when in season, is the ackee, the national fruit. It grows on a tree with distinctive lime-green leaves; the fruit looks like a red pepper. It's inedible -- actually toxic ("pizen") -- until the leathery red shell pops open, revealing creamy, thumb-sized fleshy morsels, each with a black seed the size of a grape at its tip. Canned ackee is a major export, recently admitted to the U.S. (whose FDA worried about toxins from premature picking) but long sold to Jamaicans in Canada and Great Britain. We learned to use it the way one uses tofu, adding texture to a stew and absorbing its neighbors' flavors.

Some stalls will have star apple -- a sweet fruit, softer than our apple, named for the pattern when cut in half -- or avocado, called Spanish pear. Another stall may have sweetsop, a fist-sized fruit whose ugly artichoke-like exterior hides a nest of black seeds the size of almonds, each thickly coated with a sweet, custardy pulp. At other stalls one may find soursop, its astringent relative.

Somewhere in the shed, unless out of season, are pineapples. They're natives of this part of the world, and we think are sweeter here than their cousins transplanted to Hawaii – certainly sweeter fresh-picked here than those shipped to markets at home. There are mangoes, both the stringy natives and larger, fleshy hybrids. We have a hybrid Julie mango in our yard in Treasure Beach, the fruit dangling from long stems, weighing down the branches as they fatten to sweet ripeness. There are bunches of naseberries (sapodilla), twice the size of grapes; canteloupe and watermelons, and of course coconuts.

Almost every stall-keeper has bananas; some have a tiny yellow or red variety, like sweet pudgy fingers. Elsewhere are plantains, the oversize relative that's inedible until cooked. Fried with copious amounts of oil, plantains make a soft egg happy for the company. There are almost always grapefruit, limes, lemons, tangerines -- and oranges, the best of which is the Ortonique.

In the early 1960s, aluminum companies began buying up the island, assuring bauxite reserves into the next century. The newly-independent government enacted a law requiring them to make productive use of the land while waiting to strip-mine it. To their credit, the companies hired botanists and agronomists to experiment and propagate new crops: forage grasses, tropical pines, fruit. The Ortonique, a cross between an orange and tangerine, is exceptionally sweet and juicy. In our early years, it was hard to find; nowadays many Jamaican oranges are Ortoniques.

Oh, yes, and Bligh's breadfruit: green, nubbly-skinned fruit the size of bowling balls that hang improbably in tall trees with deeply-lobed leaves. I'm not sure why the British went to such effort to inflict it on Jamaica: It's starchy and almost tasteless. Our cookbook says breadfruit can be substituted for potato in any recipe, but that would be a mistake; it has none of the flakiness of a good Irish. Only when sliced into rings and fried in enough fat is it worth bothering with.

Enchanted by its history, I tried planting a breadfruit tree at Treasure Beach; its early demise for want of rainfall spared me endless meals.

At home we're frugal shoppers: We clip coupons, make lists. We brought lists to Jamaica, but were impulse-buyers, too, wanting to try everything.

Each purchase was weighed out on a scale; the stall-keeper would tell us the price per pound and the total, and usually would round down or throw on one extra.

No vendor had everything we wanted. "Wait a bit," she would say, and call to a neighbor: "Yu' got Spanish pear? Gi' me two, please. Yu' got cho-cho? Gi' me a ha'-dozen, please." She or the neighbor would thread through the busy aisles to exchange the produce and establish the price. (Miss Joy had gone scouting and bought that forgotten watermelon from a lady five tables away.) She would collect from us and settle up later with her neighbors, keeping it all in her head. I would fussily write it all down and check that my total agreed with hers. It always did.

That was soon to involve even more awesome mental gymnastics. After our first vacation with Jim and Cynthia, Jamaica abandoned shillings-and-pence and adopted dollars-and-cents, casting its lot with the more numerous tourists and more accessible markets of North America. When we went next in 1970, Miss Joy was calculating values she knew instinctively in the old currency, translating them to the new, and keeping a tally!

Hand-held calculators were unknown; she didn't even use pencil and paper. Probably none of the stall-keepers had finished high school -- a portal to better jobs than market vending -- and it was unlikely many had even finished elementary school. Shopping is a constant reminder that intellectual gifts are no guarantee of prosperity in a developing country.

●

Folichon having been unavailable when we could come -- Brad and Cynthia were both restricted to school vacations -- we rented places a mile apart in 1970, and converged on one another during the day; we repeated the arrangement a year and a half later.

We were at Treasure Cot, a charming two-bedroom house owned by Basil and Joyce Densham, who had come years earlier from New

Zealand to run a dairy. Jim and Cynthia were at Sparkling Waters, a mile up the road, a squat bunker with a few windows cut into the concrete walls, built by a Jamaican who ran a Mandeville dry-goods store. It was a graceless structure, but was served by a phenomenal cook, a tiny woman smaller than most of our children, Miss Dinah.

Basil and Joyce came to see that we were well taken care of: They worried that their Miss Doris might hurry our dinner hour. They never dined before 8, but knew that unless told differently she would serve us at sundown. With young children, we preferred an early dinner, but would in any case have hesitated to add two hours to her already-long day.

It wasn't our first encounter with casual, unintended exploitation. The Third World was still largely in thrall to its former masters; Jamaica, although now an independent member of the Commonwealth, was no exception. Acceptance was more common than resentment, let alone rebellion. Of all the countries we've visited, we were least comfortable in India, whose caste system put all whites into the highest social order, even us in sandals and backpacks. Jamaican self-esteem was a happy contrast with Indian servility, but people still knew where their bread was buttered.

Basil and Joyce were a generation older, accustomed to the colonial order. When we suggested that eating late must make their cook's day harder and longer, they assured us that Doris (not "Miss Doris") didn't mind, and was glad for the job. A lecture on human rights would have been pointless.

The Denshams brought their pampered parrot, Horace, who went swimming with them, clutching a precarious perch on the rubber tassel atop Joyce's bathing cap. One day, when she body-surfed ashore, he fell off; she rescued him, sputtering, from the foam. Poor parrot; he hadn't learned the swear words appropriate for a near-drowning. In late afternoon, when we played croquet -- they said it "CROAK-ee" -- on their sparse lawn, Horace fluttered from hoop to hoop to await the next play.

●

Our deal for Lancel and Wilton's land had come undone. The will wouldn't be probated for another year. It would take at least another year to get a title. Besides, we had second thoughts about the remoteness and the unfriendly beach. They let us off the hook gracefully, but kept our deposit.

I'd meantime concocted a plan to buy a piece of land large enough to farm. We would find a farmer short on capital but long on ambition, build him a house behind ours, and have him grow crops, looking after our place while his wife cooked; in time he would earn title to half the land. In retrospect, I was trying to persuade myself we weren't neo-colonialists. In any case, we never found such a collaborator.

So we were looking again, in a desultory way. We celebrated Christmas with Jim and Cynthia and our friend Tom from Quaker Meeting. We swam, walked the beach, played chess with our children, and read. (Looking back at journals, I am amazed that I read a half-dozen books on every vacation. Nowadays, I'm lucky to finish one a week. Being lord of a Jamaican manse does nothing for literary habits.)

The hotel had been revived; the Swiss couple put on a New Year's Eve party with music and dancing that the children thought fabulous. Next morning we walked up the beach to visit a couple we'd met at the party: Felice (Phil) and Ianthe Manzelli, he a native New Yorker, she born in Jamaica, both working in New York City schools. They'd recently built a handsome seaside villa, Coyaba, on Major Moody's Point. My journal is full of sketches.

On our next-last morning, John Todd's cook came from next door. His brother Richard had bought a piece of Moody's land next to Mister Arthur, thinking to replicate his older sibling's weekend getaway. Now he'd decided it was too far from Kingston.

Brad and I walked two miles down the dusty road to have a look. For the first mile, people helloed us by name. Passing Coyaba, we knew we'd reached Billy's Bay when the dirt road abruptly turned to pavement for a hundred yards in front of a few shops. (Incumbent governments always did a little paving just before elections, impressing voters with improvements that not coincidentally provided some paid work for nearby residents.) We asked about Mr. Todd's land.

Elbert James walked us across his yard to show us the land -- an acre, a rod and a perch in Jamaican measure, about an acre and a quarter. We liked the view from the sandy knoll, which flattened as it neared the beach. A sprawling calabash tree below the crest bore gourd-like fruit. It was calm; the barrier reef looked like an irregular narrow walkway paralleling the shoreline, washed by gentle waves. The ocean horizon was so wide one had to turn one's head to take it in.

Richard Todd had hired men to "bush" the land (clear it of brush), and had planted a line of coconut palms, still barely knee-high. He'd also had a well dug, five feet across, lined with limestone and coral. Peering in, I dropped a pebble; we could just make out the ripple in the water 30 feet down.

Back at Treasure Cot, we walked over to chat with John about his brother's land. We had time next morning to walk up with Emily and Ken for another look before Hedley Gayle, a village building contractor with an ancient Morris sedan, would take us to the airport.

"What do you think?" I asked. "We might put a lot of money into this place, and build a house of our own."

With the sagacity of children 9 and 7, they said, "Oh, yes, Daddy!"

# 8

## Joshua

**A** tree had been felled across the road when I came down to get the house ready for guests in the fall of 1978, soon after parliamentary elections.

I stopped for a close look. A big thorny-branched acacia, it had obviously been taken down with a chain saw, apparently to block the road. Then two more chain-saw cuts had removed about eight feet in the middle, re-opening the road.

I knew of only one chain saw at Treasure Beach: one I'd brought Mister Arthur for his boat-building. I went over next morning to see him.

"Yes, sah!" he said. "It was me took down that tree."

Why?

"Well, sah, there was s'posed to be a big political rally down here. And it seemed like every time either party had a rally, the other party sent people down to bust it up.

"We didn't need that kind of violence here in Billy's Bay. So I went and cut that tree down across the road."

His strategy worked: With the road blocked, the rally had been moved somewhere else.

"The day after the election, I went back and cut the tree to open the road again. I guess it was a bit of hardship, people not being able to get their vehicles through for a few days, but nobody objected."

My admiration for the dean of the village grew. Billy's Bay is a peaceful little community; he'd taken matters into his own hands to keep it that way.

Jamaican politics have had an edge of violence in all the years we've been here. The worst is usually in Kingston. Each party has a stronghold in two adjoining slums, and there are periodic episodes of gunfire, especially in election seasons. I have in my files a newspaper photo of the JLP's Edward Seaga leaving a political rally, ducking behind a bodyguard of thuggish escorts with drawn guns.

But election violence occasionally spreads to other parts of the island. Mister Arthur made sure that didn't happen in here.

I've gotten ahead of myself. The 1978 election was one in which the PNP's Manley won a second term as prime minister. Our first introduction to the political scene had been six years earlier, just as we were finalizing our purchase of the land that would become our hideaway.

●

To almost everyone in Jamaica, admirers as well as critics, he was just Michael. A hero to some of our Treasure Beach neighbors, Michael Manley was a villain to more -- including most of the landed gentry, who – drawing no distinctions among left-wing philosophies -- saw him as a Communist who threatened their way of life.

His rhetoric briefly gave even us pause. We were on the verge of buying land when he proposed, in the 1972 election campaign, that foreigners be barred from owning land: If elected, he promised a law allowing only 99-year leases.

It was one thing to be sympathetic to the Third World's chafing under First World dominance, but this struck close to home. We were about to invest a lot of money, to say nothing of time and effort, in an enterprise that might not be wholly ours.

After soul-searching, we decided that 99 years is a very long time; not only would we be long gone, but so would Emily and Ken, before such a lease expired. There remained a niggling doubt: If Michael and his PNP could revoke our right to own land, what other radical ideas might follow? Nonetheless, we went ahead.

We would soon have fresh reason for doubt: The PNP won by a wide margin, and Michael's swearing-in as prime minister in March

1972 was followed by an unprecedented exodus of the well-to-do. Having barely finished the house, we kept meeting landed neighbors who were about to leave. A physician emigrated to start his career over as an orderly at a Pennsylvania hospital; a judge retired to Australia.

Others were poised to bail out. Fearful that their wealth would be expropriated -- Michael had talked of freezing bank accounts -- many shipped their treasured colonial-era antiques to Canada, where they might be sold to raise cash if their owners decided to flee. Visiting the Kingston docks to collect a shipment soon after the election, I saw trailer-sized containers stacked high, waiting for outbound shipment. "Dey be full of furniture," a dockhand told me with a knowing grin.

Our friend Ted, who played a role in the new government's reforms and was one of the few Manley admirers among people of means, persuaded his wife to stay, and talked her out of shipping her family treasures.

Olive Smalling, the wonderful woman who was to be our housekeeper for two decades, turned out to be a stalwart of the Jamaican Labour Party, which had governed in the first decade of independence. She was a kind of ward captain: When the JLP's Seaga came to Treasure Beach, he checked with her to be sure he shook hands with the right people. Seaga and the JLP had been swept out of office by Manley's PNP shortly before she came to work with us, and she couldn't understand our failure to perceive the threat in Manley's socialism.

By American standards, both parties were left of center. Both were based in trade unions -- one led for years by the PNP's Norman Manley, Michael's father; the other, by the JLP's Alexander "Busta" Bustamante. It was on the "conservative" JLP's watch that Jamaica forced aluminum companies to invest in agricultural improvements on their bauxite-reserve lands.

The first contest to choose a fully independent government in 1962 was between Busta and Norman Manley, who had been premier under British suzerainty since 1959. On the eve of voting, the Soviet Union sent a naval vessel on a courtesy call to Kingston Harbor. Politically-inspired rumors swept the island: If Manley won, the Communists would take over; the Soviet ship was a harbinger. Bustamante won handily.

It is a telling anecdote that says a lot about the Jamaican entrepreneurial impulse. With Fidel Castro's Cuba some 90 miles to the north, Jamaicans were -- and remain -- paranoid about Communism. For a decade, the JLP government kept Cuba at arm's length, although never breaking diplomatic relations.

Manley promptly changed that, welcoming Cuban delegations and accepting Cuban aid: two trade schools, one in Kingston and one in Montpelier that we passed on our trips to Treasure Beach. The rumor mill had them both as hotbeds of subversion. A planned state visit by Castro in the spring of 1978 -- later postponed until fall, after Manley's re-election -- fed the rumors.

Michael at 52 was a lean, handsome, light-skinned man. (Seaga, of Lebanese extraction, was equally light; it would be more than two decades before Jamaicans elected a leader as dark-skinned as most of the population.)

Manley had served in the Royal Canadian Air Force during World War II, then spent four years at the London School of Economics, where he studied with socialist Harold Laski. He worked as a freelance journalist and with the BBC in London; came back to Jamaica in 1951, worked for a leftist weekly newspaper, and became a union leader. In 1962 he was appointed to the senate – like Britain's House of Lords, a relatively powerless body – and in 1967 was elected to the House of Representatives. Two years later he succeeded his father as president of the PNP.

Before taking on that role, he made a well-publicized trip to Ethiopia to meet with Emperor Haile Selassie. The visit delighted Jamaica's Rastafarians, an underclass sect that calls marijuana a "sacred weed" and Ethiopia the homeland to which all Jamaicans will one day return. The sect took its name from Selassie, whose title in Ethiopian was "Ras Tafar." Following his pilgrimage, Rastafarians began calling Manley "Joshua," after the Biblical hero who succeeded Moses. They became a core element of his electoral majority.

●

One of Manley's first acts was to begin acquiring majority ownership of the bauxite companies, and to abrogate the existing tax schedule, which was based on the profits of various wholly-owned subsidiaries. One company mined the ore; another refined it to alumina; another shipped it by rail to a seaport; another shipped it to North America. It wasn't hard to manipulate the profits of subsidiaries to minimize taxation.

I asked my Dad, a vice president of Alcan Aluminum Corp., about the economics of the industry. Bauxite, he said, represented about one percent of the cost of a finished ingot of aluminum. Manley could have doubled the effective tax with only minimal impact on the price of aluminum products.

The companies fulminated, then hired former U.S. Supreme Court Justice Arthur Goldberg to negotiate; he eventually cut a deal not far from Manley's original goals.

Intrigued by the success of the OPEC oil cartel, Manley explored -- unsuccessfully, as it turned out -- creating a counterpart aluminum cartel. Aluminum, however, was a small part of Michael's agenda. He was more successful as one of the founders of the Caribbean Community and Common Market, Caricom.

He rammed through his overwhelmingly PNP parliament a minimum wage law that rattled not only employers but the small middle class, and even aspiring village folk like our friend Sheila Hamilton. He set about nationalizing some key industries. He created state farms and a state-managed system of small-farmer cooperatives. He borrowed Ted Tatham from Alcan to create a "Land-Lease" program, settling landless farmers on unused farmland leased for five years from wealthy owners, trying to lure rural folk back from joblessness in the cities.

Although faced with declining exports in a world recession, he pressed on with New Deal-like programs to offset brutal unemployment, running up a $100 million deficit that was papered over with bookkeeping gimmicks or printed money. When some North American hotel owners bailed out, his government bought the hotels to keep them running until the tide of foreign investment turned again.

He also initiated a program of low-cost housing projects – we passed several on the drive from MoBay -- that gave thousands of families their first house with electricity and plumbing.

(The JLP's Seaga was scornful of the new housing; his supporters echoed his complaint that Jamaicans wouldn't like small plots without room for a few chickens, goats or pigs. He was wrong; those houses are prized. Seaga also criticized the hotel purchases; but when he became prime minister a few years later, and another American chain abandoned a hotel, he was quick to buy it and keep it running.)

As the exodus of well-to-do and middle-class Jamaicans began soon after his election, Michael greeted their departure with scorn. I sat by the radio in Treasure Beach one night in his first year to hear a speech in which he said, in effect, let 'em go; we don't need 'em.

I was appalled: Jamaica needed both the capital of its small upper class and the talents of its somewhat larger educated middle class. Manley had gotten into his head an Algerian model of state-run supermarkets. He seemed not to understand how much of Jamaica's commerce was carried on by mom-and-pop entrepreneurs who worked long hours for minimal profits. Replacing them with state-paid workers would have been an economic disaster.

Years later, when he was re-elected prime minister after eight years of a JLP government, Manley recanted his more extreme views, and welcomed capitalist investment. Although much of his program in those early years was of enormous benefit to the new nation, he might have spared the island the loss of much talent had he toned down the rhetoric.

In retrospect, we had little reason during that first election campaign to assume that Michael's most radical ideas – including barring foreigners from owning land – wouldn't come to fruition. We went ahead anyway.

# 9

# The contractor

Lester Lyn's contribution to tropical architecture was a flat, cast-concrete patio roof that I'd admired at the house next to Treasure Cot and more recently at the Manzelli's Coyaba. The thick concrete assured a cool shaded haven from the sun.

In neither house, however, had he used that vast expanse to catch rainwater. Both adhered to traditional Jamaican usage, catching water in gutters around the pitched roof, with a long pipe directing it to an underground cistern behind the house. I thought I had a better idea.

In a flurry of correspondence on returning home after the new year of 1972, we'd agreed to buy Richard Todd's land and engaged Mr. Lyn to build our house. I'd borrowed the Manzelli's blueprints, modified their layout and sent him drawings. Now, in late April, we'd flown back to finalize arrangements; he came from Mandeville to meet us at Billy's Bay.

He was a small man with a ready smile. His forebears had Anglicized the original *Lin*, and his face showed so slight a hint of his Chinese heritage that I had to ask to be sure. Later, we would meet his daughter, in whom that mix of Asian and African genes was stunningly beautiful; she was a stewardess with Air Jamaica.

(The British, like the Americans, imported Chinese laborers to build the railroads; Chinese-Jamaicans are a significant part of the country's heritage. Jamaica's motto – "out of many, one people" – is not merely a knock-off of our *e pluribus unum*, but an acknowledgement of Jamaica's own history of immigration, both forced and voluntary.)

He liked my plans, including my innovation of putting the cistern under the patio, rather than excavating a separate structure to the rear. And yes, catching rain that fell on the flat patio roof made sense; surprising no one had thought of it. This was a house, he said, that he would be proud to add to his resumé.

With one exception: I'd drawn that deck over the patio to be not quite horizontal. I wanted it pitched slightly to one corner, so rainwater would flow to a downspout leading to the cistern.

We stood in the morning sunlight where the house would rise, the plans spread on the ground. Mr. Lyn's hands traced the patio ceiling in the air. "If I build it that way," he said, perfectly deadpan, "someone will stand at the rear of the patio looking out, and ask 'Who was your builder?' "

We laughed aloud, but got his point: A tilted deck would look like shoddy workmanship. He proposed instead to make the patio ceiling dead-level flat. On top, he would pour the concrete extra-thick to the rear and one side, thinner near one corner. The roof would still pitch toward the downspout, but the pitch would be invisible.

His draftsman would re-draw my plans to get structural elements right with exact dimensions for windows and doors, and make working drawings. His foreman, Roy Reid, joined the conference, a muscular dark-skinned man, a carpenter and mason who inspired confidence.

The front of the house would in a sense be cantilevered off the knoll. But instead of being perched on columns, it would rest on a long retaining wall, perhaps five feet tall when viewed from the seaside. In fact, though, that wall would be a massive 12 feet, seven feet into the ground, creating the outer shell of the cistern beneath the patio.

Assuming a concrete-block wall, I'd drawn a small protruding ledge just below ground level, so that when we could afford it we could face it with the cut limestone I'd admired at John Todd's.

"Why not build the whole wall of stone?" Mr. Lyn asked. Can't afford it, I said. "Labor and materials are still cheap," he replied. "It will add maybe $200 to your cost. I'll keep track of it; trust me." We trusted him. That cut-stone wall, 45 feet long, is one of the beauties of the place, and it cost about US$300 more.

We asked that when possible he employ some of our village neighbors for unskilled tasks; he gave us a promise so vague that we doubted it would be fulfilled. The plain fact, we would learn, was that he could find men in Mandeville willing to work harder for less money than our Billy's Bay neighbors -- who could earn more by going to sea, despite the risks.

Getting a building permit, Mr. Lyn said, often took months. But if we approved his spending a few hundred dollars, he could "expedite the process." Nothing that wouldn't pass muster eventually, he assured us; just speeding things up. We agreed to reimburse him for whatever was appropriate, and pretended not to notice that we were authorizing bribes.

Lester Lyn would build our house for US$24,000, plus the stone wall, roof gutters, a small maid's quarters to the rear and other extras that would cost another $4,000 or so.

In 1965, we'd bought our Hartford house, in a changing neighborhood where the presence of black neighbors depressed values, for $20,500. We were about to build a vacation home that including the $17,000 we paid for the land would cost twice as much as the home we lived in year-round. We were awed: It would take a lot of rentals to defray the cost.

We agreed to send a first payment as soon as Mr. Lyn had a permit. John Todd would look in occasionally, see that benchmarks were met, and authorize four more payments. Mr. Lyn would have the house ready for furniture at the end of August, so Brad and I could camp in a bedroom to see the progress. The house would be ready for occupancy November first!

•

A lot of work had gone into those plans.

Soon after we came to Connecticut in 1957, I'd built a Japanese-style house in a rural town, both designing it and doing most of the construction myself. Brad had acquired considerable skill, too; we both looked at building plans with a practiced eye. I sometimes call myself a would-be architect who fell from grace into journalism. I had a notebook full of sketches of houses I'd admired at Treasure Beach.

One was Doubloon, next to the Densham's Treasure Cot. On one of our visits, Mr. Lyn's workmen had been adding that shaded patio.

I'd poked around inside, too, and liked the layout. On returning home after the new year, I wrote Peggy Iver, an older woman who lived in Mandeville: Would she let us rent the house for a week so we could try out her design?

She didn't rent the house out, she wrote back promptly, but we would be welcome as her guests whenever we were ready. Meanwhile, she offered a few pointers.

It was a charming letter, two long hand-written pages filled with details: Put in louvered windows, to take advantage of the breeze, but don't fall for the frosted-glass louvers then in vogue; the glass would amplify the sun. Use redwood louver blades; they block the heat.

The local lore was that if you were high enough to see Great Pedro Point, as we did, you'd never have mosquitoes; with the view came near-constant breezes to keep them away. Although there's some truth to that, she wrote, screen the windows. There aren't many mosquitoes in this dry climate, but they're a stubborn subspecies whose eggs or larvae survive drought and emerge after occasional heavy rains.

And most memorable: In the bedrooms, she wrote, install tall windows whose foot is at the level of the beds, and have those louvered windows on both sides of the room for cross-ventilation; nothing beats a breeze across the bed on a warm evening.

We never got to stay in her house, but we made good use of her pointers. I designed the windows as she said; the circulation across our beds is wonderful. At sunset the sea breeze dies; after an hour or two of calm, the air inland – cooler now, and so heavier – flows back downhill to the sea. Many a night, when the temperature drops to a "chilly" 72 degrees, I've cranked the rear louvers closed as I came to bed, an amazingly easy climate control. We would later put in overhead fans for those few still hours, but we've never even considered air-conditioning.

●

Like Coyaba, our house would be a very wide V, two wings embracing the patio. Coyaba had three bedrooms, reached by hallways inside the patio. We wanted four bedrooms; hallways took up needed space and seemed a barrier to the cross-ventilation Peggy Iver urged. Out went the corridors. The Manzellis' dining area and kitchen were a single room divided by only a counter, providing privacy to neither cook nor guests. I walled the kitchen off, and put in a pass-through serving window such as I'd built in Connecticut.

It took several laborious drafts to have the wings accommodate four bedrooms while keeping the central area where they met -- living room, dining area and kitchen -- well proportioned, but I found the right fit.

A one-inch pipe brought water to Treasure Beach from wells at the foot of the Santa Cruz mountains. The line stopped a mile short of us, though, and even at that point there was barely an overnight trickle; people accused each other of hogging water up the line. Although an extension was planned to Billy's Bay, we couldn't count on its carrying enough water to meet our needs: We would pump from the rainwater cistern and from Richard Todd's well.

Phil and Ianthe had a system typical of most American rural homes, a small pressurized tank. If one drew much water, the pump turned on automatically to replenish the tank from the cistern. Jamaica at this time suffered frequent power outages, however, and they were frustrated: There would be no water after a few flushes.

Learning from their experience, I was inclined to opt instead for a water-storage tower; once pumped to that tower, water would flow by gravity even when the power was out. Richard Todd made the decision easy: He threw into the bargain a steel water tower and tank he'd commissioned before deciding to sell. It would be trucked from Kingston when Mr. Lyn was ready. For $50, Richard had the Kingston fabricator weld in a plate, dividing the tank in half, so we could separate brackish well-water from drinkable rainwater.

The house would be piped with a dual system, brackish well-water to irrigate plantings, flush toilets and serve showers; sweet water at all sinks, drawing from the cistern side of the tower. All piping, much of it buried in the floor and walls, would be PVC plastic; galvanized iron wouldn't last long in this saline environment.

There would be no hot water. Cold showers, in this climate, weren't really very cold; none of the places we'd rented had running hot water. A water heater would add to our costs and to Jamaica's imbalance of payments, since all fuels were imported. In this sun-soaked country it seemed unpatriotic to consider anything but free solar energy, even though that technology was still in its infancy. But at Mr. Lyn's urging, there would be space and piping in a little storage closet in case we later changed our minds.

In a pinch, if there weren't enough rain, one could buy water by the tanker-truck load from the Parish Council. I drew in a four-inch plastic pipe buried beneath the concrete floor from the driveway to the patio cistern to make such deliveries easy.

I wrote the University of Connecticut Ag Extension people about wastewater. We were ahead of our time; it would be several decades before Americans focused on recycling "grey water," but it seemed profligate to drain scarce water from sinks and showers into the septic system. Would trees and plants mind a little soap? I asked. It would take a lifetime of soap build-up, they wrote back, before plants were bothered. Reassured, I drew in shower and sink drains leading outdoors, where I could direct the grey water to planting-terraces.

The house I'd built in Connecticut had been one of the state's first all-electric houses. To win reduced power rates, I'd put in switched lights in every room, and lots of electric outlets. I did the same for the Jamaica house. Phil and Ianthe's patio reading lamps had extension cords trailing from bedrooms. In addition to electric outlets around the patio, I specified an outlet and a pair of bullet-style lights in the ceiling where one might read at night; no trailing cords for us! There would also be floodlights facing seaward at the outer edge.

I toyed with windmill electricity to harness that onshore breeze. An Australian manufacturer mailed a thick packet. The notion appealed to my Connecticut-Yankee gadgeteer's impulse, but the system would require huge batteries, and the prospect of keeping it in good repair without skilled tradesmen nearby was daunting. Reluctantly, we decided on Major Moody's power.

Phil called in late January to say he'd rented a week to a family from Hartford. I phoned: Would they take my Boy Scout compass, and walk over to our building site at dawn one morning to determine exactly where the sun rose? I wanted to angle the house so that early-morning sun would flood across the patio -- inviting the tropical dawn into all the bedrooms – while the western bedroom wing would shield the patio from late-afternoon sun and heat.

It would be their first trip to Jamaica; they invited us to dinner to pick our brains. By now old hands, we had a detailed shopping list of what to buy in Montego Bay and what to bring from home. We made them purple-ink Ditto copies (which would soon become part of our packet for people renting our new house) and told them to ask for Miss Joy.

They came back with my compass reading, and I laid out the house facing south by southeast. Happily, that's also the direction from which our onshore breeze comes. The sunlight behaves just as I'd hoped, and the breeze on the patio keeps it cool even at mid-day.

We explored a building loan and mortgage with banks in Black River. Interest rates were upwards of 30 percent, reflecting the uncertainty of devaluation and exchange rates, and a ten-year mortgage was the longest available. We had by now moved into Hartford, and our loan for the country house we'd built was about paid off. We re-mortgaged it.

Jamaica, short of foreign exchange, required a permit to change money into U.S. dollars. I wrote the Bank of Jamaica, filled in forms, and eventually got a letter promising that if we sold, we could repatriate any U.S. dollars we'd brought to Jamaica to build the house.

●

In an earlier time, most Jamaican houses were of lath-and-wattle construction. A frame of stout posts was filled in with a light mesh of split bamboo, onto which an adobe-like slurry was plastered. Many such houses had roofs of thatch palm fronds. After World War II, concrete block became the standard, and thatch gave way to zinc-plated corrugated steel, always referred to as simply "zinc".

In an uncertain economy, everyone bought materials a little at a time as money came to hand, lest inflation make them more expensive later. We often saw concrete blocks stacked on vacant lots, and piles of marl, which is used in Jamaica instead of sand. Construction often began with just a few rooms; if a second floor was intended, foot-long stubs of rusting reinforcing bars poked up into the sky, a declaration of grander plans.

Our house, too, would be of filled concrete block, finished with a light smooth cement coat that Jamaicans call "rendering," and painted flat white – keeping the house cooler, Mr. Lyn said.

The more expensive places nowadays had wood-shingled or tiled roofs. Mr. Lyn recommended the new corrugated aluminum sheets with bright anodized colors. He'd brought a color chart; we liked the light blue.

I gave him the Kingston fabricator's plans and dimensions for concrete footings for the tower. In building our Connecticut house, our first steps had been to bring in a temporary electrical service, drill the well and install a pump. Mr. Lyn was to have an electric pump in the well and piping to the tower before we took possession; I assumed that he'd do that right away, so he'd have pumped water with which to mix what would be tons of mortar and concrete.

If I'd listened more carefully, I might have detected the non-committal quality of Mr. Lyn's polite response. When I came to see progress on the house in August, I learned what he might have told me in April: In a land of low wages, laborsaving steps weren't a high priority.

# 10
## Brother Elbert, Miss Hilma

Elbert James, Mister Arthur's older brother, was deacon of a church a mile down the road, he taught Sunday school and often read the Bible lesson. He was "Brother Elbert" to his fellow parishioners; it suited him perfectly.

He was one of the gentlest souls I've known. When I was impatient with some task not done as I'd expected, his patience – "Oh, Mist' Don, tell me please how yu' mean it to be" -- would shame me. He was as light-skinned, tall and thin as his brother, with the same remarkable strength in his skinny frame and big hands. He and Mister Arthur went to near sea Tuesday and Friday mornings, with their mildly retarded neighbor Goof.

He added to that meager income with his casting-net. Accompanied by Goof, he would walk the barrier reef when the sea was calm, twirling the 10-foot circle of mesh so it landed flat and its weighted circumference sank uniformly, then hauling it back to see what he'd caught. He made it look easy, but it was dangerous work: Coral outcrops beyond the barrier reef might snag the net; neither he nor Goof could swim.

His land, like Mister Arthur's, abutted ours. He and his wife, Miss Lethe, lived in one little house; they'd built another for their daughter Cislyn, her husband Valney Ritchie and their so-far four children. Mister Valney captained a far-sea fishing boat on the equivalent of a sharecropping arrangement, splitting the catch with the boat's owner.

It had been Brother Elbert who showed us the land when we first saw it at New Year's. Now, during this busy April 1972 week to get the house started, we hired him to be our gardener: $12 a month to look after the place during construction, $5 a week once the house was finished.

Although he had little experience in growing flowers or trees, he would prove to have a green thumb. He was an eager learner, and a prodigious worker.

●

He was also a resourceful man, ready to improvise when unexpected problems arose. The birdbath was an example:

One of our early projects, as soon as the house was built, was a rock garden of exotic cactus on a terrace to the side of the patio. In Black River I found a pretty cast-cement bench and a birdbath with a concrete pedestal. There were rarely puddles where birds could drink or bathe; we were sure to attract a varied flock that could be watched from the patio. I left instructions to clean and refill the birdbath when he watered plants daily.

It soon became a ritual that the day after our arrival he and I would take an early-morning inspection walk. (Brother Elbert would rather have shown me everything the moment we got out of the car, but all I wanted after a long travel day was a sea-bath, rum and relaxation; he indulged me. At sun-up next morning, however, he would be waiting to walk me around the property.)

He would proudly show me fences or walls he'd built, and flourishing new plants coming into blossom ("That one lookin' very bright; it goin' to blow flowers soon") as well as ruefully showing me the failures ("It began to quail, sah; I did my best, but it die") and would point out problems that needed attention during my visit.

The visit after we'd built the Cactus Terrace, I could hardly have missed a new problem: The birdbath was perched atop an ugly, rusting wash-bucket full of concrete.

Birds weren't the only creatures that lacked places to drink, Brother Elbert explained. The birdbath was low enough that village dogs could stand on their hind legs to lap the water; it was becoming a haven for thirsty dogs. He'd found the discarded wash-tub, set it into the sand, mixed up concrete to fill it, and planted the birdbath atop the fresh concrete, more than a foot higher and out of the dogs' reach.

It was ingenious, but unbeautiful. We cut the rusty metal away with tinsnips and chipped the concrete to blur the ungainly washtub shape. Mixing mortar and using our hands instead of a trowel, we completed the disguise, molding the mortar smoothly into the column supporting the birdbath.

Painted white, it looks to this day like a miniature of a Buddhist stupa one might see in Burma. And the dogs can't reach it.

●

A fence, he'd told us on that April 1972 visit, was essential. Richard Todd had been lucky that his young coconuts escaped the ravages of wandering goats, and we had more ambitious plans. We'd been scouting flowers, shrubs and fruit trees. We commissioned Brother Elbert to fence in the property -- for $3 a day, which we later learned was half again what Mr. Lyn paid his workmen.

We ordered barbed wire from Southfield; Mr. Lyn would bring "proper" fence posts from Mandeville – sawn timbers, pressure-treated against rot, instead of posts cut out of the surprisingly dense scrub of the hills behind us.

(The sawn posts were prettier and theoretically longer-lasting. In this dry, sandy soil, however, rot wasn't a problem, and they cost four times as much as having Brother Elbert cut our own. He was eager for the work; we soon abandoned proper posts. He would go up into the hills, sometimes with Goof, in search of stout saplings. They were armed with that ubiquitous Jamaican tool, the machete. (In the United States, it's a *mah-SHET-ee*, close to its Hispanic origin. In Jamaica, it's a *MAH-shet*.) He used it not only to cut and trim the posts, but also to dig post-holes.

Although a novice gardener, he explained to me the "sea-frost" ("sea-frahst"). Waves break over our reef much of the time, throwing up a salty spume that drifts inland. One chooses plantings near the sea for their salt-tolerance.

Together, we sketched a plan to guide his gardening once we were protected from goats and Lyn's workmen were no longer trompling the yard. We drove inland to Hounslow, where the manager of a government-sponsored nursery had his own adjoining private plot with many of the same plants for sale. Erwin Hamilton would fetch them when Brother Elbert was ready.

American nurserymen pot their stock. In Jamaica, even cheap plastic flowerpots are too expensive; plants are universally grown in thin black plastic, pot-shaped bags, perforated for drainage. It's easy to tell when a seedling is ready to plant: A few roots poke out. The flimsy bags are a plus. One can minimize transplant-shock by cutting a few more slashes and then planting bag and all, confident that all the roots will find their way out.

We would plant bougainvillea along the fences, a dozen to start, in a variety of colors -- vivid red, coral pink, orange, violet -- for something like 25 cents each for a well-established plant. After watering for six months to get them established, we could virtually ignore them; they would thrive in the arid climate and shrug off sea-frost.

The bougainvillea is the splashiest of tropical plants. It blossoms year-round: little dry, paper-like blooms that seem to stay on the branch forever, clinging stubbornly against the breeze. It grows quickly to a sprawling bush, or can be shaped by pruning. Given a little support, it climbs to second-story height. It is a riot of color.

A head-high thick hedge of a native cactus called candlestick stood between our yard and Philip Gordon's. Brother Elbert thought it unsightly, perhaps because it was so common, and would cut it down when he strung the fence. In its place he would plant oleander, a pink-flowering, quick-growing shrub that also would need no watering once established, and wouldn't mind the salt air.

That may have been the only bad advice he gave us; we would soon miss the candlestick. Engine parts and fish-trap materials were scattered about the Gordons' bare-ground yard, youngsters toddled with only shirts on, and Miss Blossom built her morning cooking-fire near the fence. The ground turned out to be hardpan that only the native cactus found hospitable; it took years for the oleander to grow into a passable screen.

We would have to postpone landscaping directly in front of the house until Mr. Lyn built the terrace walls. Brad and I wanted on that terrace a sea-almond tree such as we'd elsewhere. Its natural shape is a wide umbrella. Left alone, it grows new, taller umbrellas, like a layered Asian temple. But it can be pinched back to make it spread horizontally and not block the view.

Brother Elbert and I carted up pail after pail of sea-sand, building a hillock to the planned terrace level. Atop that mound we planted an almond slip. With his careful watering, it flourished; by the time the terrace wall was built and filled in two years later, the sea-almond was a sturdy young tree that quickly grew to make the pool of shade we'd envisioned.

We would plant more sea-almonds partway down the slope where the land fell from the house to the hollow adjoining the Gordons, more umbrellas of green to hide their yard.

Near the foot of that slope we would plant three poinciana, or flame trees. We knew it as the *flamboyant* that lines the boulevards of Cambodia -- a tall, spreading tree that in early spring bears masses of red blossoms. Dorothy Harris, a plant-hobbyist neighbor at Calabash Bay, sold us three of a hybrid orange-red. "Put them below the house," she said, "so you can look down on them when they are in full blossom." It was hard to imagine the foot-high whips growing to the height of the house, but we did as she said, and have not been disappointed.

In heavy rains, the hollow behind the house collected water from the neighbors' hardpan yards; the resulting pond sometimes took a week to seep into ground. We would try a few bananas there; he thought they would tolerate occasional drowning, and would appreciate the water. Bananas proved one of our failures; that is indeed the wettest soil on our land, but not wet enough for those thirsty plants.

Mr. Lyn would build our septic system halfway down that back slope. When he finished, we would plant a few paw-paws -- papaya -- taking care that their roots not crowd the septic field. They would get sunlight much of the day, and begin bearing fruit in about a year!

The rest of the back yard was heavily shaded by a grove of lignum vitaes, between which -- an unexpected delight -- several sweetsop grew scrawnily upward, seeking sunlight. They were so ugly – twisted, thin trunks and scant foliage -- that I would have cut them down had not Brother Elbert told me they produced that lovely custardy fruit. We would in time find open places back there for an avocado, two native limes, a hybrid Julie mango and a few ackee. Only the ackee and limes survived.

Along the drive we would plant a line of casuarina trees, Australian pine in some books but "willows" to all Jamaicans, tropical conifers with long needles and tiny seed-cones. Fast-growing, with a narrow shape like a Lombardy poplar, they would shade the parking area but not take up too much space. On the inside of the driveway we would try that ill-fated breadfruit tree.

Near the house, we would plant allamanda, a short shrub with golden trumpet flowers, and another shrub with bright red pom-poms, the ixora, a favorite of hummingbirds. Brother Elbert wasn't sure how they would tolerate the sea-frost; we'd find out. Our gardening had an element of trial-and-error.

Everything would grow well, he assured us; the sand was strong soil ("strahng sile"). But the sand would need help to retain moisture until plants were established. Erwin Hamilton would bring him a truckload of the heavy "red sile," halfway to being bauxite, that is found in pockets everywhere in Jamaica; he would mix it into the sand to make the starter-holes less porous.

We'd admired the tall thatch palm planted on Windsor and Simone's terrace; beneath which the setting sun plunged into the sea. We wanted one of those.

"Hard to find, Mist' Don. Yu' have to catch them ver' young." But seedlings occasionally volunteered beneath mature trees; he would tell a friend in a nearby district where thatch palms were common -- Thatchville -- to watch for one.

●

There was more to do this busy April week. We would begin renting the house in November; we needed to hire a cook-housekeeper now. Miss Sheila at Folichon, where we stayed one last time, put out word that we were hiring, and helped us interview a stream of applicants.

Some were young and inexperienced. Some had worked at the Treasure Beach Hotel, and a few in private homes as well. Miss Sheila gave each the same admonition: "You will be cooking and waiting on people from the United States who work hard and have come for a complete vacation. You must take pride in making everything perfect for them."

Despite its slightly scolding tone -- it was the voice she would use, if she could, to tell young men they must take pride in not making unwanted babies -- it was wonderfully reassuring. All the candidates said oh, yes, they agreed. We tried to gauge the enthusiasm and sincerity with which they said it, suspecting that Miss Sheila was unique.

We also needed someone who was literate. We planned a weekly exchange of letters in which our housekeeper would tell us village news, report problems that needed fixing and tell us how each set of guests fared. That eliminated half the candidates.

We finally chose Hilma Clarke, a slight, soft-spoken young woman with a timid but engaging smile. She didn't have the take-charge personality we'd hoped to find, but seemed capable of growing into that role. One sister, Katurah, was housekeeper at nearby Coyaba. Another, Daphne, was the Todds' housekeeper who had first told us about this land. Miss Hilma had worked with both sisters; she would have plenty of advice, and helping hands if needed.

She worked at the hotel, and could continue there until we were ready for guests. We would pay her a small stipend to look in on the building's progress from time to time and send us letters.

We would pay her $10 a week when there were guests -- more than any other domestic worker in Treasure Beach -- and would encourage guests to tip her directly and generously, rather than adding a service charge as many Jamaican places did. We would pay her $5 a week when there were no guests, a radical departure from the local practice of offering no regular wage when a house was empty.

This was more than American egalitarianism. We would rely on Miss Hilma to manage the house, take care of guests, and be our surrogate for six months at a time; we wanted her to have a stake. Although we were consciously pushing up the Treasure Beach pay scale (which some of our landed neighbors would predictably resent) we were embarrassed to pay her so little, and promised a raise once we'd established a clientele.

When the house was ready, Harvey Clarke with his pickup would truck down a fridge, stove, washing machine and mattresses that we ordered from a Mandeville store.

Phil and Ianthe had bought all their linens and towels in New York and had Bloomingdale's ship them direct -- and had been appalled at the customs duty. Used household equipment, they had belatedly learned, was allowed duty-free. We profited from their experience:

We would buy sheets, blankets and towels, use them a week or two in Hartford, launder them, and send them in duffel bags. Miss Hilma's brother Wilford, who looked after Folichon, would find a place there to store them until our house was ready.

●

Our first stop this week had been to commission a houseful of furniture in Highgate on the North Coast, where our friend Tom knew of a Quaker-run furniture factory. (The early missionaries, we were told, divided up the country so they wouldn't confuse their proselytes with competing versions of Christianity. Midwestern Quakers, more evangelical than New England Friends, brought not only their faith but their woodworking skills to Highgate.)

I'd corresponded with A. M. Eslom, who ran Friends Craft Industries. From Montego Bay we drove a rented car to Port Maria, four hours on a narrow paved road that snaked along the coastline through the best-known tourist areas. We spent the night at the seaside Casa Maria, one of the historic "inns of Jamaica," hardly busier than the Treasure Beach Hotel, and next morning drove inland to find the furniture factory and meet Abe Eslom, a big, dark, friendly man.

The Highgate craftsmen built mostly from the native maho tree, whose wood is handsomely streaked in dark and blond; once cured, it is iron-hard. The chairs, drawer-fronts and bedsteads were finished in tightly-woven raffia. The "factory" had a few power saws, fed by a generator, but it was mostly hand work. The open sheds swarmed with men cutting and sanding and women weaving raffia.

Their furniture, its open grain glistening with varnish, would be not only sturdy, but an ornament to our new villa. Our Hartford house was furnished in what we mockingly call "early attic" style, hand-me-downs from our parents; we'd never bought more than a chair at a time. Now we ordered a houseful of beds, dressers, chairs and tables for $1,800, an incredible bargain. Everything would be trucked to Treasure Beach when Mr. Lyn declared the house ready for furniture, probably in September.

●

There had been, in the months since we saw the land at New Year's, more correspondence with Richard Todd, his lawyer in Kingston, and our lawyer in Black River, Nathan Curtis.

Nat's office was a bleak suite above his wife's meat-market on the main street, with a single (electric!) typewriter, a telephone and a few desks. He assured us that Manley's proposed bar on foreign ownership had been abandoned. We handed over a check on the Bank of Nova Scotia Jamaica, signed papers, and became owners of the land. (It would take two more years to get our registered title from the Jamaican bureaucracy; soon come!)

Our vacation home was under way; we flew home making lists of things to do.

# 11

## Telegrams; the hammock

In the era of e-mail, it's hard to remember when people used telegrams to communicate speedily. In 1972, telephone service in Treasure Beach wasn't even on the horizon. A single pay phone in Black River was often broken.

Mail took at least a week each way. It came to the Calabash Bay Postal Agency in a little red van still marked -- a decade after independence -- "Royal Post." The P.A.was a ten-by-ten-foot concrete cubicle with a barred front window and a back door kept wide open to let in some breeze. Two miles from us, it was open from 10 to noon and from 2 to 4, weekdays only. The postmistress seemed always to have someone with her in the tiny box, chatting away idle hours.

Telegrams went to the Treasure Beach Post Office (P.O.), a slightly-bigger building a mile farther away, open all day weekdays and Saturday mornings. Wires arrived by a dedicated line -- the only telephone line to this area -- over which a clerk in Black River spelled the message out letter-by-letter, using the Jamaican equivalent of our army's "Able-Baker-Charlie" code, while the postmistress copied it down. She spelled outgoing messages to Black River the same way.

Overnight telegrams, "night letters," cost half as much and arrived at our house just as quickly. The reason: An old man riding a burro came to the post office every weekday morning to collect any telegrams and take them to recipients, paid only by tips. Wires arriving after mid-morning would wait a day; those arriving Friday afternoon would wait until Monday. We were at the end of the burro-route, so delivery was usually in late afternoon.

●

Having a house built 1,600 miles away, by a builder one has met only once, is no recipe for peace of mind; sluggish communications made it more nerve-wracking. In retrospect, our house was completed in an amazingly short time, but it wasn't always easy. Lester Lyn was a fine builder -- and a terrible correspondent.

I wrote in early May, two weeks after our return, asking what progress he was making.

Silence.

We endured another two weeks, then wrote again, the first of several "fill-in-the-blanks" letters I tried: I'm sure you're busy, so just check off how you're doing: Plans re-drawn? Approved? Power line brought in? Site bulldozed? Tank and tower delivered?

Ten days later still, Mr. Lyn's first letter arrived, having crossed in the mail. "I had the opportunity of speaking with the Building Officer, and he has given us the go-ahead." The "expediting" money had worked; only much later would I appreciate the extraordinary speed with which bureaucracy had moved. The final plans and a formal contract would be in the mail shortly, he wrote; he would start work May 30$^{th}$.

It was by now early June; work must be under way!

He would first truck in coarse marl, a crumbly limestone gravel with some cement-like properties. Our land was reached by a public right-of-way from the Parish Council road to the sea. The same hardpan as Mister Arthur's land; the rutted track was turned into a slippery clay mud by even a passing shower. The marl, spread out with Mr. Lyn's bulldozer and packed down by trucks, would become a semi-permanent pavement.

He would then level the top of the knoll, stake out the corners, and begin construction.

A letter from Miss Sheila arrived; she'd gone to inspect. The roadway was done, the site flattened, the corner batten-boards in place. A small bulldozer (a "tractivator") was parked at the site, but no sign of workmen. The first copy of the *National Geographic* we'd sent her children had arrived; thank you. Mister Erwin had gone to the agricultural station at Hounslow, to find that the helpful man was no longer there, but he'd find someone else to sell us fruit trees. I began to wonder if we would be buying government stock.

Letters from Miss Hilma and Lancel Graham, dated early June, reported that concrete block, fine marl, re-bars, cement and lumber had appeared, but still no workmen.

I sent Mr. Lyn an overnight telegram:

CONTRACT NOT ARRIVED YET WORRIED ABOUT NOVEMBER COMPLETION PLEASE REPORT PROGRESS BY RETURN MAIL.

My impatience was unmerited: The contract, promising a finished house by October 31, arrived two days later. There were a few minor changes we could live with, but a few important details he'd overlooked. He'd forgotten to include the final blueprints, and made no mention of having a bedroom finished by the end of August. I wrote again. His reply reached us a few weeks later: He would fix the oversights and send copies of the blueprints. He was under way, making progress, but wasn't sure about a bedroom by August.

Another letter: "Almost up to belt course."

Building on a sand dune, he'd explained, required deep, wide footings, from which the foundation and walls would rise to roof level. There the re-bars poking up would be tied into a horizontal girdle of re-bars cast all the way around, the "belt course."

(A pitched roof pushes walls out. Early European cathedrals like Notre Dame solved the problem with heavy "flying buttresses." American houses have 2x6 stringers, a horizontal platform to which the pitched rafters are nailed, absorbing the lateral stress. Lumber is expensive here, so builders cast a belt around the top of the walls to hold them upright.)

Oh, yes, he wrote, the roofing company had stopped making light blue. We could have white, red or deep green; "please let us know which of the three you will settle for."

Pleased at the progress, we settled by return mail for red, along with another fill-in-the-answers questionnaire. Before he started the roofing, red would be out of stock too, or else our letter arrived too late. We got deep green. It was just fine.

●

Meanwhile, apart from worrying -- and pursuing professional lives, taking children to music lessons and helping revive a Cub Scout troop -- we planned an advertising campaign. Who might be attracted to our out-of-the-way paradise? People like ourselves, we hoped, who read the same egghead publications. We explored classifieds in *World*, *Saturday Review* (remember them?), *Atlantic*, *Harper's*, *The New Republic* and the Sunday *New York Times*, at 60 cents to $1.70 a word. Penny-pinching, we wrestled with wording, finally decided on

MODERN VACATION VILLA on Jamaica's unspoiled southwest shore. Four bedrooms, two baths, maid-cook, $250/ week (203)247-0759

and ordered one or two insertions in each for early fall. We spent about $150; cheap enough, but we would sell stock from Brad's inheritance to pay Mr. Lyn.

We would name the house *Hikaru*, from a Japanese word meaning "bright, shining." The ideograph was simple enough that I could write it and incorporate it in the piece we would mail inquirers, an identifiable (if incomprehensible) logo.

This was BC, BK -- before computers, before Kinko's. I typed out the elements of a two-page brochure and pasted them onto a dummy, fitting in black-and-white photos we'd taken in April. The pictures artfully showed the view from a house that wasn't there yet. Two views from the beach hid the house site behind trees. One of the new instant-printer places produced 50 copies.

We bought linens and towels, used and laundered them, and sent them off. Miss Hilma wrote that she'd received them, but offered no other useful information.

Covering a Democratic nominating convention, I encountered a former newspaper colleague, now the incumbent congressman's administrative aide. He wanted to take his young family on a long holiday right after the election, as far from politics as possible. A place with no telephones sounded perfect. Our first paying guest! We rented him three weeks, and planned to join him for the last of those weeks, at Thanksgiving.

I wrote Mr. Lyn that we counted on him to stay on schedule. No answer.

My latest questionnaire came back dated August 5. He was still "almost" at belt course. He was having trouble building the patio cistern. The prospect of having a bedroom for us in August was (he crossed out all but my last choice) "hopeless." The driveway gate wasn't built, the tank and tower weren't up, no electricity yet nor well pump; all that would be completed by the end of September.

I'd asked about weather in October -- nominally hurricane season -- in case we had to postpone our planned inspection trip. "Not able to tell," he filled in, "it goes and comes."

We decided I should go down alone in late August.

In our attic was a jungle hammock, Army-surplus camping equipment I'd used two decades earlier while touring the United States in a Model A Ford; I packed it into a duffel bag.

I would stay the first night at an inn at Bluefields, halfway to Treasure Beach. I didn't want to find a campsite after dark; and perhaps subconsciously I wanted a retreat if things weren't going well at Billy's Bay. A young American, Joe DeLuca, and his Jamaican wife had restored a former "great house," or plantation mansion; they hoped to make a living as innkeepers despite the paucity of South Coast tourism.

They and their inn were charming, but they had tales of woe about getting things done in Jamaica: bureaucracy, lack of skilled workmen, the soon-come syndrome. It was a conversation I would gladly have skipped.

Their only other guest was a Texas oilman exploring reserves with dynamite-and-echo equipment. The entire Caribbean, he said, had been a vast shallow sea -- from Venezuela to Texas and Louisiana -- in the Carboniferous era. There must be oil here, too, although he so far hadn't found enough to be commercially viable.

On one hand, I was sorry: Except for bauxite, Jamaica had little but low-profit sugar and bananas to sell in world markets; even a modest oil strike would have been a boon. On the other hand, I didn't want a busy port, spills and oil slicks on our pristine South Coast.

●

By noon next day I was at Billy's Bay.

There was a house, sure enough, and no need to retreat. The walls were up to belt course; the roof was yet unframed. The cistern was a huge concrete box sunk into the ground behind a handsome cut-stone wall; from its floor, two stout square concrete pillars rose to the level of the patio floor, and then on up to the roof-deck.

Mr. Lyn said they had dug it out -- with hand labor -- and quit for a weekend, during which the dry sand slid back into the hole. They'd dug it out again; the sand slumped back in overnight. They finally put up plywood sheets as they dug, and cast concrete walls up to ground level before the sides gave way again.

Save for the pillars, it would have made an adequate handball court. I climbed in to measure it and do the math: It would hold 16,000 gallons. The roof area would collect a thousand gallons in a one-inch rainstorm. In a typical year, we'd have enough rain to fill the cistern at least once, perhaps twice -- ample for drinking water, with a reserve if the well pump failed and we had to use rainwater for showers and toilets. (I'd designed a set of valves so the entire system could draw from either side of the tower -- foresight for which I would more than once congratulate myself.)

Roy Reid and a few men were building the flat triangular form into which the patio roof would be cast. It was awesome: 48 feet on the hypotenuse, a complex of plywood boxes and re-bar skeletons, including the horizontal beams that would rest on the cistern columns and support the whole deck.

Meanwhile, other workmen mixed and poured cement into the cavities of the cement blocks, from which re-bars poked up, tied into horizontal re-bars that would soon be cast into the long-promised belt course. An electrician, a slight, very dark-skinned man, was staying just ahead of them guiding wiring down those cavities into wall boxes and into Roy Reid's patio deck form for the overhead lights and outlet.

The busy electrician, we learned later, found time to father a child with our neighbor Miss Blossom, presumably while Mister Philip was at far sea. The dark-skinned boy would unmistakably not be Philip's, but would be accepted; Philip's oldest son wasn't Miss Blossom's. Few thought this scandalous. "He's a bastard," our neighbor Endley Parchment (with whom I'd sung "me donkey want wah-tah" at the Putnams') once told me in describing someone's parentage. It was a statement of fact, not a pejorative. He had a bastard child of his own in the village.

A bunkhouse stood by the driveway. It had been trucked down from Mandeville, a plywood box into which some ten workmen stowed themselves at night, the way the mutinous slave workers disappeared below decks in Melville's *Benito Cereno*. One man was also cook, preparing the standard Jamaican peas-and-rice plus fish from the beach. None of our neighbors was in the work crew, but at least they were making a little extra money with a hungry demand for seafood.

After dinner, the men played dominoes by lantern-light. It's a noisy game; they slapped the tiles down hard on a plank table. I watched, trying to understand why my childhood pastime engaged grown men. They held the tiles fanned in their hands like cards; the strategy seemed like poker, although their heavy patois -- heavier than usual for my benefit? -- made it hard to follow. They invited me to join the game. I declined, and went to my hammock to fall asleep to the sibilance of the sea.

Mr. Lyn came down every other weekend to truck them home to their families; I was reminded of progressive American prisons that allowed connubial visits. Most of the men were paid the going rate for "common labor," the equivalent of about US$2 a day. None of our neighbors would have worked for so little money, let alone worked so hard.

When I'd built our Connecticut house, I'd run a little concrete mixer from that temporary power service. There was still no electricity here; everything was done with muscle-power. Two workmen spent the day mixing cement, marl and water on what had become a huge flat concrete apron in the driveway, using short-handled square shovels to scoop up the ingredients until they were well mixed into a thick slurry. Two men heaved pailfuls of concrete to a man atop the walls to fill the block cavities.

Two others were kept busy wheeling barrows of marl, carrying 100-pound sacks of cement and fetching water. They tossed roped buckets into the well, and lugged them back up the hill through sand so loose it was like walking through an uphill swamp.

When they started pouring the patio roof deck, they would do nothing but lug, wheel, mix and carry for several days.

Richard Todd's tank-builder had tired of waiting and had trucked the tank and tower -- heavy angle-iron legs and braces, an out-sized Erector set contraption -- from Kingston. Both were stacked beside the driveway. The tank was divided in half as I'd specified.

The Kingston man would have used his truck-mounted crane to set the tower on footings, had they been ready, and would then have hoisted up the tank. With power and a well-pump installed – which would have to be done eventually -- Roy Reid's crew could have pumped water to the tower and drawn it with a garden hose; the concrete could have been mixed far more efficiently.

Yes, that might have saved later work, Mr. Lyn said, but they'd been too busy. Cheap labor, as I'd sensed when we signed the contract, is no incentive for labor-saving.

The tank was a massive box of half-inch steel, the stuff ships are made of. Four feet wide and deep, eight feet long, it must have weighed a ton. I pushed to see if I could rock it; it didn't budge.

How would they get it up now? They would use ropes to tip the tower into place, Mr. Lyn said, and get the tank atop it with jim-poles.

Jim-poles? He explained: They would set the tank beside the tower, and nudge it gradually upward with stout poles of increasing length, inching it up the slightly-inclined framework of the tower until finally the massive tank was at the top of the tower and could be levered into its steel cradle. I blanched to think what would happen if it fell.

When I came back in November, the whole thing would be in place exactly as specified; Mr. Lyn and Roy Reid would be nonchalant about what it took to get the job done.

●

I had supper with Erwin and Sheila. She urged me to stay with them, but I'd already tied my jungle hammock between two lignum vitaes thirty yards below the house, where I could absorb as much as possible of this maelstrom of activity.

That proved a happy choice: It made my reputation as the crazy American who slept in a sling.

Our natural windbreak is the sea-grape, whose fruit is only remotely like vine grapes: a huge nut-like seed, a tough skin and very little pulp. It was in season. On my first morning, three neighbor children arrived soon after dawn with gifts, cones of folded newspaper filled with grapes they had picked down by the sea.

I unzipped my netting to accept their offerings with elaborate gratitude, and ate a few. They were bitter and astringent; I smiled my thanks with a puckered mouth. "You're welcome," they said, and stood somberly. I finally told them I was going to get up and get dressed now, and they must run along. They did. Given only slightly more privacy, I dressed, washed my face and brushed my teeth by the well, and drove off for breakfast from Miss Sheila.

Before the day was out, a dozen more children had brought me paper cones of sea grapes. After dark, when I came back from dinner with the Hamiltons, I walked down to the beach and disposed of them in a retreating tide.

I slept well in the hammock. Summer sunset in this latitude is at 6:30. After watching dominoes after dinner, there wasn't much to do but sleep. First light was before 6:00. I rose early, and after that first morning made a breakfast of bananas and oranges, but I was never ahead of the hard-working construction crew.

The ani were up early, too, looking for insects in the trees around me.

Named for its screechy *AH-knee, AH-knee* call, the smooth-billed cuckoo has a bill with a huge hump, like a pugilist whose nose has been broken too many times. Glossy-black, long-tailed, almost as big as a crow, it flies in a series of flaps and glides. It's so heavy that branches bob up and down as it hops out in search of breakfast, what became one of my favorite morning performances.

On my way down the beach for a morning swim, I caught sight of a crab-catcher, and froze almost as still as the bird. Two feet tall, with grey plumage and a feathery head-tuft, the yellow-crowned night heron often stalks our beach, moving with glacial slowness. One long, jointed yellow leg reaches for a new footing, the claws outstretched, the very definition of tip-toe.

It brings its weight forward, one step every minute or two, head cocked to one side. It is listening for the rustle of hermit crabs; silence is its camouflage. If I'm lucky, I see it suddenly jab forward, plunging its thick, pointed bill deep into the sand, bringing up an impaled crab.

Craning skyward, it gulps its prey down. I applaud, breaking the spell; it flies 50 yards down the beach to resume its stalking.

●

With the house now a concrete shell, I could visualize its setting better. The calabash tree below the house would impede the view. Brother Elbert and his son-in-law helped cut it down with a Swedish bow saw I'd brought, and cut it into stove lengths; they were glad for the fuel.

After three days, I'd learned all there was to learn. Mr. Lyn was fulfilling his contract, and insisted he could meet his October 31 deadline. Brother Elbert, waiting for posts, had done no fencing and so no planting. Mr. Lyn, unembarrassed at having forgotten, promised posts early the next week.

I rolled the hammock back into the duffel bag, left it for Mister Wilford to stow with our linens at Folichon, and drove west to Negril. I had an utterly relaxing day at The Sundowner, another of the "inns of Jamaica," before going on to MoBay and flying home to report to Brad that our house was on its way to completion.

# 12

## Miss Esmie, Mister Endley, Merrick

**W**ilford Clarke's October 23 letter arrived November 2, 1972 -- eleven days before our first guests -- Mal, my former colleague, with Mary and their two children -- were to arrive:

"Hilma got the opportunity for Canada as she had rote and tell you so she left on the 21st of October." Not to worry, he wrote: He and his sisters Daphne and Katurah would clean up behind Mr. Lyn's workmen, arrange the furniture and take the bedding and linens out of storage. They had a successor to our chosen housekeeper.

Miss Hilma's letter didn't in fact arrive until several days later. Mister Wilford's letter, however, took the mystery out of a telegram that had arrived that morning, from Miss Katurah:

GOT WOMAN TO WORK FOR HILMA SISTERINLAW IF OK GIVING HER UNIFORM REPLY.

We wired back:

GRATEFUL FOR YOUR AND WILFORDS HELP PLEASE PROCEED FURNISHING WAIT UNIFORM GUESTS ARRIVE THIRTEENTH LETTER FOLLOWS.

We wired Lester Lyn that someone other than Miss Hilma would take charge of the house.

●

People have long been Jamaica's most important export. Like other nations such as Ireland and Lebanon, the island loses some of its most able citizens: They go to earn more, and enjoy a better living standard, in the United States, Canada and Great Britain. They usually send some of their earnings to family left behind, but Jamaica loses some of its best go-getters.

Miss Hilma had a job as caregiver to an elderly Canadian woman. We could hardly blame her for leaving us in the lurch: She would make more than we could offer, and could probably apply for citizenship. She might have given us some hint, but she doubtless wanted to keep our bird in hand until the other came out of the bush.

There had been the usual silence from Lester Lyn after my August visit. In early October, I wrote querulously: Miss Sheila had written that it seemed unlikely he would finish on time.

He wrote back just as testily; I should pay no attention to neighbors. He hadn't been ready when the furniture was trucked over from Highgate when Abe Eslom tired of keeping it in his limited storage space. Mr. Lyn had shuffled some of it from room to room as his workmen finished up, and had stored some in his Mandeville home, but it would all be in place by the 13th.

Sure enough, he sent a full-rate wire November 11th:

CONSTRUCTION COMPLETE FURNITURE AND APPLIANCES INSTALLED NOW AWAITING PUBLIC SERVICE CONNECTION HAVE BEEN BADGERING THEM SINCE TUESDAY WILL CONTINUE TO DO SO TILL CONNECTION IS MADE WILL PHONE AS CONNECTION IS MADE.

Our letter to Miss Katurah, saying we'd like to meet our new housekeeper before finalizing her position, arrived after Mal and Mary did; I should have sent it with them. We'd sent material to Miss Hilma to have uniforms made, and didn't want to have the cloth cut to fit someone who didn't fit our expectations.

Mal and Mary weren't our only booking: We had the house occupied during most of December and January -- some friends, but some who responded to our early ads. Great start in the rental business! But could we be sure they'd be well taken care of?

Our fears were unnecessary. Hilma's sister-in-law who had stepped into the breach was Miss Esmie, whose husband Don, a far-sea fisherman, was one of the seemingly innumerable Clarke siblings. With Katurah, Daphne and Wilford, she had unpacked our duffel bags of linens and made the house ready. Mal and Mary felt well received.

Nonetheless, we arrived two weeks later to find a stranger in charge. We got acquainted, and were pleased to find her a good cook and an amiable person. She wasn't as articulate as her sisters-in-law, and would prove to be barely literate. She was a pinch-hitter, but she would do.

We set to work instructing her in how we wanted the house run: Turn back the beds while guests are enjoying happy hour; ask if they want their rooms sprayed for stray mosquitoes; discuss with them at breakfast the next few days' menus; ask if they want their meals spicier or blander.

In retrospect, we would wish we'd spent more time with Miss Esmie, but there were other demands on our time.

●

We placed the Highgate furniture; some had been piled in a bedroom, awaiting our decision. It was beautiful stuff, and it didn't take us long to distribute it where we'd intended.

The house was finished, but raw: It looked naked on its sandy knoll. The sea-almond I'd planted with Brother Elbert, however, was surviving nicely on its sand hill, and had fresh growth. The land was at last wholly fenced in. Mr. Lyn had built a handsome driveway gate, but we needed a proper gate instead of the barbed-wire-and-hook closure at the beach.

Walking down to the beach was a struggle through loose sand. Brother Elbert agreed that we ought to have concrete steps and a walkway. He returned with Endley Parchment.

Mister Endley would become one of my favorite neighbors, a short, stocky, light-skinned man, a charming reprobate. In another society and economy – that is, if he'd had capital – he might have been a successful home-builder. In Jamaica, he was a competent jack-of-all-trades, a carpenter, mason and cabinet-maker. Even in that he might have prospered, but he was a man who worked in fits and starts.

He not only did the outdoor work I've mentioned for us; a few years later he also made some impressive furniture for one of our neighbors.

He and others were reminders that our success was in large part the result of picking American parents.

Mister Endley loved his rum, and I supposed was a ganja user. In later years, he would get religion and go on the wagon for a time, declining such earthly temptations as singing with The Buccaneers. He soon fell from grace, and I was not sorry. The fishermen's band wasn't the same without his sly raunchy lyrics and showmanship.

Yes, he said, he and Brother Elbert could build a steps and walkways from the house to the sea. We walked down together, calculating what was needed. I suggested paying them by the day. Mister Endley countered, proposing a contract: They would calculate how many days it might take, and agree to do it for a fixed price; their risk if it took longer.

They came back next day with a price. I agreed, and paid them in advance. If I'd been more alert, I might have seen Brother Elbert's raised eyebrows, but I was new at this.

Mister Endley listed materials they would need: cement, re-bars, nails, marl, a few planks to form steps. We walked back to the driveway to see how much material Lester Lyn had left. Not much. Just as well: We wanted to begin landscaping that area, the "gateway" to our Hikaru, and didn't want piles of marl greeting guests.

Brother Elbert's yard was wide enough that a truck could get past his house and Mister Valney's. He would cut a wire gate through the fence he'd just built, so a load of coarse marl, followed by another load of fine marl, could be dumped in our yard. I made the half-hour trip up to Southfield to place the order.

●

One comes on Southfield suddenly. The road twists and turns, not quite switchbacks but tracking up a steep grade to an elevation of 1,500 feet. A final turn reveals perhaps 200 yards of a shopping district. Gayle's Supermarket and Hardware dominates the inland side, set back to allow head-in parking, creating the illusion of an open square.

A barn-sized open door leads into the hardware side. Several kitchen sinks are stacked to the right of the doorway, a plastic-laminate counter stands on end. In a horse-sized stall to the left are rolls of chicken wire, hog fence, barbed wire and binding wire. In the next stalls are scoop shovels and rakes and garden hoses; beyond them are shelf-alleys of paint, mostly in gallon cans.

A 40-foot wooden counter, with the scratches and patina of honorable service, runs the length of the right-hand side. The entire wall behind, from floor to twelve-foot ceiling, is a grid of wooden boxes, most the size of a shoe-box, filled with every imaginable plumbing or electrical part. This was at the time the best-stocked builders' supply house in this half of the island.

Three clerks – my favorite is old Mister Mac, but his younger colleagues are almost as able – climb up to retrieve an item and set it on the counter: "That be the one? Somethin' else?" When my list is exhausted, it is written up in triplicate in a receipt book, and the entire book is handed over to Miss Cynthia, a pretty young mother in a little cashier's cage. She checks the math and has me sign.

This was always our destination when we came to Southfield; any other shopping need could be met in Black River, which was also home to most government agencies and, at that time, the only banks. Although the store has gradually modernized – Merrick Gayle was first on the Internet, first to computerize his bookkeeping and inventory – the basic layout is unchanged.

Merrick himself was even in those years seldom in the store; he had a backroom office no more pretentious than the hardware section, where he planned the expansion of the small family empire he'd taken over from his parents. He wanted to make Southfield a center of commerce.

In his early 30s when we first knew him, he soon took a pretty young wife from Kingston who helped in the store, but they remained childless. He was a justice of the peace, a moving force in South Coast tourism, an upland game hunter and leader of a sportsmen's club, and on the side raised German shepherd guard dogs. He would soon begin offering horseback rides along the high bluff of Lover's Leap, but there wasn't yet enough tourism to sustain it. An entrepreneur.

The supermarket, next door to the hardware, was like those anywhere in Jamaica, recognizably patterned on an American model, but much smaller. One picked up a plastic basket rather than a push-cart, and slipped through a quaint turnstile near the door. The long rows of display shelves were wooden, stocked with a meager variety of staples: sugar, flour, canned vegetables and fruit and stew; bottles of bleach; boxes of laundry soap; rum and gin and beer; paper goods; baby oil and baby nutritional supplements – a very big item in Jamaica -- and pots and pans.

One could usually find most of what one had come for, but rarely everything; shortages were chronic. In the rear of the store was a small open freezer with meat and chicken, and a very small display of vegetables and fruit; in a farming town, one didn't come to the supermarket for produce. One could pick up the *Daily Gleaner* near the checkout.

The supermarket side was cheerfully presided over by Merrick's mother, a light-skinned, bespectacled woman with her hair tied back in a prim bun. Always in a baggy print dress, she might have stepped out of Grant Wood's *American Gothic*. She often sat at one of the two checkout cash registers; otherwise one was checked out by an indifferent young woman. Purchases were usually packed into used cardboard boxes, which cost the store nothing, rather than in paper bags. A young man eager for tips would carry the boxes to the car.

Next door to Gayle's complex was the post office, no busier than the one at Treasure Beach. There was a nondescript little restaurant, a minimal gas station, and beyond that the furniture store owned by D.R. Ebanks, scion of another of Southfield's entrepreneurial families.

On the east side of the "highway" from Mandeville to Black River (but not a very busy road) were a few unpretentious shops, including a pharmacy, a hair-dressing salon, a bar and a public library. There were often a few street vendors on that side, selling fruit and vegetables.

A half-mile farther up, 50 yards off the road, was the concrete block plant run by the Parchments, the third of Southfield's major families. (Parchment is a name more common here than Smith or Jones; Mister Endley was no kin to the Southfield family.)

At the "plant," a few men shoveled marl and cement into a gasoline-powered mixer, and then poured the concrete into molds set up on benches. They barely kept ahead of demand, so there was rarely much cured block. More often than not – especially if I wanted four-inch block for wall-building – one of the Parchment sons would promise to make and send my order in a few days.

From time to time they made decorative block to dress the top of walls, choosing whatever pattern they fancied at the moment. We have at least four designs of decorative block atop our walls, a motley mix.

In the coming years, as Southfield's cool climate attracted a growing residential community of successful Jamaicans, the Parchments would open a hardware store to compete with Merrick; Ebanks would expand his furniture store; and one of the Gayle brothers would modernize and expand the gas station. Merrick himself would open an ice cream store, a better restaurant and a farm-supply store, and would persuade Worker's Bank to open a branch across the street – making Southfield a more important commercial center than Black River.

That was all years away.

●

Lester Lyn came down. We made final payment, and commissioned him to build a cut-stone terrace wall below the house, embracing our young sea-almond. He would do the work after our spate of high-season guests; we'd fill it with beach sand, after which he would build a little cut-stone well around the tree. He was obliging, setting aside our testy exchange of letters and telegrams.

On the road from Black River I'd noticed a wrought-iron shop. The owner, a gentle man with a deaf-mute daughter, agreed to make a gate for the opening in the sea-fence. Brother Elbert and Mister Endley would build concrete posts for the gate -- on contract, of course.

The "wrought iron" was in fact, -- as it is to this day in Jamaica -- welded re-bars. Only later would we learn how vulnerable reinforcing bars are to sea-frost. The re-bar gate would last only two seasons before deep rust appeared; we held it together two more years with thick coats of RustOleum paint brought from home. With advice from my metallurgist father, I learned to prime wrought re-bars with zinc oxide paint to slow the rust -- but nothing would stop it.

One more piece of work: After my August visit, we'd envisioned a Jamaican-style thatched hut gazebo near the sea-gate. A wonderful idea, Brother Elbert said. Would it be durable? Oh, yes: A good thatched roof would last 20 years or more. He couldn't build one himself, but he could with Mister Endley. He would go to Thatchville for the raw material.

As the thatch palm grows taller, its lower branches die off; the dead fronds can be tugged off, although with some care because mud-wasps nest in them. Then the fronds must be "pressed" -- ironed flat by piling on boards and stones. He would have his friend pick and sell him 50 or so fronds, and hire someone with a pickup truck to bring them to Hikaru.

We gave him money to buy the fronds and get them to Billy's Bay, but postponed the actual construction until our next visit when I could supervise the hut's location -- and see the process.

●

Although my list of needed embellishments grew daily, it was a lovely house, and the natural surroundings continued to delight us. One afternoon, sitting on our patio with Mal and Mary, we watched a pair of man-o'-wars give a fishing lesson to their three youngsters.

Properly called the magnificent frigatebird, the man-o'-war is one of the most aerial of ocean-living birds, with a huge wingspan -- almost four feet -- in proportion to its light body. Like other pelagic birds, it spends 24 hours a day at sea, coming ashore only in mating and breeding season. The male has a red neck-wattle, not unlike our turkey's, except that it's an inflatable organ it can blow up to nearly the size of a football in its courting ritual.

We see them only occasionally sporting that bright red sex symbol, but in drabber attire they are often at Treasure Beach, soaring high over the ocean. They come closer as fishermen return from far sea, grabbing an easy meal as the men sort out the catch and throw runts overboard.

Unlike most ocean birds, the man-o'-war can't rest in the sea or even dive into the water, because it can't take off from the ocean surface. Always airborne, it must snatch its dinner from the surface -- or rob other birds of their catch.

The sea was calm; a school of fish must have been driven to the surface by predatory bigger fish below. One of the youngsters would swoop down, spear a fish in its talons, and try to get away to eat its catch. Its siblings would abandon their own scan of the ocean to chase after the successful nestmate in an avian dogfight worthy of World War I biplanes, trying to snatch the fish from the sibling's claws.

The mid-air tussle often produced a zero-sum game: The fish would fall from the competing talons back into the sea.

This comic show went on more than an hour; the parents soared about screeching advice, while the juveniles, almost as big as their parents but with distinguishing white bellies and heads, tried again and again to catch a fish and keep it long enough to cram it into their beaks while in flight. We sat together, laughing aloud.

On our last night, we sat on the patio as evening fell, sipping a rum drink. On the horizon, perhaps eight miles away, were the thick cumulus clouds that form most evenings as moisture, drawn up from the sun-warmed sea, cools and condenses. A few flashes of lightning illuminated the distant clouds, but overhead the stars and Milky Way began to appear in a luminous clear sky.

Miss Esmie seemed competent and obliging; we told her to have her uniforms made.

# 13

# Customs and customs

We had not until now dealt with Jamaican customs. Like most vacationers arriving at Montego Bay, we'd followed the green "Nothing to Declare" signs, and were waved through without even opening a bag. November 1972 had been our first visit as homeowners, but since we'd shipped the linens down earlier, we'd even then had nothing to declare.

Most Jamaicans, returning from an American holiday or coming to visit relatives, arrived with hundreds of dollars' worth of acquisitions, from technological gadgets to clothing much cheaper in U.S. discount superstores than in Jamaica. They dutifully headed for the red-flagged booths to open their bags – I hadn't known one could buy such huge soft-sided suitcases --and taped-together boxes.

An agent would rummage around, more often than not making them take everything out. They paid stiff import duties before repacking their booty (trying but seldom succeeding in making everything fit the way it had) and leaving the customs area. We'd observed the process with detached amusement.

Now, on our first February vacation at our new home, we were overdue for a reality check.

We collected our luggage from a late-afternoon flight and innocently headed for the green lines. There were eight of us: Emily and Ken each brought a young friend; my mother and father had come from Phoenix to meet us in Miami.

Mom, in retirement, had taken up painting, and discovered a gift. She'd brought a dozen framed oils of tropical and desert flowers to decorate our new house; Dad had carefully packed them with plastic bubble paper and cardboard. It didn't occur to us they were dutiable.

We'd also brought a new, inexpensive bicycle for Miss Esmie's son Lionel; we assumed it too, as a gift, would be duty-free. One can hardly hide a bike. The customs agent stopped us. Sorry, he said, you'll have to pay for that; and by the way, what's in the cardboard wrappings?

We showed him Mom's paintings. Works of art! he said, starting to thumb through his guide to determine the tax rate.

No, no! I said. We'll pay duty on the bicycle, but the paintings are surely personal possessions; my dear old mother painted them herself, and they have no real value. (Untrue: to this day we hear them praised by guests.)

Mom stepped up to take credit for her works. Her white hair carried the day. The customs officer waved them through, but sent me to the cashier to pay for the bicycle, duty amounting to about a third of the bike's value. He'd been distracted enough not to open the two duffel bags, which had more towels and linens and other barely-used household equipment.

There is a travel addendum to Murphy's Law: Once things start going wrong, they keep going wrong. I'd planned to have our neighbor Hedley Gayle meet us to carry four of our group; I would load most of our luggage and the other four of us into the station wagon I'd reserved.

Our car rental agency didn't have a wagon; nor did any other. I settled for a compact Japanese sedan. I'd brought clothesline, anticipating that the bicycle might have to be tied on. I ended up with the bike on the rear bumper and the duffel bags on the roof, tied down through the open windows of the rear doors -- which of course couldn't be opened once the ropes were knotted. We looked a bit like John Steinbeck's Joad family setting out from Oklahoma.

It was by now clear that Hedley Gayle wasn't going to arrive. At 9 p.m., I dickered a price with a taxi driver. He wasn't sure where Treasure Beach was, and would follow me.

Halfway over, I realized that I'd lost him, and doubled back. He'd had a flat tire. We mounted his spare, got under way again, and arrived at midnight.

The house was dark; Miss Esmie hadn't waited up for us. I had a key and let us in, only to discover that she hadn't understood we would be a full house. After making up the beds, we stubbornly went for a moonlight swim in a calm sea before collapsing.

●

I'm usually up at first light in Jamaica, even after a late night. Brother Elbert was up ahead of me, ready for our ritual walk.

I'd noticed one problem as we walked down for our night swim: Endley Parchment had only half-finished the concrete steps and walkway to the sea. Brother Elbert scolded me tactfully for having paid the full contract price before the job was finished. I now remembered his raised eyebrow. The custom here, he explained, was to pay when the job was done. If I felt generous, I might pay half up front, but no more than that.

Once bitten, twice shy: Reserving final payment until the job is done is a custom I've faithfully observed ever since. After breakfast, Brother Elbert fetched Mister Endley, who went back to work and finished the walkway within a few days. He'd been busy, he apologized.

I also learned, on our morning round, that the well pump had quit a few days earlier. (Another addendum to Murphy's axiom: Things break down just before Mister Don arrives. I guess that's a plus: I can deal with problems and not inflict them on paying guests. But it's always a jolt to arrive and discover unexpected chores. "Why didn't you write me that this needed fixing?" "It jes' happened, Mist' Don.")

I drove to the post office to wire Lester Lyn. The plumber-electrician he sent down -- that afternoon, miraculously -- spent several hours tinkering, and finally took the pump back to Mandeville for repair. Until he returned a few days later, we skipped showers, settling for sea-baths.

Brother Elbert pointed out the planting failures: The Spanish pear hadn't made it, nor the bananas; too little consistent moisture even down in the hollow. The breadfruit tree by the drive was barely surviving, "quailing, sah, despite my best effort." (I'd looked the word up the first time he used it. Webster allows it: "to lose heart".) Breadfruit, too, wants lots of water, and loses heart in our dry climate.

The rest was doing handsomely. Brad and I both enjoy gardening at home; the tropics provide almost-instant gratification. In a mere six months, one of the flame trees had grown from a knee-high stick to a three-foot promise. The oleander, bougainvillea, ixora and allamanda all showed signs of vigorous spring growth. (Despite its relatively uniform climate, Jamaica has a season of blossom and growth as the sun moves north from its winter retreat. At 18 degrees latitude, three-quarters of the way from the Equator to the Tropic of Cancer, spring comes early.)

Apart from the fecund climate, we credited Brother Elbert, who spent hours every day watering. He drew by the pailful from the well when the pump or power failed, one or the other distressingly often. I'd left him 100 feet of hose, but that didn't reach all the new plants, so he was still carrying bucketfuls to the most distant trees and plants. I made a note to buy him more hose from Gayle's.

When I praised his work, Brother Elbert blossomed like a spring flower. He was a fisherman, with far less gardening experience than I, but he reveled in learning new skills, and took enormous pride in the grounds left in his care.

●

After getting Mister Endley back to work and wiring Mr. Lyn, we resumed landscaping. Although the retaining wall for what we'd begun calling the Almond Terrace wasn't built yet, we could begin work on cactus-filled rock gardens on either side of the terrace.

Brother Elbert and Mister Valney went down at low tide to the shallow sea in front of the house with a sledgehammer to break off chunks of coral (the dead remains of what once was the barrier reef, which was now 10 or 20 yards farther out) and lug them up. Together, we arranged them on the sandy banks. Brad and I went back to our neighbor Dorothy Harris at Calabash Bay, who'd sold us the poinciana, to buy a carful of cactus, including some exotic Yucatan succulents she recommended.

One of them, to this day among my favorites, is a low-growing thornless cactus, a *stapelia*, like nubbly green hot dogs poking out of the ground. Almost every day it produces a blossom that looks like a wide-tentacled starfish, bigger than my hand, a buff color with intricate red veins.

There was also a tall, thick, spiny cactus with angular, almost square columns. It would be several years before we would fully appreciate our night-blooming cereus, which produces a cloud of huge, fragrant trumpet-shaped flowers on one midsummer night each year. On that night, the entire terrace is permeated with its sweetness.

Toward the end of the week, we laid out and started a series of steps and terraces in back of the house, where the sand threatened to slide away and expose the deep foundations Lester Lyn had built.

Like gardening, these were all new skills for Brother Elbert and Mister Valney; they obviously enjoyed the work and were eager to please. Imagine busting nondescript coral out of the sea and arranging it into a place of beauty! Imagine learning to lay up stone, mix mortar, and build a retaining wall! I left after ten days confident that they could finish the rear terraces to my satisfaction -- and be paid when they'd finished.

●

Even if I'd been able to tolerate the sun all day -- I got a good sunburn the first few days -- I couldn't spend all my time outdoors; there were chores inside the house.

Mom, Brad, Emily and her friend Lizzie became an expert panel to decide where to hang paintings. Mindful of the hard walls, I'd brought along a gadget to hammer in hooks with tiny concrete nails. We put up two paintings in each bedroom, and had some left over for the living room and dining nook. Mom's Arizona flowering cactus models were entirely at home here. She began sketching some uniquely Jamaican blossoms.

Other indoor chores: Several switches to overhead lights were mis-wired; dismayed at the slap-dash style of Jamaican electricians, I corrected them. I hung a small ship's bell outside the driveway door in lieu of a doorbell; drilled stops into the terrazzo floor so doors wouldn't bang against the walls; built shelves in our storage closet; wrote Mr. Lyn to have a missing tile cup-and-toothbrush holder put in the west bathroom.

The doors from each bedroom into that bath still didn't work as I'd planned. I wanted them hinged so their knobs nearly met when the doors were closed. An oversized hook from one to the other would assure the occupant privacy, but would have to be released on leaving, so one couldn't lock one's neighbor out. Mr. Lyn's workmen had hung them backward. I'd gotten that reversed last November, but he still hadn't managed the hook. I improvised one out of welding-rod. Eventually, I paid a shop in Hartford $10 for a wrought-iron hook.

In the midst of terracing and repairing and swimming, we found time for a committee meeting to plan the blasting of the reef opening described earlier. Mister Arthur would cudgel up money to match the grant, and would get fishermen to buy Ja$10 memberships in the co-op, which would manage the money. Bunny Delapenha promised to find a dynamite expert. We expected the job to be done long before our next visit.

●

It wasn't all work. Our son Ken, his friend Rollin, Dad and I drove up to Mandeville one day to get a close-up look at the bauxite industry. As a vice-president of Alcan, Dad had arranged a welcoming party.

The "red earth" that is bauxite must be strip-mined in awesome quantities. We saw it dug up by monster steam-shovels and transported by huge dump trucks, or loaded onto miles-long conveyor belts.

Some bauxite was sent by rail to a seaport such as Alligator Pond, 10 miles east of Treasure Beach, to be loaded as raw ore and shipped to the United States or Canada. Jamaica was even then, however, trying to capture more of the value of its principal export by managing the first-stage reduction -- from bauxite to a white powder called alumina - before it left the island. In a deceptively simple process, water is added to make a slurry of the red earth in huge tanks; then chemical agents make the alumina settle to the bottom of the tanks, later to be dried.

The left-over — a vast quantity of sterile red mud -- is one of Jamaica's major environmental problems. The mining companies buy up mountain valleys, dam them, and pump the mud to depths of several hundred feet. In later years, we would acquire a U.S. satellite color photo of Jamaica, on which the red-mud lakes are unmistakable, blobs of rusty red among the verdant mountains.

(During this decade, Jamaican authorities explored having bauxite processors pump their residue to deep underwater trenches off the coast. A howl from environmentalists and fishermen persuaded the government that ruining a few valleys every decade or so was better than risking its fishery or its tourist beaches.)

One of our guides at Alcan was Ted Tatham. British by birth, Ted had been educated in the United States, where his father was a diplomat. During World War II, in a Canadian uniform, he'd been stationed in Jamaica, where he met his wife-to-be, a third-generation Jamaican citizen of British origin. They'd spent a few years in western Canada, where Ted worked acquiring land rights for a Canadian mining company, and then came back to Jamaica.

Ted, like Joan, was now a Jamaican citizen. That wasn't just a legal technicality; he obviously cared about his adopted country. Over the years, he would again and again help us with village improvement efforts, not least of which was getting that reef opening blasted.

●

Dad and I joined the near-sea fishermen one morning to see what Treasure Beach fishing was all about. We got up before dawn, had a cup of coffee, and donned the life preservers I'd brought, conscious that none of the fishermen had them, even though we could swim and they couldn't. It was a wonderful introduction to the way our neighbors made their living.

And we swam every morning. The sea, when we arrived, was flat calm, hardly a wave breaking on the reef, which is why we'd been able to swim at midnight when we arrived. The water was crystal-clear, and what seemed like perpetual low tide made perfect snorkeling.

"The current be down and in," Brother Elbert and Mister Arthur both said. Fifty miles south, just beyond the shallow Pedro Banks, a deep-water ocean current sweeps westward toward the Yucatan Peninsula and then swings around Cuba, at which point it is called the Gulf Stream. It's that current whose nutrient-rich waters make the Pedro Banks a productive fishery. When it shifts a few miles north - - "down and in" -- it somehow flattens the waters on our South Coast. I've never found an oceanographer who could explain that phenomenon, but it occurs several times a year.

The sea remained calm the first week, and a nearly-full moon gave ample light for midnight skinny-dips. One night, we lucked into one of those rare moments when the sea is full of phosphorescent creatures that glow when disturbed. At the surfless surfing beach 300 yards to our west, we splashed the lazy sea into a luminous frenzy, and swam beyond the sandbar.

Such quiet water, however, is atypical. Even with calm-sea mornings, it is more usual to have waves on the reef by mid-day. As snorkeling deteriorates, bodysurfing improves on the sandbar. Before our ten-day vacation was over, we got to try that, too.

Among my childhood memories is learning to ride a wave on the New Jersey shore, where the folks rented a cottage for several summers. One year Dad took me to a lumberyard to buy a length of pine plank. Back at the cottage, he shaped it into a surfboard, a long version of what nowadays is called a flutterboard. The first time I used it, I let the point drop into the underwater sand shelf, catching my gut and knocking the wind out of me.

It was the kind of event one doesn't forget; I thought for a time I'd never catch another breath. Eventually I learned to use the board to prolong a ride, but also learned to body-surf without props; Dad was a skilled teacher.

By 1973, Dad's 70-year-old legs were failing him; getting down Mister Endley's new steps and walkway to the sea was an obstacle course, and even walking along the wet strand was work.

Once we reached the surfing beach, however, his age dropped away. He waded out onto the sandbar confidently, knowing the water would catch him if he stumbled, and was soon out where the waves were breaking. His timing hadn't failed him: He caught a wave and rode it in handsomely, and went back to do it again and again.

There are few pleasures in life comparable to seeing one's father resurrect one's youth.

●

In November, we'd paid little attention to how the house was run or how clean the kitchen was. We hadn't spent enough time working with Miss Esmie and her new second maid, our near neighbor Miss Geraldine.

Before the house was built, we'd patiently explained our wishes to Miss Hilma in great detail. In February, as in November, there were enough crises and distractions that training her successor got short shrift.

A letter from returning guests the next July would bring us up short. Miss Esmie had proved a less-than-perfect housekeeper and hostess, and had alienated some of our neighbors by flaunting her new status. They also said she had lined up a job as caregiver for a former guest of ours in the United States, and had applied for a passport and visa.

We would have a different kind of work to do on our next visit.

# 14

## Miss Olive

"**S**ah," said the small man in front of me, "you must hire my wife." He was an unlikely salesman, but much to my astonishment, we did indeed hire his wife a few days later. Miss Olive came to us the way Mary Poppins arrived at that English household: miraculously.

We had arrived on Saturday. On Monday, after consulting with Brother Elbert and having the major complaints verified, we parted company with Miss Esmie, explaining only that we couldn't risk her suddenly taking a U.S. job and leaving us in the lurch. Brad would take over cooking for the four of us until we found a replacement.

We began again interviewing applicants, some of whom we'd talked with a year and a half earlier. We were enthusiastic about only Hilma's sister Katurah, housekeeper at Coyaba, who'd taken charge and helped Miss Esmie get ready for our first guests. She was interested. Phil and Ianthe seemed on the verge of selling; by stealing their cook, we would merely hasten that decision. But Miss 'Turah was reluctant to take her fired sister-in-law's job.

Tuesday Brad came down with an infection. We were afraid it might be dengue fever, "break-bone fever" to Jamaicans, which can take several weeks to pass. We put her to bed, and Emily, just turned 16, took over the kitchen.

Wednesday morning Vincent Smalling presented himself. He was a dark, unattractive man with a bit of a limp and a gimpy eye under a pulled-down leather cap. He needed a shave and a bath. He knew us from the Putnams' party. I vaguely remembered him as the rumba-box player, the one-man percussion section.

We sat on the patio steps. Olive Smalling, he said, had worked at the hotel, and more recently had cooked for the power company's Major Moody when he weekended in Billy's Bay. She'd lost that job when he sold to the Manzellis and they tore his house down to start again.

Fine, I said; have her come for an interview.

"She can't, sah." She was now a trainee conductress on the bus that ran from Balaclava and Maggotty, miles inland, to Black River and Calabash Bay.

"How am I to meet her, then?"

The bus came to Calabash Bay at 10 in the morning, and tarried ten minutes before starting back. I could talk with her then.

It seemed crazy, but we were beginning to feel desperate -- and her credentials sounded good. I went to consult with Miss Sheila, who thought Miss Olive a fine candidate, and thought Miss 'Turah should definitely not take her sister-in-law's job. I picked up Mister Vincent Thursday morning and went to meet the bus.

It had broken down, we later learned. At 11, I gave up and came back to work. Going out after lunch to see if the bus had come, I drove as far as the police station, and met the sergeant in charge. He professed to be delighted to meet me, and promised to have his men look in on us from time to time. (It was an idle promise: The station had no cruiser, motorcycle or scooter. Still, buttering up the police couldn't hurt; I bought a $4 ticket to a policemen's ball several weeks after we'd fly home.)

That night a torrential rain drove water across the patio and under the bedroom and living room doors. Emily and Ken and I mopped up Friday morning. Pondering a solution to a problem that would surely recur, I left on a series of errands, with no time for another bus rendezvous.

Saturday morning I picked up Mister Vincent and his 10-year-old daughter Margaret to try again. The bus came this time; Margaret made sure I found her mother, who had by now heard of this new job prospect.

She got in the car, and suggested we drive ten minutes up to the police station to have more time before she rejoined the bus. We hit it off; she agreed to get a ride back that night (her bus didn't operate Sundays) and come to Hikaru in the morning for a longer talk in which Brad could join.

She was slight, darker than many in Treasure Beach; a pretty woman in her early 30s with two pre-teen daughters. ("She's a ver' smart lady for a black woman," the light-skinned Brother Elbert told me; he knew her from church.. Coming from our saintly neighbor, the remark took me aback. But color bias, we knew from our travels, is a world-wide phenomenon.)

Cheerful but not ebullient, Miss Olive exuded self-confidence. She'd been the first-born daughter; her mother died before she was 10, leaving her to be surrogate mother for her siblings. A second wife was delighted to have a Cinderella to help with the next batch of children. Caring for almost a dozen, she became, of necessity, a good housekeeper and problem solver -- and, we would soon learn, a talented, inventive and resourceful cook.

It would be no surprise to learn later that her sisters thought her bossy. We saw in her not bossiness, but a welcome take-charge personality.

She'd borne a daughter, now 12, before she settled down – it was hard to imagine why -- with Mister Vincent. Jennifer, already as big as her mother, presumably looked like the father we never met; she was an attractive, studious girl. Margaret, Mister Vincent's daughter, showed signs of becoming a beautiful young woman; to her mother's distress, she wasn't much of a scholar.

We hired Miss Olive on the spot Sunday morning. She earned more on the bus than we'd been paying Miss Esmie, but she could expect tips from guests, and we promised a raise as soon as she completed an undefined trial period. Brad, recovered – it wasn't breakbone fever -- would drive her to Maggotty that evening to collect her belongings from her rented room at that end of the line.

One problem: She wanted one of her sisters as her second maid. We wanted to keep Miss Geraldine, a near neighbor who had served capably.

"No, sir, I must have my sister." It wasn't so much finding work for family members as trusting only kinfolk. Both are common attitudes in developing countries. At the governmental level, we call it nepotism. It occurred to me that high officials who surround themselves with well-paid family members are just doing, on a grander scale, what the rest of their society does.

Miss Olive feared that Miss Geraldine would undercut her and try to take her job, especially, because she was an "outsider" -- from a whole mile up the road!

It wasn't our first encounter with such parochialism: When we told Lancel about our new land two miles from Calabash Bay, he warned that our new neighbors weren't as open and honest as those we had come to know. Our Billy's Bay neighbors say much the same of people in Fort Charles, the fishing bay three miles west of us.)

We were reluctant to disappoint a near neighbor who'd become accustomed to occasional income from Hikaru. We consulted again with Miss Sheila, who spoke up for nepotism: "Of course Miss Olive would want a sister!" We relented, had a tearful interview with Miss Geraldine, and accepted Miss Olive's choice of Ida Smith as our second maid.

It proved a happy choice. Miss Ida was a big-boned, strong woman with a sunny disposition and ready laugh, as outgoing as her older sister was reserved. She had a young family of her own with Ukie Hill, one of the hardest-working of the fishermen, whom she would eventually marry. Her older children could look after the youngsters when we had a full house and needed a second maid.

The two sisters went to work Tuesday morning of our second week -- the start of a two-decade-long collaboration and friendship.

●

It didn't take Miss Olive long to become part of her new village. She began helping with Wednesday evening vesper services in a little concrete-block church that sprang up at the end of our access road, and then began after-school programs for children there. It was a games-and-crafts program, but she also taught reading. Too few of the children went to school; she hoped at least to instill basic literacy, and perhaps to lure some of them to ask that their parents send them to school.

We sent down coloring books, crayons, craft materials and children's books. Guests often brought such materials, too – especially repeat visitors – and of course came to see the little school, talk with the children, and often came to services in the church.

She enlisted some other village adults. When that volunteer effort sputtered, she took under her wing a very bright 12-year-old, Richard Thompson, who became a proxy teacher and organizer when she was busy with guests. Before long, a short children's dance or dramatic performance was added to parties on the terrace. (Richard wasn't the only youngster she semi-adopted; after bringing up her passel of siblings, she just couldn't stop mothering.)

When Hurricane Gilbert hit Jamaica years later, in 1988, we got a sense of how much that village contact had meant to our guests, and I saw first-hand how well Miss Olive knew our neighbors.

Gilbert, a Class 5 storm, the most intense category, came ashore in the east, in Kingston, and left Jamaica after tearing up Negril at the west end. Had it had followed a straight line, it would have done major damage to Treasure Beach. Instead, it took an arcing path over Montego Bay. Ted Tatham went down next day to see how his Blue Marlin had fared, and looked in on our place. As soon as service was restored – another two days – he phoned to say that there was no damage to Hikaru, and only minor damage in the village, but that the fishing economy was disrupted.

We wrote all the guests who'd been at Hikaru in the previous decade, inviting them to chip in to an impromptu relief fund; we would match their contributions up to $1,000.

The response was wonderful. Three weeks after the hurricane hit, I flew down with $2,600.

Most hotels in MoBay were still closed for repairs. That's the major market for the catch from Treasure Beach; everyone was suffering from a sudden loss of income. Those who went to far sea and found their pots – some had been torn loose from their moorings -- brought home seafood they couldn't sell.

After dinner together, Miss Olive and I drew up a list of needs. One family needed a few sheets of zinc for the roof. Almost everyone else could use some help to make new fish traps, or to tide them over until the market for fish recovered. The disrupted fishery also affected live-alone seniors whose diet usually included the runt fish given them when men came back from far sea.

We wrote down how many mouths each family had to feed, and who had other part-time work or income. We divvied up the money as best we could to meet those needs into 60 envelopes, each with the name of the intended recipient. (I noticed that where there were husband-and-wife families, Miss Olive carefully put the wife's name on the envelope, and it was the wife we called for next morning. She wanted to be sure none of the money got drunk up.)

Next morning we walked the village, stopping at every house. I developed a little speech:

"Our guests who've come to Hikaru remember how you and the village welcomed them and helped them get to know Jamaica," I said at each doorstep as I handed over the envelope. "They've sent this to express their appreciation, and in a small way to return the welcome you gave them."

They were surprised and grateful. There were a few tears; my eyes weren't always dry, either.

Because it was true. Over the years, guests have told us how warmly they felt received, and how much they admired folks they met on the beach, in the village and in churches. For many, it was a first experience in a community of color; some undoubtedly came with a bit of trepidation. Helped by our staff, they quickly felt at ease, and in varying degrees came to know the life of Billy's Bay. Given an opportunity to express their warm memories, they gave generously.

Our morning round certainly solidified the view in neighbors' minds that Hikaru and its guests were a plus for the village. It may have enhanced Miss Olive's reputation, too, although by then she hardly needed any help from us.

●

Back to August 1973. We'd arrived to find the well pump was -- again -- not working. Mr. Lyn had a new plumber, A.J. Carroll, who had been at the house a few days earlier, bringing a substitute pump and taking back the other. I drove to Mandeville Monday morning to have him come back. (I also scouted out the Manzellis' electrician to send him down; they'd come over Sunday to report that their fridge and pump had both quit, and we'd sent them home with ice.)

Mr. Carroll came Wednesday, re-installed my repaired pump, and departed -- soon after which Brother Elbert reported that it had lost its prime. I was less than cheerful at the news. We fussed for an hour, opening the plug atop the pump, pouring in bottlefuls of water to prime it, screwing the plug back down, flicking the switch, repeating the process.

Pumps are simple devices, jet pumps only somewhat more complex. An impeller, a plastic wheel inside the housing, hurls water down the smaller of two pipes, through a U-turn at the bottom, and back through a nozzle into the larger pipe. The Venturi principle, to which we're all exposed in high school, says the nozzle will suck and send up more water than was sent down.

When one stops pumping, a foot valve must close so water stands in the pipes; if it leaks, the pump "loses its prime"; one must re-fill the smaller pipe. A bubble of air in the wrong place -- wherever that is -- ruins the lift.

Anyone familiar with quantum physics or Einstein's theory probably understands why pumps fail. That lets me out.

I went to the post office Thursday morning to send Mr. Carroll a telegram, only to discover that postal workers were on strike. Murphy again.

Water was beginning to be a serious problem. There had been a long drought, and the under-patio cistern I was so proud of was nearly dry. I'd already gone to Black River -- oh, for a telephone! -- to order a tankload of water; it hadn't arrived yet. We began rationing, and Brother Elbert resumed watering by laboriously drawing bucketfuls from the open well.

On Friday I drove to Mandeville again -- oh, for a telephone! -- to summon Mr. Carroll back; he started down while I did other errands. By the time I returned, he had the well pump working again.

I thought I'd covered the likely water contingencies: If the rainwater side of the tower tank ran dry, we could shut a valve -- "lock it off," we say -- and send well water to the whole system, or vice-versa. Brother Elbert had already done that on several occasions. But that was no help if both sides ran dry or both pumps failed. I asked Mr. Carroll to come back later to install my repaired second pump as a spare, to replace what he suspected was a leaking foot-valve, and to lengthen the pipes, setting the intakes deeper into the well.

Friday night those torrential rains swept under the doors and partly refilled the cistern; there had been three inches of rain, so 3,000 gallons in the tank. Water emergency over! I drove back to Black River to call off the tanker truck. Oh, for a telephone!

●

Also, in this frantic two weeks, we had our thatched-hut gazebo built down near the sea.

Brother Elbert, as promised, had bought a pickup load of palm fronds from Thatchville; they were waiting on our arrival, pressed flat. He and Mister Endley proposed to do the job on a contract; we settled on a price that amounted to three days' work for the two of them, and on one of my pump-repair trips through Southfield I had lumber and nails sent down.

They finished the job in one day.

Although annoyed at the small swindle, I enjoyed watching the process. They set up the posts, nailed in beams at head level to tie them together, and put up a low teepee framework for the roof. Brother Elbert softened the palm-frond stems with water, and used a sharp knife to peel a flexible quarter-inch sliver down each side, like a pair of long, natural-fiber shoelaces, handing each up to Mister Endley astride the roof frame. He started at the lower edge and worked his way around and up, tying each frond into place with the slivered stems, using no nails or wires.

"This roof last forever, mon," Mister Endley assured me. At the end of the day he found a length of barbed wire to loop on top of the finished roof -- to hold it down against the sea-breeze, he explained, until the sun had baked the thatch into place. When we came down next, the wire had been removed, and the roof lasted years. The gazebo is a pleasant place to read, or to keep an eye on youngsters playing on the beach or in the shallows.

And in the midst of all this we blasted the reef. Mister Arthur had come along on two of my supply trips to wheedle contributions (or renewed contributions) from hardware store owners who had some Treasure Beach connection. I'd enlisted Ted's help in Mandeville, and had visits with the beach control agent and then the sea-blaster. But there was so much else going on that after the first day I only looked in on the blasting from time to time, marking each detonation by the siren Ashmead was so proud of, and lending my tough-cop voice to keep him on the job.

The place was beginning to look less raw. The coconut palms Richard Todd had planted were now more than waist-high along the new walkway. The first bougainvillea and oleanders were established. The little cactus garden with its stone bench under the lignum vitae tree was a pretty little haven; Brad sat there most mornings, still enough that the birds became accustomed to her and splashed happily in the bath.

●

We left Saturday morning for a late afternoon flight; I wanted to explore the vast sugar-cane fields west of our usual route. Emily protested, preferring the security of an early arrival at the airport.

She was triumphantly right; Murphy's Law hadn't been rescinded. Halfway through the sugar plantations, a thunderstorm engulfed us, wetting the spark plugs or coil. I tried to dry out the ignition system -- leaning in over the open hood, drenched by the downpour -- while our daughter reminded me that she'd told me so. I considered suggesting she walk the rest of the way, but held my tongue, and finally got a passing jitney van to give us a tow.

It took several miles of occasionally slipping the clutch before the engine started under compression. I honked the van driver to a stop, had Brad hold down the accelerator while I paid him off, and then drove to Lucea, 25 miles west of Montego Bay, and finally along the coast road to the airport.

Too late. Eastern's plane (remember Eastern Airlines?) was still at the boarding gate, but our seats had been sold to stand-bys. As it took off without us, I tried unsuccessfully to get a hotel coupon, and finally went on our own -- by taxi, having turned in the rental car -- to a modest hotel on the beach almost under the airliners' approach.

Once there, even Emily made the best of it. We had an evening swim in the hotel pool, slept well despite the occasional rumble of jets a few hundred feet overhead, and swam in the bay in the morning before flying home -- setting aside thoughts that this enterprise might be more than we'd bargained for. The pumps should both be working soon. We had a gifted cook-housekeeper in whom we were confident. God was in his heaven, and all would be right with this Jamaican world.

# 15

# The plumber

The only plumber I've known whose fingernails were never dirty was A.J. Carroll. A big man, light-skinned, he usually wore a white, loose guayabera that concealed a bit of a paunch. A growing bald spot hinted at an age of perhaps 50. He had less patois and more British in his accent than most Jamaicans, although his speech was drawled rather than clipped; he pronounced his name "Carl."

We visited him several times him at his rabbit-warren of a Mandeville office, whose file cabinets held the specifications and parts list of every job he'd ever worked on.

Even had Mr. Lyn not chosen him as his new sub-contractor, Mr. Carroll's self-assurance would have inspired confidence. Having found more than one sloppy piece of work by previous subcontractors at Hikaru, we were eager to believe the new man more competent.

Mr. Carroll was a deacon of his church. We several times waited in his office while he made phone calls arranging for Sunday vespers or church visits to some needy institution. The charitable work seemed real enough, although the timing of the calls seemed staged for our benefit.

Despite his drawl and his deacon's demeanor, he often snapped at his secretary. Miss Thomas, a middle-aged woman, seemed occasionally on the verge of tears. He directed other subordinates with a combination of curt orders and mild sarcasm. A "please" or "thank you" crossed his lips only rarely.

And he traveled -- at least when he came to Treasure Beach -- with a retinue worthy of a potentate. He typically arrived in a compact pickup he had rented, with a driver, for the day. He often brought along his 8-year-old grandson, Miss Thomas -- purportedly to enjoy a day at the beach, but in fact to look after the boy -- and no fewer than four helpers, who rode in the back under a tarpaulin against the morning wind-chill. The driver, Mr. Carroll, the grandson and Miss Thomas squeezed into the cab.

A tall young man introduced as "Organ," who had worked at the Alcan bauxite works, was his principal helper. A second man, Wade, although a technical high school graduate, was a plumber/electrician-in-training; A.J. seemed to take pleasure in riding him for not knowing what he should have learned in school. The other two, Peart and Richards, were apparently on-the-job trainees under a government program. Mr. Carroll had difficulty remembering any of their names.

His visits weren't cheap: He charged Ja$100 just for transportation each time he came. In addition, I paid Ja$50 a day for his services; Ja$25 (slightly above the island building trades council scale) for Organ; Ja$20 for Wade, and Ja$10 each for Peart and Richards. The latter two were paid a government training stipend, so my payment was a bonus they probably didn't get to enjoy. Mr. Carroll acknowledged that he took 20 per cent of each man's wage to cover his "training costs."

Altogether, it cost me Ja$215 -- about US$165 -- every time he came, no matter how long he stayed. (The Jamaican dollar had by now been devalued by about 50 percent.)

At those rates, I saved up projects so there was a full day's work when I called on Mr. Carroll; otherwise I did the work myself. Nowadays there are reasonably skilled tradesmen nearby. In those early years, it was either an expensive Mandeville crew or do-it-yourself. I accumulated an awesome set of tools and spare parts, and improved my building-trades skills.

I could never keep my hands clean. Mr. Carroll did: He ran the job by peremptorily ordering one or the other of his helpers to take each next step. Meanwhile, he often would carry on a conversation, but break off to inspect a piece of work and often order it done differently.

The work setting the well-pump deeper, during that hectic August week, was one occasion when I got my money's worth. It was also an early example of the master plumber's technique.

Ivan Elliott, a neighbor who had dug this and most of the wells hereabouts, had stopped about three feet after he hit water. He knew his business: He was down almost to sea level. Some salt water would infiltrate, mixing with the freshwater flow of the aquifer from inland; our well water has always been slightly brackish. I couldn't dig deeper without even more salt intrusion; but setting the intake lower would help. We set it this time a foot from the sandy bottom -- two feet below the surface when the well was full – enabling a half-hour's pumping before sucking dry.

Lengthening the pipes was harder than it may sound. The heavy, flexible plastic well pipe used in the United States was unavailable here, so we'd used polyvinyl chloride. PVC is relatively fragile; the twin pipes, lashed together, were heavy with water, increasing the risk of breaking them.

With Mr. Carroll calling out orders like a coxswain, six of us hauled the pipes up hand-over-hand, guiding the tops into the branches of the maturing poinciana tree – "Easy now, mon, keep them straight up and down!" -- until we had the full length out. "All right, boy, now turn back the foot-valve," he ordered Organ. The water drained off; we could then safely lay them down, cut each pipe, and splice in a short extension.

"Mind you get it glued all around!" PVC is joined by applying a cement that briefly dissolves the plastic and then hardens to create a solid bond. "Now wait, mon, don't strain it until the glue set!" Finally we hoisted the upper end back into the poinciana tree – "Mind, now, don't let those pipes bend too much!" – and lowered the whole apparatus into the well. "All right, then, now thread the couplings back onto the pump."

It was a long day. I was tired; Mr. Carroll was still fresh.

●

"Scratch a successful middle-class Jamaican," a Jamaican friend in Hartford once said, "and you'll find someone who is one generation away from a pit latrine."

It is not uncommon for Jamaicans who rise from humble origins to flaunt their new middle-class affluence -- and to show an almost-colonial lack of concern for those left behind, if not indeed to exploit them.  Mr. Carroll was uncharacteristic of that class only in being a strong supporter of Manley's PNP, the more liberal of the two major parties.

"The Gleaner," he once began a conversation vehemently as his crew started work, "is the worst paper in the world."  He bent over Organ to have him loosen a pipe fitting, putting me on hold.

"Mind you," he added a few minutes later, "what they say is half-true.  But only half.  And the columnists are the worst."

The *Daily Gleaner*, Jamaica's largest newspaper, was a sharp critic of the PNP government.  With elections two months away, it sometimes seemed the paper was more "the opposition" than Seaga's JLP.  As an opinion writer myself, I gave columnists and editorial writers more leeway than Mr. Carroll would allow them.  Nonetheless, I had to agree that The Gleaner's opinions spilled over to the news columns, and its disdain for Manley was palpable.

Most literate middle-class Jamaicans shared that dislike with a passion, not least for Manley's cozying up to Fidel Castro; they found The Gleaner a soul-mate.  Not so A.J. Carroll.

The Gleaner had recently reported that Dudley Thompson, Manley's foreign minister, had accepted a ride to Cuba in a small plane with that country's ambassador.  A third man, a Cuban who was implicated in an illegal small-arms shipment and had been denied an exit visa until the gun-running was cleared up, was aboard the plane.  He was removed by an alert immigrations officer -- while the foreign minister, The Gleaner said, tried to hide behind his newspaper.

"Oh, mon, Thompson's a Communist, that's clear!" Mr. Carroll said.  "But that business in the plane was innocent enough:  He was going to Cuba, and his plane was late, so he accepted a ride.  Nothing more."

And the incident with the newspaper?

"He went to sleep, mon.  Simple thing; happens to any of us in the car."  I imagined Mr. Carroll dozing in the jam-packed pickup on his way down from Mandeville.  "Same thing in an airplane, I expect.  Just covered his face with the newspaper and dozed off. Not hiding behind it; that's The Gleaner."

He abruptly turned back to supervise the job. "Here, boy, tighten that another turn."

●

When he tried to call his workers by name he got them mixed up, so most of the time he didn't bother; he also called Mister Valney "boy," to my embarrassment.

If his crew was dispersed -- at either end of a pipeline, for instance, or two of them at some indoor plumbing repair -- he would make the rounds, giving them curt and not-always-clear directions. He would then return regularly enough to spot any error and correct it -- usually with caustic humor at the errant worker's expense.

In mid-afternoon, Miss Thomas would appear with a cup of tea she had prepared in our kitchen. He would accept it with the briefest thanks, and sip it contemplatively without apology to anyone for taking tea alone.

He ordered me around, too. On one occasion, it appeared the work would last beyond sunset. "You'd better rig up a light, mister," he said. "This job's not going finish without a light."

As I hurried up to my fortunately well-stocked tool closet to get an extension cord and a light socket, it occurred to me that a plumber-electrician might be expected to bring along his own drop light, rather than count on an American homeowner who was only occasionally in Jamaica.

It also struck me that I couldn't remember when he had last used my name.

The cord I found was long enough to bring the bare bulb within only about 15 feet of the pumphouse. "That's not good enough," Mr. Carroll said curtly. "But we don't need that extension," he added. "Just give me the light, and we'll wire it up to the pump switch right here. Boy, loose back the screws on that switch."

He might have saved me effort by explaining that he could hot-wire the light to the switch, and wouldn't need an extension cord. But that wasn't his style. He was the master tradesman, whose needs or orders were to be intuited by lesser beings. He had achieved middle-class status largely through his own wit and will, and had little patience for those who had not done so -- or in my case he presumed had not.

Over the next several years, he was a frequent visitor. The pumps needed constant repair; it would be two years before we had a reliable spare pump to which Brother Elbert could switch confidently when the first failed.

I would get letters from Miss Olive reporting that the pump had quit, and that she'd wired Mr. Carroll to come fix it. A week or two later, she would write that he still hadn't come. On several occasions, she wired me in panic as guests' arrival neared. He had a telephone; I'd make a long-distance call from the U.S., and he'd promptly go down to solve the problem.

He apparently didn't much like being summoned by our staff; they weren't his equals.

I never quite reconciled that person with the deacon who arranged for his church to visit an orphanage, and apologized for a government that most of his economic class despised.

●

We'd flown into Kingston this 1974 visit, taking a late-afternoon flight with Emily and Ken, and stayed the night at the Blue Mountain Inn on the city's outskirts, one of Jamaica's premier hostelries. Our destination: the famous Royal Botanical (or Hope) Gardens, where we'd been told we might buy exotics not found in Black River or Mandeville.

A 200-acre tract, originally part of a sugar estate awarded Major Richard Hope for his part in driving out the Spanish in 1655, Hope Gardens is both an amusement park and a remarkable compendium of tropical flora. It did indeed have the promised unusual species -- but there was little for sale.

No problem: We were approached by a hustler who called himself "British." He said private nurserymen nearby could sell us everything we wanted. We planned to tour the east end of the island so we could tell our guests about Jamaica's attractions if they wanted to extend their stays. No problem again: The obliging British would meet us here Saturday morning.

We drove along the coast east of Kingston, bone-dry arid, then turned inland toward the shoulder of Blue Mountain, which gets an average 300 inches of rain a year. The land turned suddenly lush. One road was lined with wild mango trees in full fruit; the roadway was littered with ripe mangos so puny and stringy they were hardly worth picking up -- which was why no one had.

(One of Ted Tatham's farm-improvement projects, while on loan to the Manley government, included teaching men to graft buds of the plump and fleshy hybrid Julie or Bombay mango onto native trees such as these. It seemed an eminently sound idea, a kind of tropical WPA. Ted claimed some success, but the project didn't survive the next change of government.)

We stopped briefly at Bath, a mountain resort and Jamaica's best-known hot springs, and then back down to the coast at the eastern tip of the island. The Long Bay Beach Hotel was a reminder that a tropical climate and salt spray make maintenance a constant necessity. The bathroom facilities were rusty; paint was peeling. It had a sandy beach -- with a coconut palm so close to the sea it was washed by waves, a nice touch I've tried but failed to replicate at Hikaru -- but the surf was rough. We swam only briefly, and carefully.

Next morning we rounded the northwest tip of the island, passing abandoned coconut groves whose decaying boles, stripped of foliage by a disease called lethal yellowing, stood like a forest of telephone poles. An immune hybrid, the dwarf Malay, was readily available, but the absentee owners hadn't yet replanted. For the landed class, lost production was of little importance. For villagers who had made their living in the groves, it was a crippling economic loss.

We drove through Port Antonio, and finally up a steep valley to the crest that overlooks Kingston to the Casa Monte, a government-sponsored hotel training school. The service was as slow the Treasure Beach Hotel's, but they put on a good barbecue and had dancing on the terrace. We put the kids to bed and stayed up until midnight.

Next morning we met British outside Hope Gardens, bought most of what we'd come for, and by late morning were on our way home, Emily and Ken squeezed amongst greenery in the back seat.

# 16

## Eco-tourism

**"Y**ou really must see the potoo," said Robert Sutton. "It's getting dark enough now." He pointed to a broken, ten-foot tree-stub barely discernible in the gloom. "It likes to perch on that. Wait here a minute."

The potoo ("poe-TOO") is a rare bird not found in North America. Two cousins are found from Guatemala and Nicaragua south to Argentina and Peru; the Jamaican potoo has a narrower range. It shares owls' nocturnal habits, but at 16 inches tall is bigger than most owls. A nondescript brown, it would be hard to spot even in broad daylight.

Robert returned with a battery-pack and spotlight that he aimed at the tree-stub. There – although it took some imagining –was the potoo: as erect as a soldier, long tail flattened down the bole of the tree, neck and short bill upthrust as though baying at the moon. It looked like part of the tree, the very definition of "plain as a stick".

We had only a few seconds to recognize the potoo before the light made it nervous; it flew off in a light thunder of wingbeats, ducking and bobbing as Robert tried to follow it with the beam.

Robert Sutton was Jamaica's most distinguished ornithologist, author of *Birds of Jamaica*. Tall, lean, bespectacled, with blond hair that fell over his forehead, he looked like an absent-minded professor. He and his pretty wife Anne were among the leaders of Jamaica's growing conservation movement.

We'd spent the afternoon traipsing through the meadows and woodlands of the family farm outside Mandeville, Marshall's Pen (the name a holdover of colonial sheep farming.)

My high point had been a long look at a chestnut-bellied cuckoo – as big as the potoo, but boldly painted, with a long, brown-and-white barred tail. It waited patiently while I hurried over a barbed-wire fence for a closer look. A handsome bird, well worth a pair of pants torn on the fence. Brad missed it, but kept her clothes intact.

All work and no play makes Jack a dull boy. We're amateur birders, and bird-watching is one of my diversions from the insatiable demands of managing a vacation home. Brad has knack for spotting something unusual in the flight pattern or perch, a flash of color. I'm more likely to notice a different song.

Serious birders keep life-lists, and travel hundreds or thousands of miles to add one *rara avis.* We keep lists when traveling with a group in new territory, but have never started life-lists. Birding for us is an occasion to go for a walk – usually leisurely, usually in unspoiled terrain.

What makes such walks special is the company of a serious birder who lives in the area, knows where to look and can identify birds by their calls. When on our own, we thumb through a bird-book trying to decide which of a dozen very similar warblers, orioles, euphonias or flycatchers we're looking at.

One year we joined Robert and Anne for World Birdwatch Day. Every serious birder in Jamaica (and presumably in other countries) went out to see as many different species as possible; everyone's lists, turned in and compiled, would be a kind of report card on the health of the avian population.

We met at dawn at swampy ponds near Parottee Point (where Anne was working with a new Peace Corpsman to enforce laws against filling in wetlands). There were seven of us.

Brad and I had been to those ponds, and could count on seeing herons and egrets; perhaps a grebe or coot or a Wilson's phalarope; often a flight of blue-winged teal showing their patches as they landed in close-order formation. With seven pairs of binoculars at work – the two most important being the Suttons'– we identified 46 species in less than two hours.

Having wrung every known feathered denizen out of that habitat, Robert led us a half-hour west of the Black River to Luana Point, a rocky beach behind which lay a swampy forest.

Two centuries ago, European tapestry artists and fabric-makers got their red dye from a Jamaican tree called the logwood. We saw one cut down once: Its heartwood was a coppery scarlet. Logwood was shipped from Black River, making it a major commercial port. Great plantations were set out; the soggy ground at Luana Point was apparently just right. German commercialization of aniline dyes from coal tar in the 1860s doomed the logwood trade, although it lingered several decades.

The logwood forest was overgrown, but we walked along the remainders of orderly paths and berms. In an hour, the Suttons found us 23 more birds, including seven kinds of warblers. Stopping at Thatchfield and Pondside on the way to Hikaru for lunch, five more were added to the list.

A project with Mister Valney needed my attention after lunch. Brad and the others went on with the Suttons to Great Pond and then to an upland forest at Elim where they recorded 42 sightings. The catch for the day: 90 birds, including two considered rare or threatened, the West Indian whistling duck and the yellow-breasted crake.

●

For those who favor armchair birding, nothing beats Rocklands Bird Sanctuary outside Montego Bay. On the road to Treasure Beach, it's a stop we've long urged on our guests. The high point is hand-feeding hummingbirds.

Lisa Salmon, a Britisher, built a house on the shoulder of a mountain overlooking MoBay and began inviting paying guests to come help her feed the birds.

An ornithologist whose skills must have matched Robert's, she knew what every species wanted, and put it out. An overripe banana in one corner of the wide patio invited the Jamaican oriole and white-winged dove; tiny hanging baskets of sugar drew the black-and-yellow banana quit. She'd invite a member of her audience to sit in a straight-back chair, hands on knees with open palms into which she'd sprinkle millet. In a few minutes, a half-dozen gray-green grassquit with yellow eye-masks would be eating out of one's hands.

"Hold still now!" she would scold. "Flatten your hand, now!" A short figure in a baggy housedress and slippers, old enough to retire when we first knew her in the 1960s, she alternated between crankily complaining and amiably chatting with guests.

The hummers are the top draw. Jamaica has only three, but they're distinctive. The tiny vervain is among the smallest of the world's hummingbirds, less than three inches long. The mango is one of the largest, a bright purple. The male of the streamertail –the "doctor bird" –has spectacular tail feathers eight inches or more long. Air Jamaica wraps that long streamertail into a circle to make the doctor bird its logo.

Mornings, Miss Salmon kept a dozen little airline liquor bottles filled with sugar-water hanging around the patio and house, tipped-down as though pouring, bottle caps in place but with a hole drilled through each, small enough not to drip but big enough for a hummingbird's straw-like tongue.

At noon she took the bottles away. By the time guests began arriving at 2:30, the hummingbirds were having a sugar fit. Emboldened by withdrawal symptoms, they'd come to where she had guests sit holding a bottle. "Mind now, tip it down!" The hummers would begin to flick around the patio, and air buzzing with their wingbeats. "Hold it out a bit, now. Relax!" and then, addressing the birds, "Come sir, come! Come now!"

Maybe they'd learned to obey her. One by one – often quarreling about whose turn was next – the hummers would come to drink. "Point your left forefinger! Now raise it gently. Gently, I said! There!" If one were lucky, the tiny creature would stop hovering and perch on one's forefinger for five seconds or so, gossamer-light, close enough that one could see it swallow as it sipped through that long tongue poking out from the long bill.

She had to give up directly supervising the guests a decade ago, and has since died. But she trained a small staff of Jamaican young men who've taken over, albeit not as colorfully.

●

Lisa Salmon pioneered what nowadays is called eco-tourism; the Suttons were champions of the idea that visitors can enjoy the natural wonders without spoiling them. The North Coast tourist spots have grown so rapidly that ecology takes a back seat, and many Jamaicans must get over a bad littering habit, but there are many areas that lend themselves to eco-tourism.

One such: the John Crow Mountains northeast of Kingston. We visited in 1993, on a drive around the island with Bill and Trudy. The road grew narrower as we left the city, and then began climbing, up narrow valleys and winding switchbacks with few houses, until we suddenly came to the Pine Grove Motel, a plain but comfortable hostelry with spectacular views from an elevation of some 3,500 feet.

To the west, we looked down to the sprawling metropolis; tiny airliners winged across Kingston Bay to land at Norman Manley Airport. To the north and east, tree-clad mountains swelled upward to Blue Mountain, 7,402 feet, shrouded in fluffy clouds most of the time, but majestically in the clear each morning.

We of course went birding. We had trouble identifying one flock in a bottle-brush tree below us on the steeply-terraced grounds, and worked around to get a view looking up. Ah! black-throated blue warblers!

One afternoon we drove down a dirt road to find the jumping-off point for a hiking trail to Blue Mountain. (The guidebooks advise hiking up in late afternoon, spending the night in a shelter, and being at the peak at dawn, something we've talked of but never done.) As the road deteriorated, we quit at Mavis Bank, and spent an hour at the coffee plant.

Jamaica's Blue Mountain coffee is among the world's most coveted – and priciest. The real thing is grown only at these altitudes; the Japanese, famous coffee-fanciers, have invested heavily in new plantations up here.

As we watched, farmers dumped baskets of their red, grape-sized berries into a tank to float off immature or wormy berries. A crusher then revealed an inner bean with a pulpy film. After several days' soaking, the pulp and husks could be scrubbed off, and the beans were spread on concrete aprons to air-dry. Most of the beans, after grading, were packed into 10-gallon wooden barrels, the best headed to Japan; but some were roasted here or elsewhere on the island.

Jamaica grows coffee at lower altitudes, too; not the same quality, but we're blessed with lower-priced palates. Miss Olive regularly bought green beans in the Black River market, and roasted them by simply stirring them in a cast-iron frying pan on the stove. We've often brought home a bag of coffee beans to grind them, as she did, in the blender.

We'd planned to drive down to the North Coast by a narrow track ("other secondary roads," the map legend said) that would take us through more of the John Crow Mountains. "You know we had an earthquake?" the proprietress at the Pine Grove asked. Part of the road had been closed by landslides; she thought it had been re-opened by now, but wasn't sure.

It was open, sort of. In a half-dozen places, rock and earth had slid down to cover the roadway for a dozen yards at a stretch. A bulldozer – or strong backs and shovels -- had cleared the slides just enough for a car to ease through. With no guard-rails, we often looked over the edge into steep valleys. It took us two and a half hours to get down to the coast– 27 miles on the odometer.

# 17

# Survival at sea

We had a fireworks display for July 4th, 1974. (Jamaica's Independence Day comes at the end of July; it was just another night for everyone but us.) I hoped the occasion would kick off a marketing campaign for a new life-saving device we'd brought, a pocket-sized flare.

As dusk neared, Erwin Hamilton set out toward the Pedro Cays, leaving Lancel and Wilton and other fishermen on the beach at Calabash Bay. Ted Tatham walked out on his beach at Great Bay with a coterie of fishermen; we gathered with neighbors on our beach, from which we could see down to Great Bay.

As full dark fell at 6:45, I touched off a flare. A tiny ball of light climbed into the night sky and burst into a star-shell pattern. Two miles east we saw Ted's flare respond, illuminating the night; then Erwin's climbed into the sky six or eight miles out at sea.

Everyone on all three beaches applauded. We had their attention.

•

Deaths at sea were all too common; almost every time we came, it seemed, we were told of another.

The original cottonwood boats almost never sank. The problem was engine failure: losing the ability to maneuver in heavy seas, or drifting under a brutal sun.

Because they started out together but then went their separate ways, captains who had engine trouble late in the day had little chance of attracting help. Everyone carried a spare outboard strapped into the hold; but if both main and spare failed, they could only tinker with the engines, trying to get one running again.

When we first came, boats were painted aqua blue inside —almost impossible to spot from the air on a blue sea. The Jamaican Coast Guard was ill-equipped, but an airplane search could in theory be mounted for a missing boat. In 1973, the government decreed that all boats have a boldly stenciled number on the prow for identification, and be painted yellow inside. The men griped that bright yellow made the boats hotter and hurt their eyes.

I joined Mister Arthur in explaining why improving the odds for an aerial search outweighed a little discomfort. Everyone ultimately complied. I never heard, however, of an aerial rescue of a disabled boat. Most whose engines failed merely drifted. If they were lucky, they fetched up in Nicaragua, Honduras or Belize on the Yucatan Peninsula.

A few years earlier, a disabled Treasure Beach boat picked up a current close in around Jamaica itself. Although the men could often see land, they were out of earshot. They weren't spotted by the Coast Guard until they'd drifted past Montego Bay, halfway around the island.

Miss Olive's brother had an even more harrowing escape. When both outboards quit; he drifted past the Yucatan and caught the Gulf Stream north of Cuba. He and his crew were picked up by a freighter near Key West, half-dead, after an incredible ten days. They had survived by catching a few fish and wringing rainwater out of their shirts.

A year before that, a captain drawing his traps stopped at the Pedro Cays, where a friend asked him to carry back an engine for repair. Although it was stormy, he unwisely agreed, and strapped a second engine into the hold -- enough extra weight, in addition to a 500-pound box of fish and ice, to overcome the cottonwood's bouyancy. Mister Arthur knew the boat: It had a weak transom on which the main outboard was mounted, with a chain to prevent the engine's being lost if the mounting came loose. He surmised that the transom broke off, and the chained engine plummeted like an anchor, dragging the boat stern-first to a watery grave. The men were never heard from.

In each case, there had been other fishermen only a few miles away when disaster struck. "We need some way to signal, sah," he said. We talked about two-way radios, but at the time they were far too fragile and expensive to be practical.

●

I read about a new, compact flare, trademarked the Skyblazer. Three flares in a packet hardly bigger than a pack of cigarettes could fit into a man's shirt pocket. They were waterproof, inexpensive -- about $5 a pack -- and were set off by unscrewing the cap and striking a flint.

In February, I'd brought down a few, and had our neighbor Philip Gordon take one to sea and set it off at midnight. An astonishing number of men saw it. "What was that light at sea?" Word got around: a new safety device.

(He also tried out a companion device, a tiny smoke-generating gadget for daytime use. In the sea breeze, the smoke dissipated before it could produce a distinctive column; we gave up on smoke signals.)

I talked with Wilton at the fishermen's co-op. Yes, he'd heard about that test firing; great idea! But – ever the cautious bookkeeper -- he was reluctant to invest in a supply; he wasn't sure anyone would buy them.

I went back to Bob Satter and the Cottonwood Foundation, reporting on our triumph of blasting the reef, and asked for $200 to buy the co-op an initial supply of flares. I wrote Wilton to ask his approval of applying for a grant.

Just then a letter from Miss Olive told how Mister Valney's engine failed as he neared home. Leslie Buchanan came in, expecting his neighbor just behind him. When he didn't show up, Mister Leslie went back out, finding him just as night fell. Miss Olive, alerted, turned on our patio lights, a trio of yellow bug-repellent bulbs that made a night-time landmark. They'd made it in safely, Mister Leslie towing the disabled boat. I wrote back hoping the incident would make people think about how useful flares would be.

Bob and the foundation came through. I ordered $200 worth of Skyblazers. They arrived, a package the size of a loaf of bread that would easily fit in a suitcase.

Then I made a terrible mistake. Fresh from our encounter with the customs officers at Montego Bay airport, I wrote the woman in charge of the Cooperative Department, asking her to send a letter urging that duty on the flares be waived as a gift to the non-profit co-op.

Because of the "explosive nature of flares," she wrote back, she had contacted the national security and justice administrations to get their approval. I by now knew Jamaican officialdom well enough to know I was in quicksand.

Survival Systems, Inc. sent a sheaf of testimony that their Skyblazer wouldn't explode. It had been tested extensively, would only burn – not explode -- even if thrust into a furnace. It was officially declared safe to carry on U.S. airliners. I sent copies to the Cooperative Department, and to Ted, who pitched in trying to budge the bureaucracy.

I had no luck. Ted struck out. The co-op lady wrote that she was awaiting approval from security and justice.

It was now late June; I'd written everyone promoting the planned demonstration. I finally said the hell with it, and smuggled the flares in. I buried them amidst my underwear and socks, and brought along my packet of testimonials to their safety in case I was challenged. I went through the green line; my suitcase wasn't opened.

The demonstration was a huge success. Wilton sold most of the stock I'd brought him within a few days.

In the following months, the flares were used at least twice that I heard of. Once, a captain lost both engines as he neared home. With the flares, he got the attention of another captain who towed him in, saving a catch that he said would otherwise have spoiled.

Another captain was farther out when his spare engine failed in rough weather. His flare brought a colleague who loaned him a spare on which he made it home -- and as he told it, saved his life.

Neither captain bought a fresh supply of Skyblazers. A year later, Wilton still had a few unsold flares.

We were up against fatalism. Few fishermen learned to swim; they argued that sharks would get them even if they tried. None wore or even carried life preservers. Despite the frequency of breakdowns at sea, they carried no more than a small bottle of drinking water, and no provisions for a longer time at sea.

If their number was up, they felt, it was up. Period.

Before the cottonwood boat ran its course, we helped Mister Valney buy one, and learned about the economics of fishenin'.

He captained a boat owned by Harvey Clarke, on the marine equivalent of sharecropper terms that justified the "Flem Snopes" tag our friend Cynthia had hung on Harvey. After paying the costs of each trip -- gasoline, fresh spark plugs and ice -- he shared his catch 50-50 with Harvey. After seven years, the boat and engines would be his. By then, however, the boat would be at the end of its useful life, and the engines would be long gone.

Mister Valney and I went over his expenses and costs laboriously, several evenings at our dining table with a pocket calculator. It was the first time he'd tried to evaluate the costs and profits of his livelihood. By the time we finished, I suspected he knew more about the economics than most of our neighbors; it was certainly an eye-opener for me.

He and Harvey had about 40 traps at sea. His best profit from a trip was $100 (about US$75 at the time); the average was only $40. Weather occasionally held him back; he made 40 trips a year.

Although the initial cost of the boat and engines was less than $3,400, he had after three years paid Harvey $5,800. The outboards needed an overhaul at least once every two years; one of his was on its second overhaul, at his expense. After a third overhaul an engine was no longer reliable for a far-sea trip. Mister Valney would bear alone the cost of new engines.

Brad and I agreed that the debt was killing him. We grubstaked him to a new boat that Mister Arthur would build, and enough money to make a new and larger set of traps. He would open a bank account and deposit part of his profit after every trip – a reserve fund for future needs – and pay us back as he could.

Harvey got wind of our arrangement before the boat was built, and unilaterally ended their contract. Mister Valney spent money on a lawyer who got nowhere. On our next trip, I negotiated a settlement to buy Harvey out. But when Mister Valney went in a borrowed boat to draw his traps, he discovered that Flem Snopes had sent a man ahead of him to cut the ropes, leaving the traps to rust on the bottom. I threatened legal action, but in fact we were helpless.

Mister Valney's independence with his own boat helped; he built up a modest bank balance and began paying off the debt. He hardly prospered, however. He finally decided he wasn't cut out to be a captain -- by then he was earning better money at Hikaru – and turned the boat over to a son. He went to sea as crew for a few more years.

We were reminded that fishenin' provides a better living than subsistence farming, but is not the route to wealth. A few men achieved a comfortable middle-class life, by Jamaican standards, but they were without exception those who had the capital to buy a boat, have 80 or 100 traps at sea, and send other men to sea on terms similar to those Harvey Clarke had imposed on Mister Valney.

●

The outboards in 1974 were 40-horse Evinrudes or Johnsons, two-cycle engines that ran on gasoline mixed with oil. To encourage fishing, the government sold gas pre-mixed with oil, at reduced rates, at seaside stations in Black River and Great Bay. We knew a trip to far sea was in the offing when we saw fishing boats coming back from Black River with the distinctive blue plastic gasoline bottles.

The government also sold the outboards on an installment plan, paid off whenever fishermen bought gas; the cost of an engine was Ja$1,100, about US$850. That was more than outboards sold for at home, and several men implored us to buy and ship down engines for them. We declined: It would have been an extra burden on every trip and a hassle with customs, and we'd have had to decide who deserved the next engine.

I succumbed, however, to pleas that I buy parts for several neighbors. "A 40-horse?" the marine supply salesman in Hartford asked. "Are you sure?" He looked it up. The Johnson and Evinrude 40-hp engines were identical, he said -- and were no longer sold in the United States. It seemed the American manufacturer was unloading outdated stock on our Jamaican neighbors. He special-ordered me the parts.

In the next few years, Japanese competition appeared: a 50-hp Yamaha that the men thought more durable. It cost more, and wasn't available through the government installment plan, but those who could afford it bought Yamahas. A few tried an even more powerful 75-hp engine, but most decided the added power wasn't economical.

Within a few years, the government dropped its installment plan for outboards.

●

The emergency flares weren't our first involvement with fishermen's problems. Before we built the house, Lancel and Wilton had complained when a bauxite ore carrier plowed through their pot-set at near sea, shearing the ropes that tethered the traps to their floats, leaving the pots in marine graves. It happened "all the time," they said; could we do anything?

Alligator Pond, just east of Great Pedro Point, is a major bauxite-loading dock, called Port Kaiser, the terminus of a dedicated rail line from Mandeville. Ships eased in from the west, staying within sight of land and the Lover's Leap lighthouse, to find the port. In doing so, they plowed through a fishing ground of which they were unaware.

I made them aware. In my Saturday *Hartford Times* signed editorial, I wrote about the problem -- and thanks to my dad, sent a copy to the right man at Alcan. I got a letter back promising to make ore-carrier captains aware of the fishing ground and have them steer clear.

They did, moving a mile or so farther out; the problem of sheared lines disappeared.

In the next few years, we tried other approaches to make fishenin' safer. I sent Mister Valney a life-vest for Christmas of 1975, urging that he wear it all the time. No luck: He found it uncomfortable on the long trip. He left the harbor wearing it while I was there, but soon began routinely tucking it under the seat. After two years it was so scuffed and torn as to be worthless.

I read somewhere about a Peace Corpsman in the Eastern Caroline Islands, in the South Pacific, who had helped fishermen build a fishing craft adapted from an Oregon design. Its engine, which drove a hydrojet instead of a propeller, was mounted in a well inboard, so the captain didn't have to sit at the back of the boat.

Mister Valney had often told me how the salt spray at the back stung his eyes, making it hard to maintain his compass course and sapping his energy. An inboard well would solve that; water-jet propulsion would avoid damage to propellers that still occasionally clipped the reef coming in to the harbor. Plywood construction would be new for Mister Arthur and others here, but would avoid the long search for ever-scarcer and ever-costlier cottonwood trees.

The South Pacific fishing sounded much like our Jamaican fishery; I wrote the Peace Corpsman for details. He sent sketches, and told me where to buy plans for the dory for $50.

I bought the plans and took them to Mister Arthur and his brother Cornelius, also a boat-builder, in Calabash Bay. I wrote for details about the hydrojet from its New Zealand manufacturer, and wrote Nicholas Sutherland, a talented auto mechanic near Frenchman's Cove, to see if he could convert a Ford Zephyr engine to power a hydrojet.

Mister Cornelius turned me down right away. Mister Arthur couldn't visualize a Pacific fishery like the Caribbean, but he would take my word about the similarity. A plywood boat didn't interest him; he couldn't imagine its being as strong and seaworthy as a dugout canoe. Looking at the plans, though, he said he could carve an inboard well for the engine out of a cottonwood log. Mister Nicholas said that if we got that far, he could adapt an automobile engine to the boat.

The men were creatures of habit, however. Even Mister Arthur's son Ernie wouldn't invest in a boat whose design had never been tested here. We were by then planning Mister Valney's new boat, but he couldn't afford to pioneer an untested design. If I wanted to commission a boat using the Oregon design, Mister Arthur would build it -- for me. I might get Mister Valney to use it, and buy it if he liked it.

The Cottonwood Foundation felt a boat would cost more than they'd invested earlier, and the outcome was less clear. I brought the drawings home. They're in a mailing tube in the attic.

●

Mister Arthur sparked our final effort to improve our neighbors' survivability at sea. When he was a child, fishermen had regularly gone to the Pedro Banks under sail. He had fond memories of Sunday regattas in which fishermen had sailed a marked course that Long Island yachtsmen would have recognized.

An outfit in Annapolis, Maryland sold brand-new or scarcely-used sails at bargain prices. With astonishing frequency, East Coast boat-owners commissioned custom sails with personalized logos for their Snarks, Sunfish and other small craft -- and then traded up to larger boats before the sails were ready.

The sailmaker mailed a monthly listing of such sails, some for as little as $35. I took a list to Mister Arthur. "Let's try it!" he said enthusiastically.

I bought a sail and brought it down. More precisely, I smuggled it, undeclared, at the foot of a duffel bag topped up with used clothing for neighbors. I'd learned from the flare episode. We still weren't making money with villa rentals, and I balked at paying a 35 to 50 percent duty that I would have to pass along to our neighbors.

Mister Arthur was just finishing a boat; he promptly stepped a stubby mast, and we went out one sunny morning to give it a try.

We nearly capsized. It was a very small boat he'd made for near-sea fishing, and the sail overwhelmed it: The boat bobbed and swayed like the proverbial drunken sailor. After a half-hour's fruitless maneuvering, we lowered the sail and came back on the outboard.

Undeterred, he stepped a mast into Mister Valney's far-sea boat. Much more successful: It moved sluggishly under sail, but it moved and could be steered. If both his engines failed, Mister Valney said, he was sure he could sail to shore; maybe not to Billy's Bay, but certainly to a safe landfall. He would be happy to carry the sail, furled up on the mast.

In the next several vacations, I brought down a half-dozen sails from Annapolis; half the boats at Billy's Bay soon had sails as emergency gear. They were nylon or other artificial fiber, relatively impervious to the elements, but the Annapolis people urged that the sails be spread out in the sun after every trip to prevent mildew.

Two years later, I asked Mr. Valney how his sail was holding up. Embarrassed, he showed me: It was eaten through and tattered. No, he confessed, he hadn't routinely spread the sail to dry; at the end of a long day, that had been a chore easily postponed. Besides, the sail and mast were in the way as his crew drew traps. As the sail rotted through, he'd given up carrying it to sea.

So had the other neighbors who'd bought sails. I offered to buy and bring down replacement sails from Annapolis; no one took me up on the offer.

If their number was up, it was up. Period.

# 18

## Patronage

**A**lthough we arrived before 9 for a 10 a.m. audience, we were not the first; two other cars were already in the yard, and others would soon join us.

I parked in the shade, and Miss Olive went to the door to announce our presence. A staff member took her name, and she came back to where we stood with Mister Arthur -- like all the gathering petitioners, chatting among ourselves and ignoring the others. We were competitors.

Derrick Sangster, member of parliament for our district, was a prosperous landowner, a nephew of Donald Sangster, a former prime minister for whom the Montego Bay airport is named. His cattle ranch and farm, a half-hour's drive from Treasure Beach, was a spread whose fence paralleled the road for at least a quarter-mile as we neared.

We drove through the gates – *Fullerswood Park* neatly lettered in the pink-painted concrete wings – and across a cattle guard into a pasture where a few Brahman cows browsed. Then the driveway led into the shaded yard in which a pair of hogs, several goats and a dozen chickens foraged. Mr. Sangster's home was a sprawling, weathered wooden farmhouse.

We had come begging.

Some of the government's public works budget was managed as pure patronage: Each MP, regardless of party affiliation (Sangster represented the Jamaica Labour Party then in the majority) was allotted a budget for his or her district. There was no bidding requirement and little governmental review: The member of parliament chose a favored contractor to do whatever work he or she authorized, and set the price. As elections neared, MPs were allotted extra public-works money.

The fact that Sangster held informal office hours one Sunday a month wasn't publicized, but party insiders like Miss Olive knew.

At 10 the MP, having finished a leisurely breakfast, began hearing from his constituents; an aide called us in the order we'd arrived. When our turn came, we were invited through a gate into a small garden and then to a glass-jalousied porch where he sat at a small desk-table facing straight-back chairs for his guests. He was a big man, in his late 20s, a bit on the pudgy side, with hooded eyes that betrayed no emotion.

I was reminded of a scene in Puccini's *Gianni Schicchi*. A rich uncle has just died, leaving his wealth to a monastery. His grasping relatives decide to have the shrewd Schicchi, posing as the old man, dictate a new will. One at a time, each comes to the bedside to whisper bribes if the imposter will name them recipients of the house, the mule and the mills. "*Sta bene*," he mutters non-committally to each petitioner; "very well."

Miss Olive wanted one of the new all-fiberglass boats made for her by the government factory in Kingston – and another for Miss Ida's husband -- with higher leeboards to make it suitable for trips to far sea. Mr. Sangster said he discouraged such requests, because the extra work slowed production, but he would speak to the factory on her behalf.

Mister Arthur's mission was the real reason we'd come. The MP had already authorized a complicated battery light to illuminate the reef passage at the fishing cove. It would cost less than expected, and we hoped the left-over money might bring poles and power lines to a big overhead light on the beach where the fish were weighed out.

The money wasn't really left over, Mr. Sangster explained; funds were limited, and there were others with requests, but he'd consider a light. *Sta bene*.

I mentioned that I'd brought a small, battery-powered strobe-light blinker that I'd thought might mark the reef opening. A different arrangement had now been made for Billy's Bay, but the gadget might be useful for other fishing coves. Mr. Sangster for the first time showed genuine interest, and gave me a calling-card so I could send him more information.

Mister Arthur, once here, decided to push his luck. He asked for repairs to the rocky road to Fort Charles. He wanted the government to investigate the high price of chicken-wire for pots. He wanted the government to speed up the next delivery of outboard engines, which had been held up for lack of foreign exchange.

Mr. Sangster waited politely until Mister Arthur paused for breath. "Thank you," he said, standing to signal that our interview was over. *Sta bene.*

●

With the reef opening wider, the men were indeed putting out more pots and staying longer, often coming back after dark when it was hard to see the passageway; they were still scraping on the reef or shearing off propellers.

Taking advantage of a few days of unusually low tides in May, Mister Arthur had rallied the fishermen to build a concrete pylon on one side of the newly-widened reef opening. They'd cut out the bottom of an empty steel drum, set it on the reef lip at the narrowest point, and hurriedly mixed concrete to fill it. The slurry oozed down into the porous reef-rock and set before the sea level returned to normal, giving it a solid foundation. Then they'd set a narrower barrel atop the first, and had filled that, too.

The result was, for Treasure Beach, a veritable Colossus of Rhodes, a thick, six-foot high column. The steel drums were already rusting off, but the concrete pylon would last – indeed, has lasted – forever.

Mister Arthur originally hoped to run a power line to the pylon so an electric light could illuminate the safe passageway. I'd talked him out of that: The line, more than 50 yards long, would have drooped across the cove and might have electrocuted any inattentive fishermen snared in it. If it broke as it whipped in a high wind and fell into the water, the whole cove might have been electrified.

I suggested a spotlight atop a pole on the beach, pointed out at the reef opening. No, he said, such a light would be in the captains' eyes, making it even harder to navigate the opening.

He reluctantly agreed that the light atop his harbor improvement ought to be free-standing; I'd promised to look for something suitable.

I found the strobe light (designed for running lights on barges under tow) with an electric-eye sensor to turn it off by day; a compact six-volt lantern-battery would last six months.

By the time I brought it, Mister Arthur had persuaded the MP to commission a light powered by an automobile battery, and had it installed.

It was a Rube Goldberg invention. A wooden dollhouse of a box was fastened atop the pylon to house an automobile battery, with a sealed-beam auto headlight pointed down into the opening. In late afternoon when men were expected home, someone would carry the battery out to turn on the light. There was a spare battery if the first ran out of juice before everyone was home; both would be trickle-charged back on shore between trips.

Most of the time, however, waves break over that reef. Carrying a heavy battery out to the makeshift lighthouse involved a precarious walk along the edge of the barrier reef. There were no hand- and foot-holds on the pylon to get up to the box; one had to also carry a short ladder. In bad weather, or after dark, getting a battery installed proved impossible. The whole cockamamie contraption was soon abandoned.

Billy's Bay always voted lopsidedly for the JLP; the MP came through. A power line was brought to the beach, and its light – even though not aimed into the captains' eyes – proved enough to make the pylon readily visible at night. My strobe light sat in our closet for several years before I handed it on to fishermen with less political clout at nearby Frenchman's Cove.

A few years later, Miss Olive got her big chance – she thought -- at the government gravy train. When the road to Billy's Bay was paved, filling in perhaps a mile of dirt roadway between the small sections that had already been paved in election seasons, her political patron named her one of several contractors, each responsible for a few hundred yards.

"But you don't know anything about paving!" I said.

"I don't need to, Mist' Don," she said. She, and each of the other contractors given these plums, would subcontract the actual work to a professional from Black River. He would bring in a grader, steamroller and other equipment, and would do the whole job from one end to the other.  She would pay for her share of the tar, gravel and other materials, and for her share of the cost of the equipment and labor.

The project nearly bankrupted her.  Each contractor was expected to pay the costs out of pocket, and to be awarded his or her fee after the work was done.

We came several months after the paving was finished, and she still hadn't been paid.  I drove her up to a government office in Santa Cruz, and after several hours' palavering she finally was given a check.

From what she told us – she wasn't the world's best bookkeeper -- it appeared she'd broken even at best, and had probably lost money on the deal.

Even political patronage is apparently not, in Jamaica, a sure way to riches.

*Sta bene.*

# 19

## Sea-frost, varmints, terraces

The barbed-wire fence along the beach was beginning to rust through. "It's the sea-frahst, Mist' Don," Brother Elbert explained. Two years after he'd strung it in 1973, the galvanized wire was heavily oxidized; it might last another year, but not much longer. He'd warned me that we would sooner or later have to replace it with a concrete-block wall. I hadn't expected later to come so soon.

The sea-frost showed up indoors, too: When I went to remove a window screen for repair, I could hardly budge the screws.

"Well, of course," my metallurgist father said when I phoned him on our return. "Your screws are steel; the frame is aluminum. Those two metals invite electrolysis, which welds them together; salt just speeds the process." I'd squirted oil on the window screws; Dad assured me that wouldn't help much. At a specialty builder's store I found aluminum screws to replace the steel on all the window screens Lester Lyn had installed -- and cursed the sea-frost.

More evidence of that invisible nemesis: I plugged an electric drill into a patio outlet for a repair chore, and found it alarmingly wobbly. When I turned the power off and took the cover plate off, the outlet fell out in pieces, all but the brass screws destroyed by oxidation. I've ever since made it a routine on every trip to check outlets. After three decades, I've replaced every one in the house at least once, and those facing the sea, several times.

The rusting fence along the sea-front would have to wait; I bought a fresh roll of barbed wire from Southfield, put it in the shed behind the house -- sheltered from the salt -- and asked Brother Elbert to tack up another strand or two if the original wire fell apart before my next visit.

●

The torn fiberglass screen I'd set out to repair had holes in it, the size of a quarter or half-dollar, right in the middle. Same thing at several other windows, especially those by the game table. What would make such neat round holes?

When the answer jumped out at me, I didn't immediately get it.

We were sitting in the living room one evening when a mouse scampered across the floor. Emily saw it first, screamed, and got up on a chair. Brad joined her.

Louie Gordon, our next-door neighbor's 12-year-old son, was at the game table with Ken, being introduced to jigsaw puzzles. "Palm mouse!" he said, and started in pursuit. The mouse ran out onto the patio and -- we hoped -- into the yard.

Within minutes, another appeared, to another chorus of screams. This time Louie was quicker: He snatched, caught the mouse in his hand, raised it over his head and hurled it to the hard terrazzo floor -- and coolly kicked the dead rodent out the front door. Another appeared. This time Ken, onto the new game, joined in a successful pursuit.

The mice seemed to have come from the small corner closet where we locked up clothes and personal possessions between visits. Ken turned on the closet light to explore. Another mouse scuttled out, and then another. The boys thought this better sport than jigsaw puzzles; their tally that night was five dead mice and two that got away. Inside the closet was a now-empty nest in the shreds of what had been a T-shirt.

Oh, yes, Miss Olive said next morning. Mice, and larger rats, too, are a constant problem. They often live in palm trees, and spoil the coconuts, but they'll come inside if given a chance. She thought she'd heard them scuttling around the attic crawl space.

In Connecticut, snakes help hold down the rodent population. There are almost no snakes in Jamaica. The British imported the mongoose – whose prowess in dispatching snakes Rudyard Kipling celebrated in *Rikki-Tikki-Tavi* -- from India. The new predators proliferated, all but eliminating snakes. Now the mongoose is part of the varmint population; it steals eggs. One often sees a mongoose streaking across the road, looking like a weasel with a squirrel's tail.

(I was driving with Mister Endley the first time I spotted one. "Oh, look!" I said. "A mongoose." "Yes, mon," he replied, combining a puckish sense of humor with Jamaican patois, "or it might have been an 'oomongoose.")

The morning after Louie's exploits, I went looking to see how the mice had gotten in -- and solved the mystery of the screens. Every window had redwood louvers. The blades were closed against rain when the house was vacant, but most evenings were left in a horizontal position to admit the breeze. Palm mice could sit comfortably on the louver blades while they gnawed through the fiberglass mesh.

Gayle's Hardware had only fiberglass or steel screening. The fiberglass was no barrier to mice, and steel would quickly succumb to sea-frost. On our next trip, I brought a 100-foot roll of aluminum screening, stapled pieces over all the attic vents to keep mice out, and began replacing window screens. It would take several trips and several more rolls to complete the job. Jamaica to this day exports bauxite, but has just begun making or importing aluminum window screening.

Merrick had lots of rodent-control materials, though. I tacked hard blocks of bait on trees near the house, and opened the ceiling trap door to chuck pieces as far as I could into the crawl space. I also set spring-loaded traps in the corners of cupboards, but Miss Olive soon made clear she didn't enjoy disposing of the dead mice they caught. In the ensuing years, we've brought from home every trap and bait known to gadgeteering America. We finally settled on a bait that does its work— usually, but not always – when rodents go outside to find water.

(When they die in the attic, they stink. If I'm there, I climb up into the hot crawl space, gagging, to dispose of the remains. I suspect that some guests must detect a strange smell and wonder what it is. Fortunately, in that heat, it doesn't last long.)

Keeping mice out of our closet turned out to be easy. Moth balls, Merrick advised: Sprinkle them around. It worked; there were no mice on our next arrival, and no more clothing torn into nests. Scattering

While at it, I dug a shallow trench, and put in an underground electrical conduit from the house so I could someday put a light at the almond tree. By late morning I had the terrace ready for paving.

Saturday, Brother Elbert and I took turns wheeling marl; by now I had a permanent construction dump in the hollow behind the well. It was more hot, hard work, and I was grateful for a sea-bath when we quit at 4. (Jamaican workmen started work at 7, in the cool of the morning, and quit at 4 if they'd had an hour's lunch break. We always took an hour's break; I needed it.)

●

I was just back from a refreshing swim when Miss Margaret appeared to say her mother was stricken by a throat blockage that left her barely able to breathe. Brad and I hurriedly drove to get her and headed for Black River Hospital.

A doctor examined her and found no apparent cause, but would keep her overnight -- hardly a promising diagnosis. Just then an ambulance arrived to take a critically-ill patient to in Montego Bay. We got Miss Olive into the ambulance, and came home for what was left of a night's sleep.

We'd sent the poor lady off in a nightgown. We made ourselves breakfast Sunday morning, had Miss Margaret assemble a small suitcase, and set off for MoBay, where we easily found Cornwall Hospital, a four-story building on a commanding hillside.

No serious problem, a doctor told us; he'd prescribed a few medications, one of which was a tranquilizer; she was dozing now, but would be released in early afternoon. We drove to the relatively-new Holiday Inn for lunch, and came back to bring her home, apparently recovered.

●

We were now waiting for the tile to be delivered, and had an excuse to relax. The sea was calm, so we went for a long snorkeling swim. I was a dozen yards in the lead, halfway to the surfing beach, when I looked down to see a shark, bottom-feeding just below me.

Don't make a commotion, the rules say, lest you attract attention. That's easy to say in the abstract, harder when one is staring down at a shark. I did everything wrong: I trod water vigorously to get my head above water, spat out the snorkel tube, and hollered to Brad: "Shark!"

moth balls inside the closet as we lock up has become a part of departure-day routine.

●

The major effort this trip was to be paving the Almond Terrace. Lester Lyn had built a low cut-stone terrace wall below the patio, and a sweeping crescent wall on the seaside to contain what would become our sunning terrace, where the almond tree was already established.

Miss Olive had then hired village women to fill in behind that wall with sand -- women, because village men would have none of such demeaning labor. Brother Elbert or Mister Valney went down by the beach, where the on-shore breeze kept adding to a sand dune, and filled five-gallon pails. A parade of women hoisted pails atop their heads and toted them up to spill into the terrace. It was hard work, for which we paid them $6 a day. They paced themselves, but the terrace slowly was filled in, several weeks' patient work in our absence.

On our next trip, I'd helped Brother Elbert level the surface, and found some plugs of Bermuda grass to plant; I envisioned an island of grass.

Disastrous! To get the grass plugs to spread, Brother Elbert watered the terrace regularly. The grass flourished, but so did a colony of ants that in this arid climate were desperate for moisture. As soon as he watered, the ants appeared -- and bit anyone brave enough to walk barefoot or even sandal-foot on the terrace. The more grass we had, the more sharp-toothed ants we would have. Grass wouldn't do; I would have to pave the terrace.

In Mandeville, I found a shop that made foot-square concrete tiles with a cross-hatch pattern and a moderately coarse texture that would be slip-proof. I ordered 600, to be delivered in a few days. Coming back through Southfield, I ordered cement, marl and framing lumber. We would cast a flat surface on the terrace, and then cement down the neatly-patterned tiles.

After lunch, we began grubbing up the grass we'd so painstakingly cultivated.

It was hot, hard work, and we didn't finish. Mister Valney went to far sea that night; I felt guilty having worked him so hard, but he insisted he never napped before a trip. Brother Elbert went to near sea with Mister Arthur every Friday morning, so I soldiered on alone

I could tell she'd already seen it: She was swimming hard for the barrier reef, making almost as much commotion as I had. I followed her over the reef, where we caught our breath, both with reef-scratches bleeding slightly -- a come-on for sharks, I thought.

"Oh, mon," said Mr. Arthur when I told him of our adventure, "that's a little inshore shark that never troubles anyone; he was more scared than you were."

If so, I told him, that was one helluva frightened shark.

(A few years later, I spotted a manta ray bottom-feeding. Mindful of my unneeded shark panic, I stayed calm, rolled over on my back and waved the swimmers behind me to come see. A half-dozen of us paddled in the clear water to watch the ray, as graceful as a ballet dancer, flipping its wing-tips to maneuver. Suddenly, it turned – perhaps it had seen us – and disappeared. When I told Mister Arthur, he said I'd been foolish: The ray has a long, raspy broomstick tail that is loaded with toxin. A man in the village had to have a leg amputated when it was raked by a ray.)

Still waiting for the tile, we left in late morning for Negril at the western tip of the island; we were still trying to visit all the tourist areas so we could tell our guests about options if they tired of our beach. Stopping at Black River post office, I wired:

PLEASE DELIVER TILE ORDER IMMEDIATELY OR WIRE US UNABLE TO DO SO.

We stopped in Savannah-la-Mar to buy a few groceries, went on to have a late lunch at The Sundowner and swim a bit, snorkeling through the shallow waters to look for conch. It began to rain; we started home early, and soon drove out of the rain.

Just past Black River, I noticed tiny thatch-palms beside the road. To my annoyance, Brother Elbert still hadn't gotten us a seedling from Thatchville to replicate the Putnams' sunset-behind-a-thatch-palm. I got out a lug wrench and dug around a seedling no more than a foot tall.

It was easy digging in the loose, sandy soil. I got down a half-foot, and tried gently to lift it free. No luck. I tugged hard. No luck. I dug more, made almost a foot, and tugged again. The taproot was still thick enough and deep enough that I couldn't budge it.

Two days later, I went back with a shovel, with which I got down two feet -- and still couldn't dislodge the tiny-looking tree. With a fresh appreciation for Brother Elbert's wisdom, I gave up. We would wait for his friend in Thatchville to find one young enough to be dislodged.

●

Still no tiles. Necessity is the mother of invention. I thought we could make a slip-proof cross-hatch pattern on the terrace floor by pressing strips of chicken wire -- from which the fishermen made traps -- into fresh concrete. I drove to the post office to wire Mandeville:

CANCEL ORDER FOR TILE. DO NOT DELIVER.

Wednesday morning we set to work: Brother Elbert, Mister Valney, and Goof, whose proper name I finally learned, Rafael Taylor.

Using two-by-fours, we laid out forms ten feet long,. We mixed concrete in a corner of the terrace, cast it into the form, and floated the surface with a home-made wooden tool to make it level but not too smooth. When it began to set, we pressed a piece of chicken wire into the hardening surface, and lifted the wire. Presto! Exactly the pattern I'd hoped for.

We finished more than a third of the terrace area the first afternoon, and went back at it next morning. Judging the right moment to pattern the fresh concrete was tricky: If it was still too soft, the lines slumped and blurred; we floated it smooth again, waited a few minutes, and again applied the chicken wire. We got better at it.

We'd just finished another section when an afternoon shower struck, softening the fresh concrete. The shower passed; we re-floated the surface and successfully struck the pattern before quitting.

We had a hard rain that night, but the concrete had by then set sufficiently that the rainfall did no harm, and in fact made the concrete stronger by moistening it as it cured.

Brother Elbert and Goof went to near sea Friday morning with Mister Arthur. Mister Valney and I mixed, cast and patterned the next-last section. We left one smaller section to be cast after my departure, and used the waning afternoon hour to clean leaves from the rain gutters.

Phil and Ianthe Manzelli came to dinner. I was elated by my terracing success. Phil was depressed: Our plantings were doing better than his, despite his two-year head start, probably because his soil was less hospitable. His pump and refrigerator were acting up. He was again talking about selling.

After dinner, we sat out on the hardened part of my new patio, lucent under a half moon, and tried to console him: You have to ride out the difficulties of a developing nation. He was not consoled; we knew we would soon lose a neighbor.

Saturday morning I turned to a few household repairs. The table at the edge of our shaded patio was loose on its moorings, thanks to guests who sat or leaned on it. I'd brought along anchor bolts, and made it more secure.

On our previous trip I'd brought down plans for Adirondack chairs, and had commissioned chairs and a chaise from Radford Taylor, a carpenter at Frenchman's Cove ("Coffinmaker," the sign above his door said). They were on the terrace when we arrived, handsome additions, but he hadn't made them rigid enough to withstand guests' moving them around; I braced them.

●

One more issue to address before we left. Our friends the Satters, after their second visit, had reported "a small problem." They'd hired The Buccaneers for a party. Miss Olive's ebullient sister Ida danced with them. Suddenly, as they told it, "an unfortunate incident occurred": A strange man appeared and attacked Miss Ida, cold-cocking her, down and out. Miss Olive, trying to protect her sister, took a blow to the face.

Miss Olive's letter had elaborated only slightly: "He punch me in the face," she wrote. "Mr. Satter take me to a Dr. next morning. I was given some tablet and ointment; feeling much better."

We got to the root of it: The attacker was Ukie Hill, Miss Ida's common-law husband, who was enraged to find his wife dancing with a stranger.

Her dancing was entirely in character, and entirely innocent. She wanted people to enjoy themselves. She laughed easily, shared in jokes – even, we would learn, when she had problems at home. She was more than handsome enough to make a man jealous.

We talked with them. Mister Ukie said he now understood that dancing with our guests wasn't cheating on him. We suggested he marry her and make it official; he said he'd think about it. He was one of those who spent six weeks at a time camped at the Pedro Cays, where he could earn enough to take care of the growing family he was siring with Miss Ida.

Brad and I sat on our moonlit terrace one more time, admiring our handiwork, and left Sunday morning for home, confident it would be finished in our absence.

●

After a better-than-expected first season, our bookings had dropped dramatically, thanks in large part to a new cartel of oil-producing nations, OPEC, that was holding back supplies to jack up prices. In a way, we were sympathetic, as was Prime Minister Michael Manley. Third-World countries rarely control the price of their raw materials; they sell cheap, and buy back finished products dear. Manley had begun exploring a similar cartel of bauxite producers.

Meanwhile, fuel shortages were playing hob with tourism. There were long lines at American gas stations; soon one could buy only every other day, sometimes only five gallons. We'd made several trips to the neighborhood station to tank up for the 200-mile trip to and from New York's JFK. We'd had difficulty buying gas in Jamaica, too.

Some domestic airline flights were cancelled for lack of fuel. Prospective guests were uncertain that they could get to airports or that their flights would get off the ground. No flight to Jamaica was ever cancelled, we told the few people who telephoned asking about our Hikaru, but they were understandably not reassured.

We were subsidizing our new tourism enterprise more heavily than we'd anticipated, and more than we could afford. We needed something to enhance our marketing and lure more guests. We began thinking about a tennis court.

That plan would be set back by a telegram a month after our return home.

# 20
## Brother Elbert's death

The telegram was as stark as it was unexpected, telephoned by Western Union on a Friday midnight:

ELBERT JAMES DIED BY DROWNING VALNEY RITCHIE

We wept for a lost friend. Dear sweet, gentle, hard-working Brother Elbert. I could see him patiently drawing pailfuls of water from the well to keep our plants alive when the pump quit; hauling a fishing trap hand-over-hand with Goof, taking turns with me wheeling marl to our terrace little more than a month ago. We weren't even sure how old he was, but surely not ready for death.

Next morning I wired back:

WE MOURN LOSS OF GOOD NEIGHBOR FRIEND AND CHRISTIAN THE NOELS

We felt helpless. There was no telephone, not even anyone we could phone to learn more. We knew little about funeral rites, but guessed that in a tropical climate interment must come soon. We weren't sure we could arrive in time even if we flew down Sunday morning. Besides, we couldn't: Brad was busy with the always-hectic opening of the school year; I was covering a special session of the Connecticut legislature.

So we mourned privately, trying to imagine the scene, recalling the keening of wives and mothers following deaths while we'd been at the house, hoping our thoughts and prayers might be felt 1,600 miles away, waiting impatiently for a letter that might tell us more than the grim fact.

●

There had been a death in a family near the fishing beach two years earlier; we heard the wailing carried up on the wind, late into the night. It had been Brother Elbert who explained that the family and much of the village would not sleep: The "duppie," or ghost of the departed, would be about, not yet settled into an afterlife; it might seize on anyone sleeping, and do harm.

That had been unexpected in a village of devout, church-going Christians. We knew that voodoo -- *obeah* in Jamaica -- is deep in the culture, but had thought Treasure Beach far removed from those African roots. On reflection, we'd concluded that staying up to fend off duppies was not entirely different from, say, an Irish wake.

The winter before last, a woman had been visiting Blossom Gordon next door when word was brought that her 18-year-old son had been accidentally electrocuted. She began to wail, joined by Miss Blossom, a quavering ululation.

Hymns were the more sustained expression. One of my favorite village sounds is the voice of Mister Valney's wife Cislyn in the yard behind us, singing hymns as she works. She is a tall, large woman with a handsome, strong face, at least 30 pounds heavier than her husband, her body sagging with the weight of a half-dozen childbirths, complaining occasionally of arthritis or other pains. Her voice is clear, and her pitch true; her hymns on a still morning are a testament of faith and a lovely way to greet the day.

There were two small churches within earshot on calm evenings; we often heard the sweet sound of hymns, on joyous occasions as well as those of mourning.

Death was distressingly common in our little village, and rarely of old age. Hardly a visit went by without our hearing of a boat lost at sea. A year earlier a young man, visiting from an inland village, had drowned when caught in a current that carried him through the reef opening.

But Brother Elbert!

●

I wondered if he'd been net-fishing, walking along the barrier reef with Goof, waiting for a lull in the waves and then deftly casting his 10-foot circle of fine mesh into the waters off the reef. He and Goof would draw the net back; pull out the fish gilled in the net, and slip them onto gaff-loops at their belts. Then he would shake the net to free the folds, walk a few paces along the wave-washed reef, and spin it out again, a flattened bubble that glistened briefly in the morning sun and dropped again into the sea.

He'd told me on our last visit that he'd nearly drowned when the net caught on a reef and he was dragged into the sea. It was a shallow place, there were hardly any waves, and Goof had pulled him up. The net was torn, though; he'd showed me how he would weave and knot nylon twine to mend it. I'd bought some twine and set it aside with the cache of things to be sent with guests or brought on our next trip.

Letters from both Miss Olive and Mister Valney confirmed that he had indeed been netting, starting several miles to our west and working his way homeward; the accident occurred less than a mile from Hikaru. A wave had apparently knocked him into the sea. Goof had been unable to help; Brother Elbert had become tangled in the net in deep water beyond the reef.

"I was at Hikaru about 9:30," Miss Olive wrote, "when I heard someone call out 'Brother Elbert is drowning!' I ran off with the intention and hope that when I got there I would see him on the shore explaining what happened. Instead I saw a crowd of people screaming and some searching in the sea.

"Can you imagine what happened to me then? The worst shock I ever had in all my life. I don't know how I can work at Hikaru without Brother Elbert. There is no other can fill his space. He was such a good man, my best friend from when I was about 11; we went to church together to teach Sunday school, and had been together two years at Hikaru without a frown on each other. My heart melts inside when I think of him as a dead body. But as he always said, he has gone to be with the Lord."

Mister Valney's letter added details. Brother Elbert's body had been wedged into the reef, extricated with difficulty, and then was drawn up on the sand and lay there about four hours until the police came to take the body to the refrigerated morgue at Black River. (I supposed that was routine until a medical examiner declared the death accidental, but a kindness, too, allowing a few more days to arrange a funeral.)

He was buried the following Tuesday. The service at the church where he had so often been lay preacher lasted from 2 in the afternoon until 5, Mister Valney wrote, and then he was buried in his own yard, as is often the practice. "There were 21 cars, vans, minibuses and a lot of Hondas [motor scooters]", Mister Valney wrote. "All were mourning the loss of a good man.

"Remember his goodbye to you when you were leaving," he added. "If we don't meet on earth let's meet in Heaven."

There was a letter from Miss Lethe, the grieving widow, too. It was in the same hand as Mister Valney's. I realized that Brother Elbert's letters had been in the same hand, too: Miss Lethe – or perhaps Miss Cislyn, their daughter and Mister Valney's wife -- was the family scribe. I've often wished I could be a fly on the wall to hear how letters are dictated or composed.

●

Mister Valney wanted to take over the caretaker's duties, and Miss Olive agreed. I sent a check to Miss Lethe, wrote consolingly to Miss Olive, exploring an appropriate memorial.

A bell for the church, she wrote back, or perhaps a striking clock. A bell sounded too ambitious, but I found a handsome wall-mounted, wind-up schoolhouse clock for $85. She said that was more than she'd expected, and approved. In early November, I wrote our former guests to tell them of Brother Elbert's death, suggesting they send Miss Lethe a card, and telling them of the planned memorial. "If you'd like to participate in a small way in that, please let us know," I wrote.

A half-dozen of them responded, sending small checks, and more wrote Miss Lethe; Elbert James had made a deep impression.

Undaunted by the experience bringing the flares, I tackled the bureaucracy again. We had time; our next trip wouldn't be until April. On an old customs receipt, I found an address for the Collector General, and wrote asking how to have duty waived on the clock. (The search for an address made me realize that telephone books are useful even if one has no telephone; I've since made it a point each year to wheedle a book from the phone company in Black River to take home.)

My letter was forwarded to the Trade Administrator's office, which sent an application for an import license. I filled it out and mailed it back. Then I heard from the Collector General, where I'd started: Furnishings for churches were exempt from duty, but I would need a declaration from the "head of the denomination" that the clock would not be re-sold. I sent those forms to Miss Olive for signature by the pastor of the Calvary Assembly of God at Calabash Bay.

In due course I received yet another set of forms -- in sextuplicate -- on which to apply for exemption from duty. But the clock would have to be "detained for inspection," and I would need the services of a customs broker. I planned to fly down alone in early April, and go back to MoBay to meet the family a week later, so the "detaining" might work out. Hiring a broker to avoid duty on an $85 clock seemed crazy. I went ahead, assuming I could bull my way through unassisted.

●

Meanwhile, life went on. There was a torrential rain -- an estimated six inches, although my rain gauge was knocked down in the rain-softened soil. Mister Valney wrote that the deluge breached some of the terraces that he and Brother Elbert had recently built. He wrote a week later to say they were stabilized, and could await my next visit to be repaired.

The heavy rain followed a drought typical of that time of year. Brother Elbert's garden planted in our bottom land suffered, and nothing but the caliloo-spinach survived; the rains came too late to rescue his beans, corn or cassava.

Miss Olive wrote that two neighbors' daughters, both pre-teens named Dawn, had made pests of themselves, bothering the guests, hoping for attention. She'd talked with them and with the parents, to no avail. I wrote our neighbors Philip and Blossom, asking them to urge their daughter Dawn to be less pushy; Philip wrote that she was only being polite when guests showed interest.

I reached the guests, who said the two Dawns had been only minor pests, and had indeed gone home when asked.

This was our first experience with a recurring problem: shielding guests from village intrusions, but understanding why neighbors intrude. A child who charms an American visitor can expect at the very least a chain of correspondence, more likely some gift on departing or mailed on return, or -- the ultimate good fortune -- an invitation to come to the United States, attend school as a resident visitor, perhaps find a job and somehow win a treasured "green card," entitling the bearer to earn U.S. citizenship.

We deplored the "brain drain" in the abstract, but understood the individual's impulse. I wrote Miss Olive to lay off a bit, make a point of greeting children by name at the door as a way of acknowledging their ambitions, and let guests say whether they welcomed a visit at that moment. I wrote asking our next guests -- repeat visitors we felt were sensitive -- to mediate.

I revised the packet of materials we sent when people booked -- by now called *Hikaru Hints*, a growing compendium of guests' questions and discoveries -- to urge that guests take a hand themselves if village children were too aggressive, and spare Miss Olive the exclusive role of stern gatekeeper – "house dragon," I phrased it.

One set of guests complained that barking dogs had spoiled their sleep. I wrote Mister Philip, Miss Olive and Mister Valney pleading that dogs be chained when we had guests, on the far side of houses from Hikaru, please. Philip wrote back: He would tie his dogs when we had guests, but they provided security for us, too; besides, Mister Valney's dogs were just as noisy as his.

(As near as I can tell, no one in the village ever gets up to see what the dogs are barking about. They sleep through the clamor, just as city-dwellers in the United States tune out sirens and other urban noises that would ruin the sleep of anyone just arrived from the countryside.)

There were continuing problems with the pumps. When the freshwater pump failed, I wrote letters looking for parts. No luck: It was German-made, and I couldn't find a supplier in either the United States or Jamaica. A typical developing-country problem: Overseas manufacturers get rid of their outdated inventory, with no prospect of follow-up service. I wrote A.J. Carroll urging him to find a replacement pump from an established company that had a service facility in Jamaica.

Meanwhile, I wrote Miss Olive: How about the hand pump? When I designed the water system, I'd bought a unit that could be used, albeit laboriously, to pump water from the cistern to the tower. It had rusted shut, and was useless.

The impact of the OPEC oil embargo had worn off; inquiries were up. Riots in Trenchtown, a Kingston slum, however, made American headlines, a new deterrent to bookings. I began a long series of letters to the Jamaican Association of Villas and Apartments. The latest thing in air travel was an "ITX" fare (for Inclusive Tour something) that bundled reduced airfares with ground accommodations. An officer of JAVA wrote back: He wasn't pushing the South Coast because of its inaccessibility. I responded that we didn't expect referrals, but that membership would let us offer our guests lower air fares. We joined.

Still, bookings were slow. We had several inquiries from people who were unsure about coming. I began writing Miss Olive about people I thought might book at the last minute, promising to wire her if they came through. One such tentative booking I wrote her about was with a colleague, Jose Santiago; a few days after posting that letter, we had another inquiry from a Mr. and Mrs. Roman from Chicago.

Both, as it turned out, came through. I wired Miss Olive: SANTIAGO PARTY OF SIX ARRIVING MONDAY EVENING FIFTEENTH TWO ROMANS COMING TWENTY-SEVENTH LETTER FOLLOWS.

She wrote back that she'd worried whether she'd be able to communicate with the Romans, and then realized when my letter arrived that Roman was their name, not their nationality.

●

I arrived in early April of 1976, declared the clock and left it for inspection. A week later I came back to meet Brad, our family, and guests, and cleared it duty-free without much hassle.

We'd arranged with Pastor Kenford Senior for a memorial service and presentation of the clock on what turned out to be Palm Sunday; I brought a dark suit.

It was a lovely service, full of tributes. The clock, installed on a wall near the pulpit, had an engraved plaque: "In loving memory of Elbert James from his friends and guests at Hikaru." It chimed the quarter-hours to everyone's delight but perhaps mine; it chimed through two and a half hours, by which time my suit was drenched with perspiration and still darker.

One of the guests who contributed to the clock wrote of the irony of Brother Elbert's death:

"One Sunday we left Hikaru for a hike toward Black River accompanied by several of the neighborhood children. We went around the first point and were on our way to the next when we heard someone calling. It was Mister Elbert and he had walked the distance to warn us about the rocks and the incoming tide. He was insistent that we return by the track. I can picture him now. 'Now mistress, it is not safe.' And any number of times he cautioned us to watch the children on the reef. Grandpop went out to the edge of the reef to fish, and poor Mr. James was worried the whole time he was out there."

●

Two years later, almost to the day, we received word of another neighbor's death. We'd learned earlier that Philip Gordon had failing kidneys. He was sent from Black River Hospital to Mandeville and finally to the University of West Indies hospital in Kingston, the nearest facility with a dialysis machine.

In Hartford, he could have lived a long and productive life with regular dialysis. In Jamaica, he would have spent most of his time shuttling from Treasure Beach to Kingston for treatment -- even if he'd been able to afford it. He had no insurance, of course, and postponed seeking help for his final bout until too late. He died soon after arriving in Kingston by ambulance.

Brother Elbert's family had grieved, but carried on. Philip's family was far less fortunate: He and Miss Blossom had never married. They'd planned a ceremony for her birthday that August, but his recurring illness postponed that; his death left her still a common-law wife. That gave her rights under Jamaican law, but rights not easily asserted without legal help.

Philip had bought the land next to Hikaru from his father -- several neighbors had witnessed the transaction -- but never applied for a title, and didn't even have a paper recording the purchase.

Miss Blossom came back from Kingston to find the house Philip had built locked up, and her meager belongings strewn in the yard. Jimmy Gordon, Philip's father, had taken possession of not only the house, but Philip's fishing boat and engines as well. She fled to her mother's in Flagamon, halfway to Southfield, taking the younger children with her. One of the engines had been brand-new; she and Philip had bought it from their bank account, she wrote. But his brother insisted Philip had borrowed $1,000 from him -- another paperless transaction, if real -- and made her pay him before releasing the engine, which she sold to raise a little cash.

She couldn't afford a lawyer. She lived for several years in Flagamon with her mother, taking a new common-law mate; her former in-laws seized on that to tell the village that she'd been unworthy of Philip. When Dawn emigrated and finished a community-college degree, she brought her mother to live with her in Florida; we still keep in touch.

Philip's first-born son Louie, who had helped our son Ken catch mice, had rights under Jamaican law, too, and tried to get a jack-leg village lawyer to help him. Having no success, he had no choice but to rent his father's house from Mister Jimmy. He lived there as tenant instead of heir and owner until his grandfather's death, when he finally inherited the house.

# 21

## Mister Valney, Michael

**S**o Valney Ritchie would now be my strong right arm. We'd known him first as merely Brother Elbert's son-in-law, a fishing captain whom we'd helped buy a boat, and an extra hand when there was more work than his father-in-law could handle.

There was much more to him. As he took over, I came to rely on his common sense and his uncommon work ethic.

He'd grown up in Flagamon. His father had played a minor role; he inherited his indomitable stuff from his mother. Although past 80, she still walked down to visit him occasionally – perhaps eight miles – and would waken before dawn to start home while the air was still fresh for the uphill walk home.

Our age difference was just enough that Mister Valney saw me as a father figure, and I took to him as a son. He occasionally addressed me as "Mist' Don," but more often called me simply boss -- "ba'as." I initially disliked the name; it reminded me of the South African usage toward white colonials. He intended no slur, however, and I came to love it as a familiarity.

"Well, ba'as," he would begin, and would proceed gently to tell me why my blunt American ideas didn't fit the Jamaican way.

He had no alarm clock, but woke to the growing daylight, up most mornings at 6:30 to pump water. He would sit smoking a cigarette -- usually tobacco, but sometimes marijuana -- listening to the sound of the pump. If we'd been sparing of water, the overflow tube I'd built into the tower tank signaled him to turn it off. More often, he'd hear when the pump began sucking dry, a subtle change in pitch that I often missed. He'd go home for a cup of coffee, and come back to pump again when the well had re-charged.

An early riser myself, I took to sharing this morning ritual. I'd plod barefoot into the kitchen to turn on the coffee-maker that had been primed the night before. By the time I'd dressed, the coffee was ready; I'd pour him a cupful, laced with sugar and a dash of salt, and sit beside the well to chat about the day's plans. We had a talk one morning about over-reliance on chemicals; his morning toke became tobacco instead of ganja, a slight improvement.

Mister Valney was too cautious to be a successful fisherman; he lacked the bravado – or was too smart -- to risk his life in uncertain weather. He told me, on one morning chat, of an incident early in his fishing career, before he married. An enterprising man had built a plank boat, twice the size of the traditional dugouts, and set out for the Pedro Cays one evening. A veteran captain inspected the boat, declared it un-seaworthy, and declined to board; Mister Valney followed suit. The boat sank somewhere during the night; a dozen hands were lost. He learned caution.

As I've mentioned, having the Buccaneers play on our terrace had become a vacation event that our guests enjoyed. They were fishermen who played, with varying skill, the banjo, guitar and rumba box, with Mister Endley the singer, performing a mix of traditional calypso and very American country-and-western. We wet their whistles with an occasional Red Stripe.

These evenings drew an audience of neighbors, including several dozen children who were easily coaxed to dance with us. (And I led them in an audience-response game, a lion hunt, that became a perennial favorite; even today grown-ups recall playing with me.) Mister Valney, nursing two beers to last the evening, would sternly prowl the perimeter, watchful for young men who'd had too much drink or ganja; he would gently but insistently send them home lest they spoil the party.

Building the tennis court would test his mettle.

●

A court, we hoped, would boost our sagging bookings. Although the land fell gradually to the seaside in front of the house, a sand dune on the east side pushed farther toward the sea and then fell off sharply to a flat area almost exactly the width of a doubles court, but not quite long enough.

Perfect! We could cut into the dune, holding back the sand with a cut-stone wall that would be a visual companion to those above. I made sketches, and wrote Hedley Gayle.

Mister Hedley, down the road near Frenchman's Cove, was a building contractor, a short, precise man, a deacon of the church where Brother Elbert had served. I'd asked him to bid when we built the house. He had no experience, however, in estimating a job, and no capital to take on so big a job on contract. "You buy the material," he'd said, "and give me the plan, and I'll build your house." I'd reluctantly decided that would entail too much uncertainty at so great a distance, and had turned to Lester Lyn.

We'd stayed in touch, though, calling on him occasionally to ferry our guests. On one occasion I'd rented a car to carry half our houseful, and had him bring the rest. I'd left MoBay airport just ahead of him, but arrived a half-hour ahead. I guessed he was that kind of a builder: perhaps a bit slow and fussy, but very exact.

I'd built typical New England stone walls, using flat slabs of gneiss and schist. Utterly irrelevant! In Jamaica, a stonemason trims each chunk of limestone – from softball- to volleyball-size – using the blade end of his hammer to reveal its natural hard faces. Sometimes he'll heft and trim several before finding the stone that fits the next niche. Although using mortar, he relies in large part on the way stones fit together.

Miss Olive made abundantly clear that Vincent was an "experienced" stone-cutter who could do the initial trimming and might even learn to lay up the stones. I was happy to provide him work, but not on-the-job training. Mister Hedley wrote that he'd learned stonemasonry working at the hotel in 1954. He hadn't done much wall-building recently, but was sure he still had the knack.

He still preferred that he and his workmen be paid by the day. He could order additional materials from Gayle's on my account, but I ordered a huge supply to start with: block, cement, re-bars, marl, two used 50-gallon drums that Mister Valney would fill with water for mixing mortar, and four truckloads of limestone.

It would all be trucked through Mister Valney's (formerly Brother Elbert's) yard, soon before our arrival. The guests who would be at the house that week had asked about fishing; Miss Olive would arrange to have them go to sea the day everything was delivered, to spare them the noise and air pollution of the Diesel trucks.

●

I was by now – 1977 – a different kind of journalist. In the spring of 1975, three years after we built our house, I had resigned my cherished position as editor of the *Hartford Times* in a policy dispute with a new, conservative owner. After four months' joblessness, I'd accepted an offer from WFSB-TV3 to learn the television news business as "senior correspondent," covering the State Capitol and hosting the Sunday morning news-interview program.

The Washington Post had recently acquired the station and was bringing a fusty, all-talking-head news program into the modern world of "Eyewitness News." Although I'd never been much of a TV news-watcher, I was intrigued to learn a new craft.

By the end of the first year, I felt confident enough to propose filming a series on Jamaica, appealing to Hartford's large West Indian population and helping the broader constituency understand the newer arrivals. I hoped to interview both Manley – then in his fifth year as prime minister – and Seaga, who was now leader of the opposition.

I flew down on a Saturday with a Channel 3 colleague. The hollow was stacked with building materials. Mister Vincent and Ivan Elliot, the well-digger, were hard at work trimming stone, with an impressive pile ready to be carried to the court site.

Monday morning Mister Valney brought around a crew of villagers: three men to start digging with him, and three women to begin carrying bucketloads of marl and cut stone to the work site. Jim would fly home Tuesday afternoon and I'd drive to Kingston for a few days' filming. By the time I got back, joined by Brad and a houseful of guests, the excavation might not be quite finished, but Mister Hedley could start work.

Ah, the best-laid plans! The "sand dune" turned out to be a stony hillside with only a thin mantle of sand.

It was a limey sandstone or a sandy limestone, fractured into thin layers that yielded easily to a pick-axe or mattock, but it would be much slower work than we'd expected. The men started hacking into the hillside. I had Mister Valney wheel the excavated stone to the seaside end of the court, where we would eventually level it out. I remained stubbornly confident we could get a good start during my remaining week, and drove to Kingston to interview Joshua.

●

With a nudge from Ted Tatham, Manley's press secretary had arranged an hour's interview; he turned down my proposal to spend a day shadowing the prime minister. (Seaga didn't respond to two letters, and wrote apologetically a month after my visit that they'd been mislaid. I interviewed him a few years later when, as prime minister again, he spoke at the University of Hartford.)

Having arranged to rent a crew from the Jamaican Information Service, I made the Casa Monte hotel school my base, and drove to the station. I had a long list of scenes to film, including -- in the "eyewitness" genre, to make clear I'd really been there -- a number of "standup" introductions, bridges, closers and teasers.

In Hartford, we worked as two-man teams: one reporter, and a cameraman who wore a headset and monitored sound as well as taking pictures. Network crews, on their occasional visits to Hartford, had both a cameraman and a sound man. (That's not sexist language: Only later would women appear in technical roles).

I was astonished to find myself with a four-man crew: cameraman, assistant cameraman, sound man and "grip" -- the man at the bottom of the totem pole who lugged equipment and set everything up for the others. He was also "clapper man." Holding up a slate that I'd seen only in old movies about Hollywood, with a few chalked words, he identified each shot audibly as "take one" or "take two," and made it official by clapping down the hinged bar.

We spent the first day learning to work together -- I learning to be surrounded by so many busy acolytes getting in each other's way, they learning an unaccustomed style of news presentation. We drove together in the JIS Land Rover, starting with the more distant scenes on my list, more than an hour out of Kingston at a bauxite works, where I did my first stand-up.

I'd drafted it as the closer of the third segment in a four-part series. "Manley, whose prime dollar earner is the bauxite that produces aluminum, sees himself as an important part of the developing Third World, a stance that has significance for U.S. foreign policy. In my final report, I'll take a look at Jamaica's role in world trade. Don Noel, Eyewitness News, Kingston, Jamaica."

We found an outlook over a cable tramway carrying huge buckets of bauxite. I wanted the camera to start tight on a moving bucket as I began speaking, and pull back to find me in a wide shot. We did several takes as my new crew got the hang of it; they seemed to enjoy the new technique.

Mostly, however, we shot what was then called -- these were the days before videotape -- "B-roll," the footage that would cover part of the "A-roll" of the Manley interview, or that I would voice over on an audio cassette when I got back to the station.

I still have the shot sheet: More footage of the bauxite works, and an Alcan processing factory; sugar-cane fields and a sugar factory; small farms; one of Ted's Land-Lease developments; a beach dotted with tourists; street scenes of Kingston; luxurious homes on the hills overlooking Kingston; shanty-towns; one of Manley's new housing projects; the Cuban-built trade school. Oh, yes, and graffiti, shots snatched as we encountered them. One read "Revolution now! Up with Socialism!" Another read "To Hell Fidel -- Cuba no!" Yet another read "CIA out! Kissinger out!"

At the end of the first day —a setting sun illuminating the city below from Casa Monte on the hilltop -- we filmed my stand-up open for the series. Next day we would get a bit more B-roll, do a few more stand-ups (I shot more than I used) and film the Manley interview.

One stand-up was to be in Trenchtown, one of two slums where each party supported a rival gang of toughs. A few months earlier, as the International Monetary Fund met in Kingston, there had been a shoot-out that seemed politically inspired to capture international attention. Manley responded by imposing a curfew and creating a "Gun Court" with power to put gun criminals away for life, a measure later struck down by a British appellate court. (Jamaica is now finally moving toward a Caribbean appeals court to take the place of the British.)

The Gun Court had only transient impact; by the time of my visit, the appalling rate of gun crimes was rising again. Jamaica most years records 600 to 800 violent deaths, including as many as 200 assumed criminals shot by police. That's several times the violent-death rate in Connecticut – with a slightly larger population – and a single death at police hands becomes a *cause celebre* in my home state.

My JIS crew was clearly not eager to film in Trenchtown. It usually took them five or ten minutes to set up, check sound levels, and clapper the scene. They were nervous about spending that long in a tough neighborhood, and feared I might prolong the stay by stumbling.

"Can you do it in one take?" the lead cameraman asked.

I could, and did. They were obviously relieved. We packed up in record time and fled the scene before we'd attracted a crowd.

●

The interview was at Gordon House, the prime minister's official headquarters. My crew knew the way -- they were, after all, employees of a branch of the government -- and were deferential as we were ushered into Manley's book-lined study (with his own two recent books prominent on a coffee table), where they set up lights and microphones.

We waited only a few minutes before Michael appeared, dressed as always in an informal grey pants-suit with a short-sleeved, open-necked jacket vaguely reminiscent of a Nehru jacket. His pretty young wife Beverly accompanied him to play the gracious hostess, then disappeared as we got to work.

He spoke easily, with an accent somewhere between clipped British and the Jamaican patois. It was a speech pattern – extra emphasis on some syllables – that I'd come to know in John Todd and Ted Tatham, easily understood by an American but unmistakably Jamaican. (I remember especially one of his favorite phrases, which I'd heard often when he declared his intent to crack down on one or another group of miscreants: "We will put them under heavy manners.")

We began with his economic reforms. "Obviously," he said, "we want to insure, to MAX-imize, agri-CUL-tural pro-DUC-tion; but we want to see that everyone has, you might put it, a piece of the ACT-ion." Where large-scale farming was most efficient, as on sugar plantations, he wanted cooperatives, with everyone "from managers to grass-cutters" as equal shareholders. Where small farming was appropriate, the Land-Lease program would help landless farmers who had fled to the cities get back to a livelihood they knew.

Fidel's impending visit had become a political hot button. There were rumors -- again politically inspired, and as near as I could learn unfounded -- that Michael planned to train the Jamaican police force in Cuba. How, I asked, did the Jamaican model differ from Fidel Castro's?

I hadn't expected his answer: "I think that Cuba is relying more on revo-LU-tionary fervor and exhor-TA-tion. We have a tradition of eco-NOM-ic incentives; that's what will work here. They follow their route, and we'll follow our route."

I pressed him: Was the relationship with Cuba special? He parried: There were many important neighbors; he had recently exchanged state visits with Costa Rica, Venezuela and Mexico, and was working on joint oil and industrial projects with the latter two. I started to go on to another question; he interrupted to make clear he wasn't retreating. "But Cuba is important, too," he added. "They're all important."

I asked about his effort to create OPEC-style cartels among bauxite and sugar producers. Manley was unapologetic. Economic growth in the Third World, he said, won't happen unless the poorer nations "band to-GETH-er and re-FUSE to sell raw materials unless they get a higher price. It's the only way that's working up to now. It's an approach that doesn't appeal to JUST-tice or REA-son, but on pos-SESS-ion of economic STRENGTH."

Those are the parts that made it into my Channel 3 series. I wish I'd kept the out-takes, but have only my sketchy notes. It was a fascinating and long interview -- the crew had to change film magazines halfway through. Several years earlier, I'd been part of a group interviewing Carlos Andres Perez, then the reformist president of Venezuela. Manley and Perez were among the most interesting political leaders south of the American border.

The press secretary stepped in to break off the interview. We shook hands, and Manley let us stay in his study a few minutes longer to film a few "re-ask" segments, as I repeated some of my questions with the camera on me to facilitate later editing. Then we went out to film a quickly-improvised stand-up on the front lawn with Gordon House behind me.

At JIS headquarters I parted company with my crew, genuinely thankful for their hard work and adaptability. I reclaimed my rental car and drove up to Casa Monte to catch up notes, have a quick dinner, and collapse into a deep sleep. Next morning I drove back to Hikaru, joined later in the day by Brad and a gaggle of house guests.

●

The crew had chopped one corner back to the point where I wanted the back-court wall to begin. They could go on excavating toward the other side of the court while Mister Hedley began laying up the wall. He arrived Monday morning.

"It don't suit." The limestone Merrick Gayle had sent down was too soft, he complained. He could start the low, largely decorative wall beside the court, but the high retaining wall would need first-class stone, "properly hard."

Where were we to get such stone?

Miss Olive to the rescue: Her late grandfather had owned a bit of land up against the coastal hills, with a seam of limestone that was easily quarried; the family had occasionally dug out building stones there. I could have all I needed at no cost; I'd be helping level the site for some future use. I could hire Mister Vincent – of course – and Mister Ivan to quarry out the stones.

Mister Hedley went to see, and declared her grandfather's stone properly hard. He could do a few days' work with what we had on hand, and then come back when a supply of the good stone had been trucked to Hikaru. I put the two stone-cutters to work.

There wasn't much I could do, so I joined our guests for several days' real vacation. On Friday, we drove up to see the Black River market, and hired a fisherman (nowadays there are comfortable pontoon tour boats) to take us up the river, that magnificent salt-water morass, considered one of the best examples in the world.

Great islands of water hyacinths were floating down, pushed by interior rains, and the jacanas were having a field day. A dark, robin-sized bird with a distinguishing patch of bright yellow on its forehead, the jacana is long-legged, with almost prehensile toes that let it balance on floating vegetation, foraging where no other bird can venture.

From ten yards away, the jacanas seemed almost to walk on water as they ran along the hyacinth-pads, dipping down to harvest insects. Quarrelsome creatures, they chased each other across the pads with high-pitched bickering sounds, fluttering to show their light green wing patches.

Herons and egrets were plentiful, too. We see cattle egrets constantly: They forage widely, and fly past us in late afternoon to roost in the Black River mangrove forests. This day we saw the rarer snowy egret, only a bit larger but with an unmistakable fluffy white crest. We also got a good look at the three-foot-tall great egret, the even-taller, stately great blue heron and a smaller cousin, the yellow-crowned night heron, the familiar crab-catcher we saw on our beach.

We looked for crocodiles, but saw none. A bauxite company upriver at Maggotty had polluted the river while building its plant, our fisherman guide said, killing all the crocs. (Fortunately, this would later prove untrue. A few survived, and as the river cleansed itself, the survivors multiplied; nowadays one always sees several sunning on the banks, disguised as logs. River tour guides bring along skinned chickens to feed them, to be sure they appear for tourists' cameras – not my favorite example of eco-tourism!)

A mangrove forest is one of my favorite passages. The mangrove is one of the hardiest of trees, world-wide at this latitude. It propagates readily: If its seed pod, floating vertically, comes to rest on a sandbar or mudflat for even an hour, it can root itself and grow into a new tree. It makes tall thickets on soggy islands where water birds roost, safe from four-legged predators. Here and there, it grows to stately forty-foot trees from whose branches long tendrils trail into the water. The tendrils, too, root easily, so a mature tree spreads, eventually choking the waterway unless cut back.

We threaded our way through one such a mature grove, marveling that the water was tannin-dark but clear enough one that could see the bottom, quite different from the muddy, hyacinth-choked river near town.

While I played, Mister Valney and his village crew hacked at the hillside, wheeling away the broken stone. It would take longer than planned; I left Miss Olive money to pay workers. They would stop when we had guests, but the retaining wall ought to be finished by my next visit, when I could supervise casting the playing surface.

On Saturday we got an early start and rafted the Martha Brae River near Montego Bay -- not as long a float as we'd had at Port Antonio, but more varied scenery. Then we flew home.

# 22

# Mister Vincent, John Beek

I followed progress through slow exchanges of letters, made worse by a postal strike. Miss Olive wrote at the end of April that she'd paid a total of 68 days. A month later, she'd paid another 48 days. Mister Vincent easily led the payroll; he and Mister Ivan had a good pile of stones, she wrote, but she still hadn't found a truck to get them to Hikaru.

I had reason to doubt the efficiency of all this work. A few years earlier, in hopes of more income but also to keep her husband gainfully occupied, Miss Olive had rented a field near the main road at Pedro Cross. It was the first of several unwise investments, an example of the unquenchable Jamaican entrepreneurial instinct. She had Mister Vincent plant it to peanuts, and sent him up daily to hoe, weed and tend the field.

The crop failed, primarily because of a drought. But I'd thought her husband's devotion to the task less than whole-hearted. I'd picked him up on the road one mid-afternoon -- he'd quit early because it was "too hot, sah!" and he had me drop him off at a bar to slake his thirst. There were several more bars along his route home; it was clear he usually stopped at more than one.

With some $250 invested in yet-unused stone, I began to think I was running one of Manley's full-employment programs. Miss Olive wrote that she'd gotten two more men to join Mister Vincent quarrying stone, and hoped soon to hire a van to fetch them. Mister Hedley wrote that he'd done another two days' work, but was waiting for better stone. An artistically gifted friend of Mister Valney's sent a very good sketch showing the excavation of the hillside near completion. But the rest of the tennis court was hung up on the rocks, so to speak.

●

I decided to make a quick visit to see if I could get the project back on track, and wrote the nurseryman just east of Mandeville to get me some plants and leave them out by his gate.

John Beek was a small, dark, wiry man, clean-shaven, with close-cropped hair showing streaks of grey. He was a devout Christian, a Bible-reader, and a mystic. He always wore jeans, a blue work shirt -- and rubber boots, since watering plants was a constant task.

He ran a government nursery, part of an admirable re-forestation project. On a football-sized area near the road were row after row of short trestle-tables, on which a crew of women under his direction planted seeds into those ubiquitous black plastic bags and coaxed them into seedlings: casuarinas, the feathery Australian pine; Jamaica's native mahogany; several varieties of tropical slash pine; and maho, the tropical hardwood from which our furniture had been made. ("Not as good as the natural-born trees," he said, "but almost.")

On the hillside above the workspace, below the little shack where he and his wife lived, he had cut terraces on which he grew more conventional nursery stock for sale to the few like me who found him. He would stump down among the rows, finding almost everything I wanted, cradling the plastic sleeves in his huge hands as he brought them up to my rented car. It took me three back-and-forth cuts to turn the car around in his tiny yard to head back down the rutted track.

"Anythin' yu need I can get," he said; he had colleagues around the Hope Gardens we'd visited in Kingston. Given a little notice, he could have any plants waiting on my next visit. I suppose he contacted them by mail, but I wouldn't have been surprised had he told me he communicated by telepathy.

"I had a dream last night that yu' was coming," he greeted me on one of my visits. "I got up this morning to have everythin' ready." And indeed, the plants I'd written for were neatly lined up near the driveway; he'd dug them up, confident I would arrive.

I had him set plants out near the road this time, because I would arrive in the middle of the night. For Independence Week, Air Jamaica put on extra flights, including an evening flight to Kingston. I could put in a day's work at the television station before leaving. I would rent a car at the airport, drive two hours up into the hills, pick up the plants, and spend what was left of the night with Ted in Mandeville; he would leave out a key.

I was hardly traveling light. Mister Arthur had begged for a chain saw to speed his boat-building; I packed up my own saw, recently reconditioned. The Denshams had begged for a supply of tennis balls and sunscreen for Basil, who was subject to skin cancers. Miss Olive, blessedly, wanted only a potato peeler.

The flight, delayed, arrived at 2 a.m.; a sleepy customs officer, eager for bed, didn't even look at the chain saw. The car-rental agent, however, was long abed. I dickered for a taxi, and talked politics with the driver on way to Mandeville. He was disappointed because Manley had promised free education, but his children still had to buy books and uniforms. We stopped to pick up John Beek's plants; it was nearly dawn when I crawled into Ted's guest bed.

After a chatty late breakfast, Ted phoned around to find me a rental car at one of the few Mandeville agencies. No luck: Jamaicans returning for Independence Week had them all. Then he remembered that his neighbors, the sister and brother-in-law of the JLP's Seaga, had just bought a car for their daughter, who wouldn't be old enough for a driver's license for another two weeks. I gratefully borrowed it, bought a few groceries at the market, and got to Treasure Beach in mid-afternoon.

The wall was less than half-built. In my original sketches, it was to be six or eight feet tall. Instead, it would now be a full fourteen feet high. Brad had long wanted a croquet court, another diversion for our guests and one of her favorite games. I planned to level out the area behind that high wall, and eventually get around to seeding it, hoping ants wouldn't ruin the game.

The wall would be even more striking than I'd hoped, a handsome mirror of the stone above, but a lot of work remained.

Mister Hedley came up Sunday after church. He'd used up all the stone Mister Vincent and the others had cut out of the hillside. A grid of re-bars was laid out in the court-to-be, exactly as I'd specified. Two fresh mountains of marl were in the back yard, ready to be carried down by the tireless women. If the well pump hadn't broken down (again!) he would have begun pouring concrete before my arrival.

Monday I went up to order materials to fence the court once it was paved. Merrick would send down several lengths of 1½" pipe, which he had on hand, and a thick roll of six-foot chain-link fencing clad in a green rubberized coating against the sea-frost, which he would order from Kingston; his truck went weekly. He would send down hacksaw blades so Mister Valney could cut the pipe into eight-foot lengths; an over-sized star drill with which to hammer holes into the concrete; and green latex paint to protect the galvanized-iron posts.

I would have to send down a special quick-setting, expanding cement to anchor the pipes. Merrick knew what I wanted, but it wasn't available on the island at present. Although he had a substitute, he recommended I bring or send the better product – not an uncommon experience.

We had time: Mister Hedley couldn't start pouring the base of the court until the pump was operating, and then it would take him several weeks to finish the job. It would all be done by hand, of course, using long 2x6 planks to level out the wet concrete, and floating each batch to a smooth surface with what looked like a wooden trowel.

I remembered pouring the floors of the house I'd built in Connecticut. A readi-mix truck used long trough-like chutes to spread the wet concrete fairly evenly. Like Mister Hedley, I'd used a plank to level it, but then I'd floated it smooth with a gasoline-powered gadget that looked like an overhead fan mounted on a lawnmower. Even with mechanization, dark had fallen and the concrete was nearly set before I got the job done.

No gasoline-powered float here; I again marveled at the resourcefulness of skilled tradesmen in a developing country. The court would be cast well in advance of my next trip, ready for me to apply a resilient surface.

●

Reassured that the work was going according to plan, if slowly, I sent Mister Vincent back to his WPA job of quarrying rock, left Miss Olive enough money to be paymaster for the next few months, and drove back to Ted's, stopping to send A.J. Carroll down to get the pump running. The short visit had been worthwhile.

It turned out to be even better. Ted had discovered that Seaga's brother-in-law whose car I'd borrowed, an Alcan executive, was flying to Miami the next morning, taking the company plane from Mandeville to Montego Bay; I could go along. Ted drove me to the little airstrip.

They let me have the front passenger seat of the twin-engine Beechcraft for a spectacular half-hour flight. The route, across the heart of the Cockpit Country, provided a birds-eye view of the up-and-down checkerboard of that verdant Karst topography of limestone hills and sinks.

It was easy to see why the Maroons had been able to defend their mountain redoubt. There was only one road in from the south; it snaked through narrow defiles flanked by high bluffs. One could imagine a few men with rifles holding off an army. That had indeed happened often during the several decades before the British made peace with their former slaves and let them set up semi-autonomous towns and farmlands.

At MoBay I thanked my hosts profusely, boarded my homebound airliner, and was back at work Wednesday morning. The tennis court would be ready for final surfacing on my next trip, and the retaining wall would be up to its full height.

# 23

## Downhill tennis

**W**hen we first came to Jamaica in 1966, we'd often seen people by the roadside -- mostly old people -- patiently chipping stone into gravel. The government came along to buy gravel by the cubic yard, to be used in road-building.

Manley's new socialist-minded government had put an end to gravel-chipping, declaring it demeaning work. I hadn't been convinced: It seemed a better way to provide an income for marginal or elderly people than outright welfare -- which hardly existed anyway -- and the work wasn't all that hard. But under the current regime, piles of gravel by the roadside had disappeared.

In their place were now piles of cut stone suitable for wall-building. Farmers on those steep hillsides quarried out rock and rolled it down to the roadside into neat piles awaiting a buyer. I hadn't paid them much attention until Hedley Gayle sent me to buy "properly hard" stone.

I was about to learn a lesson in trust.

●

In Hartford, as I began the tennis court, I'd found a helpful contractor. A court may look dead-level, he said, but it isn't: You want a court to shed rain water and be quickly playable. He showed me a design, with an imaginary diagonal line from one corner to the other. His courts pitched about one inch from that diagonal to each opposite corner.

I sketched our site. Never mind the diagonal, he advised; just make the court an inch or so lower at the seaside end. There will be an astonishing amount of water, he said; you can plant trees below the seaside end, and they'll be well-irrigated every time it rains.

He put me in touch with a Connecticut company that made a surfacing material called Latexite, a chunky mix of liquid rubber to give the surface resilience and bounce, with several thin green acrylic finish coats. I ordered four 55-gallon drums; a plastic tank of muriatic acid to etch the surface; two long-handled 30-inch-wide squeegee blades to spread the material; white latex to mark the lines, and a tennis net with steel posts and a crank.

It would all be shipped to Kingston, where with a phone call I'd engaged a customs broker Ted recommended to clear it, pay an awesome duty, and truck it to Treasure Beach. He was to phone me collect if there were any doubt it would be at Hikaru before my arrival.

We invited good friends, avid tennis players, to join us in February. I would fly down four days early. Mister Valney would have a crew of village men standing by to help me acid-wash the cured concrete and squeegee on coat after coat of materials. By the time Alby and Leta arrived, it would be done; they could play tennis every day of their week with us.

I was still learning the meaning of "soon come."

I arrived Wednesday to find that the concrete base of the court had been completed only two weeks earlier. I'd been told to let the concrete cure a month before applying the Latexite; I hoped two weeks in this tropical sun would suffice. It was a handsome job; one wouldn't have guessed it had been poured one wheelbarrowful at a time, spread and leveled and floated smooth with only hand tools.

The pitch toward the sea, however, was more than I'd expected. That turned out to be not Mister Hedley's fault, but mine: I later found the letter in which I told him the court should tilt toward the sea at a rate of one inch per ten *feet*. Oops! I should have written one inch per ten *yards*. No help now: We would have forever a downhill tennis court.

But there were no barrels, and no communication from the customs broker. I drove to the post office to send a telegram.

I'd also had no response from the Trade Administrator. I'd written asking for duty-free admission of the surfacing materials; our membership in the Jamaican Association of Villas and Apartments supposedly gave us a tax break, rewarding our efforts to increase tourism.

The retaining wall was still unfinished. Mister Valney and his crew, having wheeled most of the excavated material to the foot of the court, had begun lugging the rest up above, behind the wall-in-progress, for what would become the croquet court. Piles of stone rubble up there waited to be spread out once the wall was finished. The amount of stone excavated and hauled here or there was awesome.

Mister Hedley came Thursday. He needed more stone. He was waiting on Mister Vincent to quarry more from Miss Olive's grandfather's lot. I was growing impatient with my full-employment program; wasn't there some other place to get stone?

Up near Haddo, he said, a mountain town on the road we traveled from Montego Bay. An area with good limestone; he wanted two truckloads.

I would travel that road Saturday to turn in my small rental car, trade it for a van, and bring back Brad, our son Ken and a friend, Alby and Leta and friends from Washington DC, Peter and Sally. I'd try to commission some stone on my way over.

●

First, though, I had to find the Latexite. Up to the post office, hoping for a reply from the broker. No word. I sent another telegram, telling him to expect me in the morning. Miss Olive found a neighbor who would rent me his pickup and go with me. Meantime, Mister Valney would go to work drilling into the new court and setting posts for the fence with the expanding cement I'd brought. The neighbor and I set off before dawn Friday morning; by 8:30 we were at the broker's office.

He was utterly unapologetic as he shuffled through bills of lading. Oh, yes, the ship had docked ten days ago, but of course it took a few days to unload and stack materials in the customs shed. It must be there now; he would go down with us.

We drove through a guarded gate to the wharves and a huge shed of goods awaiting customs clearance. Our shipment wasn't as easy to find as I'd expected. Barrels are the most economical way to ship goods to the Caribbean; Jamaicans in Hartford and other parts of United States send thousands of barrels a year stuffed with everything from clothing to appliances. But we found my tennis court materials, and did the paperwork. I pretended not to notice that the broker slipped the customs agent expediting-money.

Documentation of the supposed tax break had of course not arrived. I paid duty and tax amounting to half the value of the stuff, and loaded it all into the pickup. I reluctantly paid the broker his full fee, including the bribe money; he checked us through the gate, and we started back to Treasure Beach, stopping to pick up a few more plants from John Beek as we neared Mandeville.

We arrived just past sunset and manhandled the barrels off. I paid my village trucker, left the barrels in the driveway, had supper and collapsed into bed.

Next morning, I left Mister Valney and one of our now-regular workers to roll the barrels down to the court, and set off to meet the family and guests in MoBay, hoping to stop along the way to buy stone.

●

Sure enough, as I neared Haddo, I passed a dozen or so piles of limestone by the roadside. I slowed to look them over, then went back to a pile that looked big enough to make two truckloads. As soon as I was out of the car, a man appeared from a house on the hillside. "I want to buy stone," I said. "Yes, sah," he said; "here it is."

How would I get it to Treasure Beach? I asked. No problem, he said, we'll get a trucker. Here comes one now.

He flagged down a passing truck and explained my need. "Irie (*EYE-ree*)," the trucker said, Jamaican for "just fine". He was working today, but would be free Sunday; he could come back to get my stone and deliver it to Treasure Beach. I didn't ask how the stone would be loaded, but suspected that the people who formerly made government gravel by the roadside would get a few hours' employment in the private sector.

I gave him $100 to pay for the stone when he loaded it; I'd have another $50 waiting for the transport cost when he delivered each load. It looked to be better stone than we'd been quarrying at Treasure Beach, and at less cost.

Looking back, it was an amazing transaction: I was dealing with a villager I didn't know and who didn't know me, and a trucker we'd just flagged down on the road whom neither of us knew. I would not have dared such an arrangement in Connecticut. I'm not sure I would dare it today in Jamaica. In that time and place, however, it seemed perfectly natural: We were all honorable men, doing business on the basis of trust. Our mutual trust was not misplaced.

I made a sketch map of where to find us; we shook hands all around. I drove on to MoBay, swapped the car for a van, collected the family and guests -- Alby and Leta with their rackets and a supply of balls, eager for a week of tennis -- and broke the bad news as we drove to Treasure Beach: They couldn't play tennis next morning, but instead could help surface the court.

We arrived in time for a sea-bath. Mister Valney had the barrels neatly stacked by the court.

●

We started Sunday morning after breakfast, and quickly got the rhythm: Alby and Peter dipped pailfuls of the base coat out of the barrels and spilled them onto the court; Mister Valney, Ken and his friend John and I used the yard-wide, long-handled squeegees to spread the stuff evenly on the concrete surface, starting at the retaining wall and working from side to side toward the sea.

It was watery-grey when first applied, a nubbly surface. By the time we had the first ten yards down, it began to blacken in the sun, a mark of curing. We finished the first coat before lunch, and left it to cure thoroughly. The instructions said it might take 24 hours to blacken completely; not in this climate!

Lunch was interrupted by the arrival of the trucker with the first of two loads, backing through Mister Valney's yard to dump. I offered to pay him for the first load; he declined; he'd be back in a few hours. Sure enough, by late afternoon he was back with the second load. I paid him $100, we shook hands again, and he drove off. I was still marveling.

By then we'd spread a second coat of base latex. We knocked off for a swim, allowing the undercoat to cure overnight. The sea was perfect; we played at the surfing beach, some recompense that our guests couldn't yet play tennis.

Monday morning we went back at it with the finish material. The first coat was hard to apply over the rough base, but it quickly cured and began to look like the real thing. We got a second coat down after lunch, and a final coat Tuesday morning, as smooth as a billiard table.

Before anyone could play, of course, we needed lines. I'd brought down a chalk-line, a hand-held gadget in which a long string is coiled up in a reservoir of powdered blue chalk. One drew the string out, stretching it from one point to another, and then lifted the string and let it snap back, producing a neat blue line.

That makes it sound too easy. Every line had to be carefully measured -- the Latexite folks had provided a diagram with official dimensions -- and the lines had to be squared. There's a "rule of 3-4-5" to drawing a right triangle: If one leg is three feet, the other four feet, and the hypotenuse five feet, the corner will be precisely square. I used a bigger triangle, 9-16-25, to measure and set the corners with more accuracy.

Mister Hedley's court wasn't precisely square. We shifted the starting point several times before I could be confident the lines would meet specifications and the sidelines would be more or less uniform.

By late afternoon we had it right: a grid of thin blue lines between which we could paint. I sent the gang down to swim while Mister Valney and I began stroking in the white lines. He was hesitant at first -- painting was another new skill -- but quickly got the hang of it. We worked until almost dinner-time.

Thursday morning we stretched the rubberized chain-link fencing along the new posts, tied it into place with fine wire ("lacin' wy-ah") and I left Mister Valney to finish painting the lines. After lunch, we christened the court -- Alby and Leta the polished players, Peter and I filling in an awkward doubles team.

Friday morning Alby and Leta had -- at last -- a serious set. Basil and Joyce Densham arrived in mid-morning to try out the court in a singles match and then doubles with Alby and Leta.

The breeze was up by then, affecting play. I made a note to send someone up to John Beek for more willow (casuarina) seedlings that Mister Valney could plant on the windward side. Among the plants

I'd picked up on the way back from Kingston were four of what we call royal palms, but the clairvoyant Mr. Beek called cabbage-palms. We'd set those at the foot of the tennis court. If it rained, nature would take care of them; otherwise, Mister Valney would have a lot of hand-watering until they were established.

Alby and Leta played one more set Saturday morning before we left. Although they'd been appalled, as I'd been, when they first saw the seaward tilt of the court, they reassured me that the exaggerated pitch made little if any difference in play.

●

They suggested, however, that my layout provided too little backcourt. They were right: In transcribing measurements from Connecticut, I hadn't realized the importance of space behind the back line in each court.

After our departure, Mister Hedley would not only finish the retaining wall with the new stone, but also extend the court seaward. We still had material left in the barrels; on our next trip, Mister Valney helped me apply successive coats of underlayment and green finish surface, and re-painted the lines of the entire court.

The sidelines, too, were inadequate. The court area itself is exactly right, but there's too little room to handle a shot aimed at the sideline. I couldn't see a way to fix that; we tell people to agree on ground rules about hard serves too near the sidelines.

Alby and Leta also suggested we extend the chain-link fence to enclose more of the court: It was too easy for a wild shot to fly into the deep Bermuda grass beside the court, where even a bright-yellow ball could hide maddeningly.

Although there was still work to do, I was pleased: We had the only tennis court at Treasure Beach, and perhaps on the South Coast. I would amend our magazine ads.

The exaggerated seaward pitch turned out to be a blessing for anyone practicing alone. If one hikes up the net slightly, one can stand at the seaside end and serve toward that imposing stone wall. The balls bounce off the wall, and roll under the net and back down to be served again. No need to hire ball-tenders: With a sleeve or two of tennis balls, one can practice endlessly.

My Connecticut court-builder consultant could not have imagined a layout so perfectly designed for the novice to practice service.

# 24

## Louie's cocks and dogs

Steve, our house guest, announced at dinner that he was setting an alarm and would get up in the middle of the night to catch The Rooster, armed with a flashlight, the pole hook I use to prune high branches, and a crocus sack to hold his prize.

It is a desperate man who will ruin a night's sleep to avoid having his night's sleep ruined, and I felt guilty. But neither Mister Valney nor I had succeeded, and I fervently wished Steve well.

●

Before I get to Steve's night-time exploits, let me confess to having compressed time: I've jumped ahead to the 90s. A lot has happened that I will give only passing mention.

Most notably, Miss Olive has retired. After two decades' hard work, she decided to join her pretty daughter Margaret in Miami. She finds occasional interludes of work as a caregiver to older Americans, but for the most part enjoys a well-deserved rest.

We didn't pick her successor; she did. She wrote that her sister Joyce would take over. We knew Miss Joyce only slightly; she'd filled in as second maid a few times. As we had two decades earlier, we wondered whom we would find in charge of our house. We worried if she could cook.

What joy! Miss Olive was a very good cook, but her sister is better. Miss Joyce loves to cook as much as Julia Childs. At every visit, she presents us some new recipe – sometimes from a book, sometimes learned from a guest, sometimes just invented on her own. She bakes cinnamon rolls, finds new ways to use ackee, cooks fish with a variety of sauces, serves vegetables in new combinations, tenderizes the tough Jamaican beef with marinades. Each new dish is a treat.

Just as important, Miss Joyce is a warm, loving, engaging person. Even more often than on Miss Olive's watch, guests write to say that they love the house, the setting, the village, but above all our housekeeper. We have been twice blessed.

After a decade in television – despairing of TV news' getting better – I'd jumped at the chance to become op-ed political columnist for the *Hartford Courant*, once my cross-town rival.

And we had a telephone! Unexpectedly, the phone company began stringing lines, with introductory-offer prices that persuaded almost everyone to hook up. We got in line early enough, and Miss Joyce did, but Mister Valney hesitated too long, and was put on a waiting-list; the new line's limited capacity was filled.

I skip my efforts, thanks to our frequent-visitor friend Bill, to build a solar hot-water heater of dubious merit, and our eventual decision to replace the home-made version with a professional installation that finally provides reasonably warm water to showers. I also skip over a major construction project, a new concrete water tower when the original steel-legged tower succumbed to sea-frost.

Let me, however, dwell a moment on the new water tower and its avian complement.

A jack-of-all-trades neighbor a mile up the road, Orel Hill, designed for us a ladder to the new tower – of reinforcing bars, of course – with a pair of yard-high hoops above the last rung, providing a secure hand-hold as one climbs onto the concrete deck that covers the tanks.

Those hoops have proved a magnet for birds. The vultures are sometimes up there early in the morning, drying the dew off their wings in that classic spread-eagle pose.

Our resident pair of sparrow-hawks – American kestrels – are up there much of rest of the day, harassing the pigeons that hang around looking for drips from the tank. I've never seen one caught – the protective cover of the rear lignum vitae trees is only a few yards away – but it makes a great show as the kestrel dives and the pigeons flee.

We suspect the kestrels live more on lizards than on small birds. We sometimes see one of them up on the ladder hoop with a lizard in claws or bill. They're high enough that we can appreciate the savage realities of nature without being able to see much of the blood and gore.

If only they were bigger, the kestrels might catch roosters. I'd pay them.

●

Our neighbor Louie – Philip's son, the one who taught our son how to catch mice -- raises chickens. He buys day-old chicks in Black River -- sometimes flown in from Glastonbury, Connecticut, a few miles from our home -- and feeds them in elevated pens in his yard until they're old enough to sell to a small hotel in Calabash Bay. There's little market among his neighbors; they all have a few hens in their own yards. If the hotel doesn't want his chickens, he straps cages on his motorbike and takes them inland to sell.

Michael "Louie" Gordon is a handsome man. Although like most men in the village he quit school before learning to read and write with any facility, he inherited his father's intelligence: He can do most things he puts his hand to, and is a hard worker. I'd like to think that if he'd inherited the house right away, as he should have, he would be more prosperous. I'm not sure, though: He is a man on whom good fortune refuses to smile.

Over the years, he's tried a half-dozen ways to better his livelihood, occasionally with loans from us. The first effort was a piglet that he bought as soon as it was weaned and raised to a hog that he sold at a modest profit. He didn't try another because there wasn't enough money in it. Too bad. I liked the hog; it was quiet.

He next tried turkeys. They're astonishingly fragile creatures that take sick and die if they get wet in a sudden rainstorm; and there's not a regular market for them. He gave up turkeys. Just as well: They are anything but quiet. A gobbler at dawn will waken any sleeping beauty.

Intermittently, he buys fish and lobster at the beach, and takes them inland on his motorbike to sell. (We helped him buy his first bike, a second-hand vehicle whose muffler was a rusty shell, completely ineffective. He rewarded us, on our next visit, by coming home at midnight and revving the engine for several minutes. "Hit start better in de mawnin' if I do that," he said apologetically when I complained next morning.)

He started raising honeybees in the early 1990s. My friend Steve, a companion from childhood, a beekeeper himself, sent down some equipment. I've periodically printed up fancy computer labels for Louie's honey -- *Treasure Beach Bougainvillea Honey -- Michael Gordon, Beekeeper --* that would make a very attractive tourist item if Louie, like most Jamaican beekeepers, didn't package his honey mostly in used rum bottles.

Honeybees are quiet and not aggressive, but they're thirsty, and Louie didn't at first provide enough water near his hives. When guests complained that they couldn't use the footbath coming up from the sea because bees clustered to drink the drips on the faucet, I made a ruckus; Louie promised to put out water. I finally cast a concrete trough right beside the fence, which Mister Valney fills when he waters plants.

So nowadays Louie raises bees and chickens next door. In our dry, sunny climate none of his livestock ventures have stunk. The caged and grain-fed chickens aren't a noise problem, either: They're slaughtered and sold before the cockerels find their voices.

But over the years, a few chickens have escaped to make an independent living scratching through village yards, notably ours. No one, including Louie, claims ownership. At this time, the undisputed sultan of this feral harem was an oversized rooster of apparent Rhode Island Red heritage that had taken to crowing in our yard. Guests had begun complaining regularly -- including Steve and his wife Jacquie.

●

As always, I woke at first light the morning after Steve set out to catch The Rooster, padded into the kitchen to switch on the coffee, and stepped quietly into the back yard to catch the ani act.

There was a bright yard light amidst the tall casuarinas by the parking area, controlled by a photo-electric sensor. Night-flying insects, attracted to the light, fell into stupefaction among the needles. Just as the light switched off at dawn, a troop of smooth-billed cuckoos arrived for a vigorous breakfast, bobbing up and down like clowns in a trapeze act as they worked their way along the branches. It was a daily circus.

There were also enough stunned bugs in the ground shrubs to attract The Rooster and his harem. He suffered from insomnia, and complained occasionally during the night from a lignum vitae tree behind the house. That was far enough away, and muffled enough by foliage, that only light sleepers heard him. At first light, however, he led his retinue of quietly clucking hens to join the ani in a morning meal, and soon lustily crowed his pride in being such a good provider.

The site of this performance was 20 yards from the rear bedroom windows, on open ground. Sound sleepers -- Steve, obviously, not so blessed -- might tune out his night-time crowing, but a loud "cock-a-doodle-doo" under one's rear window as sunshine streams through the front window would waken anyone.

I saw that Steve's overnight mission had failed: Chanticleer was there again. I heaved a rock in hopes of driving him away before he woke people, but he crowed defiantly in retreat.

At breakfast, Steve described his adventure. The tree in which The Rooster spent the night was stouter and taller than a typical American apple tree, but with thinner foliage. Steve had easily caught him in the flashlight beam. A bright light fixates most wild creatures; that's how one jacklights deer. Not, however, Chanticleer; he had taken advantage of the illumination to hop to a higher branch, well out of reach of Steve's pruning-hook.

It was not the first failed effort to catch the wily bird, but it would be nearly the last.

●

In retrospect, I should have put the master bedroom in the west wing. Because the house is angled to catch the morning sun, the west end is farther from village noises, closer to the sea, filled with the gentle murmur of the ocean. The east wing listens to sounds from the neighbors' yards.

I like the morning sounds. Although there is no longer the hee-haw of burros, roosters crow – most of them at a tolerable distance. Miss Cislyn sings hymns in a strong, clear voice as she starts a breakfast fire. Miss Merle, Louie's wife, scolds a child, a sound of domestic normalcy. After I've enjoyed the ani act and gotten a cup of coffee, I sit at my writing desk at an east-end window as the dawn brightens, the louvers tipped up so I can see the sun come over the mountain as the daily villagesong begins.

Guests who want to sleep in are understandably less tolerant. The lead couple in every group -- the ones who've chosen Hikaru and brought their family or friends -- invariably chooses the master bedroom. They're the ones who will decide whether to come back, or recommend us to other friends. By my design of the house, I've exposed them to annoyance and a short night's sleep.

Protecting our guests from village noises, or at least minimizing the irritation, is a chore near the head of my "to-do" list on every trip.

I arrived once to find that Louie had acquired a beat-up gasoline-engine generator, and had tinkered until he had it working. He started it in late afternoon – about the time we gathered on the patio for drinks and conversation. It ran a few electric lights, but his primary interest was to power the second-hand television set he'd bought. His tinkering hadn't included replacing the muffler.

I hurried down to the fence to remind Louie that on my last trip I'd loaned him money to buy poles and have an electrician wire his house.

"Well, Mist' Don, I run out of money before I reached to that p'int." The electrician who'd quoted him a modest price had moved away; the next tradesman he'd found was higher-priced. He hoped the next batch of chickens would give him enough profit to finish the job. The generator was a stop-gap, and he was eager to be rid of it, because keeping it running took too much effort.

Oh, yes, he said. He hadn't thought about the noise. He would move the generator to the far side of his house, and minimize its use when we had guests.

●

The one persistent village noise that gets to even me is barking. Everyone has a dog or two in the yard, bony, ill-fed creatures of unfathomable origins, short-haired Ur-dogs kept for security. Anyone walking down the road at night stirs up a clamor of curs that run snarling up to the yard fences and bark ferociously long after the provocation has passed.

It isn't only passersby that prompt the canine chorus. If a dog has a bad dream in the middle of the night, he'll waken and bark, rousing neighbor dogs who bark in sympathetic vibration, wakening all but the soundest sleepers in our east bedrooms. The counterpoint barking will die away as the dogs go back to sleep, usually after a reprise or two: Sometimes the last dog down the line yelps once after the others have settled down, setting off a fresh round.

Under a full moon, the dogs can keep each other -- and guests -- awake for hours.

"I didn't notice them," Mister Valney said when I challenged him after a night of fitful sleep on one of our early visits.

"But if they don't waken you -- if you don't get up to see what the commotion is about -- what good do they do?" I imagined a burglar stealing everything in sight while dogs barked and people slept.

"It take a brave mon step into de yard against them dogs," he replied, and of course he was right.

So we reached a compromise with him and other near neighbors: When there are guests at the house, they tie the dogs up -- on the far side of their houses. Tied dogs don't carry on so, and the noise of their barking will carom away from our guests. We tell our guests to speak up if their sleep is disturbed, and we have our staff make a point of asking, at breakfast, if folks slept well.

The first defense is to remind Mister Valney and Louie to tie their dogs. But we also keep a supply of earplugs that can be offered guests if all else fails.

Fecundity exacerbates the problem. There is no Humane Society here offering to spay females and neuter males. I would pay to have that done, but I don't know of a veterinarian within 20 miles of Treasure Beach. Anyway, most neighbors would correctly see such an offer as self-serving, addressing a non-problem from their perspective. I suspect that many of the men, having sown a few wild oats of their own, think it would be inhumane to deny a dog his day.

On one trip, I walked over to see Mister Valney and discovered a bitch nursing eight newborn pups. "Why do you need more dogs?" I demanded. "Don't need 'em," Mister Valney said, "they just happened." But his wife kinda liked them.

I was in a grumpy mood; my sleep had been spoiled, and recent guests had complained. On impulse, I made the puppies' demise a condition of continued employment. That night, after the village and his wife were asleep, the poor man put all the pups but one into a crocus sack, walked down to a reef outcrop on the next beach west, and sacrificed them to Poseidon. He hated doing it, and I didn't like making him, but neither of us saw an alternative.

Some hotels in the major tourist areas of Jamaica systematically buy and destroy every dog in town. I haven't come to that yet, but I don't rule it out.

●

I've already come to that, however, with roosters. No one pretends they guard the houses.

Goats roam, too, and must be fenced out; we've more than once lost a tender young shrub or tree to goats that got through a gate carelessly left open, or found a hole in the fence or managed to jump over a wall or fence. "Goat in the yard!" is a cry that galvanizes our household to enlist guests to run out the marauders.

People own the goats; most of them wander back to their owners' yards at night. They're a cash crop: A knacker from Black River drives through the village every few months, buying goats until the back of his truck is full of bleating creatures. And goat -- curried in a stew, or marinated and broiled or spitted -- is a celebratory meal.

Chickens roam, can't be fenced out, and no one claims them, sells them -- or eats them.

"Whose are they?" I asked Mister Valney the morning after stoning Chanticleer and his harem away from the house.

"Nobody's, Mist'. Don."

"But they must belong to someone. Who eventually eats them?"

"We don't eat that kind of fowl. They -- you know, they eat almost anything they find. We people don't care for that. Nobody here eats them."

Louie confirmed that. People in Treasure Beach were fussier than elsewhere, he said. They ate chicken bought frozen in the supermarket, or once in a great while bought his caged, grain-fed chickens, but they wouldn't eat these "wild" chickens, and neither would he.

I once lived on a farm, and knew this was nonsense: Not many decades ago, subsistence farmers in the United States raised a horse or cow, a pig and chickens, feeding grain to only the largest animal and letting the others root or scratch out what the horse or cow hadn't fully digested. I tried explaining that to Louie once; he didn't believe me.

"Can you catch this rooster and the hens?" I asked the morning after Steve's fiasco.

"Yes, mon," Louie said. He might have to make a trap, and lure them into it with grain, but he could catch them.

And what will you do then, just drown them in the sea? Oh, no, Louie said. Inland folk weren't so discriminating. He would take them to his in-laws near Newell, and they'd be happy to eat them, perhaps not realizing they were "wild."

Tell you what, I said. You catch up this noisy bunch, and any others that wander into my yard. I'll give you $50 each (at the time about US$1.50 – the Jamaican dollar had been devalued mercilessly), and you can sell them inland.

Oh, no, Louie said. As a favor to me he would set his young son Daren to catching stray chickens and roosters, but he'd just give them away as a bonus to his best customers when he went inland selling fish.

Sell 'em! I urged again. I frankly hoped that if he made a little extra profit, he might have Daren catch them without my paying. No, he said stubbornly, "I couldn't rightly do that with these wild fowl; I'll give them away. But we'll get rid of them so they won't bother the guests."

We left thinking we had solved the rooster problem.

●

We'd created a monster.

In the next few weeks, Miss Joyce paid Daren and a young pal for some 30 chickens and roosters. Guests' complaints dwindled. We specifically asked, in our regular calls on their return, whether roosters had bothered them. Most said no, hadn't noticed any. A few said they'd heard a cock-a-doodle or two, mostly in the distance.

But the bounties Miss Joyce reported in her letters continued: one or two roosters a week.

Then she and Mister Valney wrote that neighbors were complaining: Their roosters were disappearing. They all had a few hens to produce eggs, and made a point of keeping a few roosters to be sure the hens' eggs were fertile and would renew their little flocks.

It wasn't hard to figure out what was happening: Daren and his pal were cocknapping to claim my payments. I wrote Louie to keep his bounty-hunter closer to home.

By now I had an ally. Lenroy Buchanan -- one of our children's pals growing up -- went to the States, became a citizen, made some money, and has come back to open a bed-and-breakfast 50 yards from our gate, Irie Rest. We're not competitors: His accommodations are lower priced, appealing to a younger clientele. But his guests, too, complain about roosters, and Lennie has joined me in the hunt. He sets his small staff to catching them, and kills them on the spot.

"I can do that," he told me. "I'm a Jamaican. You're not. I have that advantage, and I'm going to get rid of them all."

Neither of us, however, has entirely solved the problem – and never will. Louie patiently explained the facts of life to me one morning when I'd been wakened by a rooster that was unmistakeably in his yard.

"I have she-fowl in the cages, Mist' Don. As soon as we catch up a rooster so there's no he-fowl around, other roosters gonna come by. We can't stop that."

It was so obvious that I was embarrassed. Brad and I, as veteran birders, know that the male bird sings in the morning to stake out his territory. One way to get a close look at a shy bird is to play his song on a tape-recorder; he'll call and come nearer to see if another male is intruding, defending his turf to keep his mate to himself.

Roosters are, after all, male birds. They crow in the morning to stake out territory, and their neighbors respond to delineate their own turf. It's a primal ritual. And if no male bird calls one morning from previously-occupied territory, as Louie explained, "some young he-bird goin' to come 'round to see if there be some unclaimed she-birds."

Sex and the single rooster.

# 25

## Helen and God's School

"They don't have any printed paper!" Helen said with astonishment. "They have the kids write down the problems from the blackboard – pre-school children!"

Children don't have the hand-eye coordination to copy like that until they're at least six, she explained. In schools she supervised in Bethel, Connecticut, teachers avoided making kids copy material from the board until the latter part of first grade.

Helen and Brad were just back from a morning's visit to God's School, and the catalog of horrors lasted through lunch. The teachers had one pair of scissors for 60 children. They had to alternate between teaching pre-schoolers and 15-year-olds, and hadn't been taught how to leave work that would keep the alternate group busy.

Several boxes of books that Helen had shipped down after her last visit (her school had just bought a complete set of elementary reading texts when a new administrator arrived and wanted a different publisher's texts) seemed to have disappeared, and those that had survived weren't being used. She'd brought materials to make file cards so children could take books home to read; the idea seemed unfamiliar to most of the teachers.

The object of all this attention was the brainstorm of June Gay Pringle, a sometime Treasure Beach resident, one of Basil and Joyce's daughters. She had observed that slow learners or children who fell behind had little chance of catching up in the public school system, and founded her modestly-named private school to meet their needs.

The teaching staff was not as well-trained as those at nearby Sandy Bank Elementary School, but they had smaller classes than the 35 or so common at Sandy Bank. Having children copy material from the blackboard was a necessity: They had no copier, mimeograph or even Ditto machine.

When Brad first went to visit God's School in the mid-1980s, it was down a country lane a half-mile past the end of the pavement: a single wooden shed that couldn't be locked up at night, and almost no playground equipment. In theory, parents paid tuition to send their children; in practice, they paid late or not at all, so the teachers hadn't been paid recently.

Although June Gay occasionally stayed at the Denshams' Treasure Cot where we'd vacationed years earlier, she had moved back to Montego Bay, and dropped in only rarely. The head teacher was leaving in a few weeks for an American summer job on Cape Cod.

The school was sliding toward oblivion. Brad set out to get it back on track. As a trustee of Bob Satter's small American foundation, she wangled $500 to buy some playground equipment, and spent part of our next vacation getting a local welder to put together swings, using her dutiful husband's specifications and drawings, and got Orel Hill to build a sandbox and truck up some sand.

She found a willing if overworked ally in Jason Henzell, June Gay's nephew. In the next few years, Jason persuaded the Black River Rotary Club to contribute enough for a new concrete-block classroom building with a small kitchenette, so the school could provide lunches. Another small grant from the Satter Foundation paid for new desks and chairs that Mister Orel made.

●

Helen – a veteran teacher, a gifted organizer, a leader with Brad in the state and national associations of guidance counselors – had become a frequent companion on our Jamaica sojourns, and a collaborator in improving God's School. By 1995, she was making her fourth visit, and had come prepared to offer the teachers a short course in pedagogy.

It wasn't easy. The first morning, she began to demonstrate some techniques, and the teacher left the room to take a break, thinking

Helen just wanted to teach the children. There was tension over the missing books.

Some had been given children with an aptitude for reading; others had been put away lest they disappear. The idea of a lending-library so that any child could take a book home seemed too much for the staff. Teachers' becoming familiar with the new materials and using them with the children would entail extra hours -- if not days -- for an overworked and underpaid staff.

Teaching in Jamaica is perhaps the lowest-paid position an educated person might consider – hardly a magnet to get the best and brightest into the classrooms. In recent years, Jamaica's chronic shortage of experienced teachers has been aggravated by American recruiting: New York City lured away 300 in one summer.

One of the God's School teachers, having completed a government course (but not a college degree) was certified, and in the mid-1990s earned the equivalent of US$50 a month, about the same as teachers at the official Sandy Bank school. The others, with little but a personal interest in helping children, earned less. Miss Joyce earned more than seven times as much, not counting tips.

Although school is theoretically mandatory to age 16, most children drop out long before that. There are no free school buses. By the time Treasure Beach children reach junior-high age, they face either a two-to-three-mile walk to Newell Secondary School or a dollar-a-day ride on a village bus. Attendance is spotty. It rained one morning when Brad and Helen had planned to be at God's School; one of the teachers phoned to suggest they not come, because children didn't make it to school on rainy mornings.

Whatever the shortcomings of this little private school, the children at least get some measure of individual attention. More than one visitor to Sandy Bank School has wondered how any child learns. Much of the study is still rote-learning, and some teachers seem to feel they've accomplished a lot simply by maintaining order and some semblance of attention.

My most enduring recollection of Helen's frustration had to do with lesson-planning.

"It's basic," she said one evening over dinner. "You have to plan what each group of children will do after you leave them to work with another group. They should be busy, and learning on their own. Otherwise, if they're just sitting waiting for you to come back to their group, they'll be bored and inattentive, and before long they'll be disruptive."

It's not that Jamaican teachers can't learn such skills: They don't have time, don't have experienced role models or supervisors, and don't have enough time routinely set aside, as American teachers have, for "in-service" training. And the best and brightest college graduates are hardly lured to an underpaid profession.

Helen and Brad persevered; they went back several mornings, killing their vacation time as they tried to improve Jamaican education.

●

Brad's involvement with education at Treasure Beach had begun years earlier. She'd taken an interest in two of Mister Valney's children – Malcolm, her favorite, and his younger brother Delroy.

Mister Valney and Miss Cislyn had sent their first-born child and only daughter -- Ivorine Eugenie, or Jennie -- to school with some regularity. The boys who followed, however, hadn't gotten to Sandy Bank.

That was all too typical: Boys' likely future was at sea; they could get by without real literacy and even without much basic math. School was free, but parents had to send children in a simple uniform, and give them money to buy a bun for lunch from a vendor outside the school.

The Ritchies had five boys --Patrick, Mac, Varon, Malcolm and Delroy -- and an uncertain income. Brad began to focus on the boys' illiteracy. She shamed Miss Cislyn into sending Malcolm to join his age cohort in fourth grade.

The system offered no help for children who started school late: They were put in the class appropriate for their age, not their preparedness. Catching up was mostly their responsibility: Teachers might try to give extra work or coaching, but with limited training and large classes, little could be expected.

On our next trip, Brad found Malcolm hanging around Monday morning long after he should have been at Sandy Bank. He was discouraged because he couldn't read or write. With that handicap, he couldn't understand most of the lessons – most of which, of course, were set out on the blackboard for students to write down in their notebooks.

Brad, a high school guidance counselor, had never taught first or second grade. At first she did some simple tutoring using our own children's books. Back home, she got advice from colleagues, and came next time with appropriate texts and workbooks.

The lessons began at Malcolm's home, with his younger brother Delroy joining him. Miss Cislyn sat in to be sure her sons behaved.

Behaved – and performed. Delroy, having never been to school at all, was behind his older brother. After introducing them to cat-rat-hat, for instance, she would point to the workbook and ask each of them in turn "What's this word?" Malcolm usually got it; Delroy usually didn't. Whack! Miss Cislyn produced a stick that she cracked across the knuckles of the boy without a right answer.

Brad protested, without much success. Miss Cislyn was of the school that thought learning was enhanced by corporal punishment.

Next day, the lessons moved to our Cactus Garden; mama was politely told to stay home.

Delroy soon dropped out of the tutorials, and never got to school. Malcolm, with Brad's intermittent coaching, stayed in school – more or less -- through sixth grade.

There was no program, however, to hold a child back if he hadn't yet mastered sixth-grade lessons: The next step would have been the junior-senior high school at Newell.

Malcolm didn't go on to junior high; neither do most of the kids at Treasure Beach. A new computer lab at Sandy Bank will help, and Peace Corps volunteers have recently made a real contribution, but Jamaica has a long way to go before it has a population prepared for the 21st century of global commerce.

# 26

## Murray, Tony and Henrietta

I'd forgotten, in the two decades since the house was built, how labor-intensive a Jamaican job can be. Five weeks after we'd commissioned a swimming pool, the area below the Almond Terrace swarmed with men, many stripped to the waist in the heat.

They had cut the sandy hillside, holding it back with plywood. On the sea-side below that bulging barrier was the excavation for a 50-foot pool, the walls already formed, a vertical sandwich of plywood filled with re-bars. A skeleton of re-bars lay in what would become the floor. The plastic-pipe arteries that would be the filtration system snaked through the re-bars.

To one side was a mixing platform, the size of a small dance floor, sheets of ply tacked together on the ground. A plywood chute propped on makeshift trestles hung into the pool area.

Four men spent each day wheeling marl, gravel and cement from the supply dump near the well. A narrow plank roadway made the first half of the 70-yard trip relatively easy. After that, they looked like a plowing team: One man pushed; another, in a rope harness, dragged the wheelbarrow from the front. When the wheel mired in the loose sand, the lead man slipped off the traces and pried it back up.

Two men spent the day shoveling those materials onto the platform -- "One *huh!* two *huh!* three *huh!*" they measured the shovelfuls -- then mixed, folding and turning like Bunyanesque pastry chefs. When the dry batch was uniform, they mixed in pailfuls of water from a 50-gallon drum into which the garden hose ran constantly. Mister Valney, running the pump as often as he could, barely kept ahead of them.

They pitched the wet slurry onto the chute; an intermittent chunky waterfall plopped into the pit. Reuben Murray, our general contractor, had two men with him, spreading the concrete on the pool bottom, using shovels and a wheelbarrow to muscle it to the far end, poking and tamping to be sure the concrete filled in around the re-bars.

Meanwhile, Peter "Tony" Taylor, our electrical and plumbing contractor, had two men weaving waterproof electrical cables for underwater lights through re-bars in the sidewalls, leading them to what would become a pump-and-filter-shed. Their piping, mostly now completed, included two floor drains that Murray and his men took care not to clog.

I was up as at 6:15. Mister Valney was an hour before me, getting a head start pumping. By 7, the crew – housed in a crude plywood barracks on vacant land next door – had finished a rudimentary breakfast, and work began.

When dusk fell, they worked on. Tony had strung an electric line: Two 60-watt bulbs faintly illuminating the wheelbarrow course, another over the mixing platform; two more casting a shadowy light into the pool area. Sometime after 10 they quit for the night, sloshing water out of the drum to sluice naked, muscular bodies in the half-light before turning in. (They were inlanders; it didn't occur to them that the calm, shallow sea thirty yards away would make a soothing bathtub. I suspect none of them dipped a toe into the Caribbean the whole time they were there!)

Most came from near Montego Bay. Murray, who drove over from MoBay each morning, ferried them home every other weekend. Instead of being paid by the day, they'd negotiated a contract: The sooner they finished, the sooner they could have something better than connubial visits – or go on to the next job.

Workers in the tropics, it is often said, are lethargic. Having bargained to make it worth their while, these men set a pace that would exhaust strong men in temperate climates.

●

Brad, a lap swimmer, had long wanted a pool. I'd stalled her off, arguing that we couldn't raise the rates enough to make a pool pay for itself. Besides, we had the sea just a few steps away.

She also loves croquet. I'd tried to fob her off with that court above the tennis court. After several years, we had a skimpy but smooth lawn; Mister Valney and I installed tall halogen lights so one can play croquet after dinner.

Croquet in the evening is no substitute for an early-morning half-mile in a lap pool; she kept raising the subject. Meanwhile, we increasingly had phone inquiries from people who asked if we had a pool – then said thank-you and hung up. By 1995, I was persuaded. We went down in April, armed with pictures and books Brad had accumulated.

Harry and Lucille Harris and their daughter Henrietta DeLisser, whose Water Conditioners Ltd. was the island's premier pool specialist, came from Kingston on an April afternoon, joined by Tony, their contractor-collaborator.

Harry was probably 70, but still sharp. His wife Lucille, an attractive redhead a few years younger, was obviously running the business. Henrietta, willowy, light brown beautiful, an avid tennis player who had grown up in relative privilege, was gradually taking over. Her husband, whom we never met, had a business of his own. They were old-money establishment.

Tony was new money, earned on hard work and smarts. He arrived with a nubile young lady who accepted a soft drink and stayed out of the way. He would be responsible for the project, using materials and know-how from Henrietta and her parents, and supervising the general contractor, a man with whom both had collaborated on earlier pools.

Reuben, whom we would meet as we finalized plans a few days later, had risen from laborer to construction manager by hard work, with the considerable help of a wife who kept the books and managed the payroll. His son Garth was growing up in the business; either Reuben or Garth would be at our job every day. They were new money, too, but not yet on Tony's scale.

That first afternoon we designed the pool. Brad had a picture she liked: long enough for respectable laps, with an ellipse, a half-circle, off the foot of the lap lanes, where the less ambitious could laze. The picture had an underwater bench formed in the wall of the ellipse, where one might sit, tush in the water, to sip a drink and gaze out at the Caribbean forty yards away.

A nice design, Tony and Henrietta said; we can do that.

I wanted the pool carved back into the hillside so it would only partially parallel the tennis court. That would take a lot of work to hold back the sand, and eventually a finished retaining wall. Brad wanted the entire pool in-ground, which would have required even more excavation. We compromised on having the seaside end of the pool deck two feet above ground. Its elevation could be disguised by sand carved out of the hillside and spread below.

Henrietta visualized it immediately. A pretty setting, she said.

When we got down to details with Murray a few days later, it was apparent that Tony's skills didn't include spatial relationships: He couldn't visualize the retaining wall cut back into the hillside. Murray, the least-schooled of the three, got it. We can do that, he said.

Henrietta and I sketched and re-sketched. Finally we had a rendering with which we were all satisfied. But how to replicate it so we were all – literally – on the same page?

One of my projects this trip had been to bring and install a fax machine. "It makes copies," said Henrietta. Unaccustomed to such modernity -- two years earlier we'd had no phone – I'd forgotten that. Before we parted, everyone had a detailed sketch of how the pool should look when finished. Tony would be supervisor and electrician-plumber; Murray would build the pool, with massive reinforced floor and walls against Jamaica's occasional mild earthquakes.

On the flight home, I used the laptop to write a three-page letter with elaborate detail on everything we'd agreed to. At home, I printed it out and air-mailed a copy to each of the three.

●

When Lester Lyn built the house, I'd come only once in eight months to see how he was doing. I had less confidence in Murray, and came back three times in two months. There were problems to solve each time.

I arrived in late May, my first trip, just as the crew was running out of cement; there was a shortage on the island. We'd ordered 200 bags – 200! Ten tons! – but only 50 had been delivered. Garth went to buy the last few bags that Levy's had, on the way to Black River. I drove up to Southfield to beg Merrick to find us the balance, and he soon did.

Tony arrived, with his men in the back of his pickup and a different nubile young woman in the cab. She, too, accepted a soft drink and stayed out of the way while he and his men installed a separate power line to the pool, climbing the driveway pole to hot-wire it to the 220-volt lines -- not bothering to disconnect the power.

I also hired a plumber to set the pump intakes still a bit deeper into the well, risking their silting up in order to help Mister Valney stay ahead of the cement-mixing's insatiable thirst. And I laid in a supply of light bulbs; one or two a night were broken when workmen bumped into them.

When I came in mid-June, the final retaining wall, deck and the entire pool were rough-finished, with steps down into the pool. I took several photos of the empty shell from the house, finding an angle that minimized the work areas. (Back at The Courant, a friend in the digital photo lab filled it with blue water, and I sent out postcards to past inquirers announcing the new amenity.)

Murray and his men were about to start the white-cement finish coat as I arrived. But the entire floor was level.

No, no! I protested. We agreed the lap area would be four feet deep, but that you'd taper up to a shallower depth in the ellipse, so young children could stand. Oh, yes, Murray said; there's still time to fix that. He had his men mixed up more concrete. At the foot of the steps, the concrete must now be two feet thick; good thing the cement shortage had eased. Since I paid for materials, fixing the error cost me more than it did Murray.

And there were no lap-lane tiles on the floor. We'd agreed on a strip of blue tiles down the middle. Specially-ordered tiles with a big numeral 4 were to be embedded in that strip at several points to make it evident one couldn't dive. Murray insisted that he hadn't forgotten; he just couldn't find them; maybe Henrietta hadn't sent them. She and her mother came for a job conference; she went to the temporary storage shed, opened the box and handed them over.

No problem, said Murray: He'd cement them down, and cast in a bit more fine concrete so the tile strip would be flush with the pool floor. A few more bags of cement, but who was counting?

There was also time, in June, to fix a problem none of us had anticipated:  A heavy rain might wash down from the sandy hillside, flooding the deck and dirtying the pool.  There was still time to pitch the deck away from the pool to shallow gutters and drains.

Henrietta brought solid-blue tiles and a tile-cutter that she showed me how to use.  Together, we cut and pieced together the ideograph for Hikaru, a foot and a half high.  We put it on a big sheet of paper, tracing around each piece.  As Murray finished re-casting the shallow part of the ellipse, his son Garth, the tile expert, would use the pattern to imbed the cut tiles into the final floor.  It's a handsome flourish as one steps into the pool.

Garth arrived the next day, having been held up by a road accident that totaled his car but left him unscathed.  He turned out to be expert indeed, and deftly cut a second set of cut tiles to imbed a Hikaru ideograph in the retaining wall, another showpiece flourish.

Other details:  I'd brought a surge protector for Tony – who arrived with yet another pretty young woman --to install on the power line lest a lightning strike or voltage spike destroy the pump.  With Tony's support, I insisted that Murray -- as we'd agreed, and I'd specified in my letter -- dig a deep pit in which to bury the plentiful concrete debris, not just spread a little sand over it.

And Tony promised to find several hundred plugs of Bermuda grass. For some reason called Bahama grass here, it spreads aggressively.  The excavated sand spread out below the pool was a barren moonscape. Now that the peak demand for water was past, Mister Valney could plant the plugs and water them with sprinklers I'd brought.  Once established, the long grass, a meadow rather than a lawn, would look much as it had before we began, and would need no care.  Meanwhile, Mister Valney would spread long needles shed by the casuarina as a mulch to keep the still-fluffy sand from blowing into the pool and making extra work.

Oh, yes, water!  In another week, they'd be ready to fill the pool – 18,000 gallons, Tony estimated.  The trucks that regularly fill village tanks each carry 100 feet of heavy hose.  An obliging neighbor at the National Water Commission agreed to deploy two trucks for the two days it would take to truck that much water down from the re-filling station four miles away; their combined hoses would reach the pool from the driveway area. We estimated a dozen trips, US$400 worth of water.

I also arranged to have the last truck top up the now-depleted cistern under the patio. Tony helped design a siphon line to the pool, so Mister Valney could replace water that evaporated in the hot sun – maybe an inch a week!

We couldn't count on enough rainfall to keep up with that; we'd need more from the public line. I already had a pipeline down our access road. The commission, faced with daily complaints about a dry line, was reluctant to add even a drop more demand. I insisted that we would only use it as a backup to our rain catchment system, and the top man finally agreed. I hired a local plumber to make the connection.

(For the next six years, there was no water in the line during the day. Mister Valney periodically hooked up hoses so that during the night, when a trickle of water began, he could top up the patio cistern. Finally, a long-promised four-inch line to Billy's Bay was laid, providing more than enough pressure to get water into the cistern and – finally! -- up into the tower tank.)

●

Brad came with me in early July, to sign off on the job and make final payments.

The pool was full. We christened it with a quick swim before dinner, and went back to skinny-dip under a nearly-full moon. Over Brad's protest, I tried to turn on the lights around the deck and the big underwater floodlights. Her modesty was safe: Tony had put the switches inside the carefully-locked pumphouse. First item on our new list: Relocate the switches to where guests can use them.

Murray's jerry-built bunkhouse was gone. With my permission, Mister Valney's son Varon had disassembled it –Murray might have just burned it down – and rebuilt the framing lumber, ply sheets and zinc roof into a little bar out by the road. I didn't begrudge him the materials, but I would come to regret the gift: Varon, like the other three (!) village barkeeps, attracts customers by playing loud music. We occasionally need to remind them to turn it down at night.

Tony and Henrietta had given Mister Valney lessons in tending the pool: Clean it daily with a skimmer and suction hose; keep thick hockey-pucks of chlorine in baskets in the filter line; backwash the filter regularly; test the water at least weekly for pH and chlorine balance, and add an amazing variety of dry and liquid chemicals, including one to prevent algae.

This was all just as new to me. When Tony and Henrietta came, I had them each give me a course in pool maintenance; then I joined Mister Valney every morning to go through the ritual, helping him feel comfortable in his new role as wizard of water.

Tony had arrived with yet another beauty – Mitzy, who stood out from the others as a conversationalist. While she and Brad talked, Tony and I went over the switch problem. No problem; he would put a switch at the edge of the deck. Chipping out concrete to get at buried pipes and wires is familiar work in Jamaica; construction is often imperfect the first time around. When they finished, no one would detect the repair.

Murray also agreed – as I'd specified, and he'd forgotten --to build an adequate drywell below the tennis court. Back-washing the filter is a regular event; an underground pipeline from the pumphouse was already staining the sand.

Tony suggested we finish the retaining wall with a coarse gray, "splashed-on" stucco, a durable and handsome surface that wouldn't need painting and re-painting. Murray and Garth and one of their workers did it the next day, after I put masking tape on the tile ideograph.

Meanwhile, I turned to landscaping the new addition. I had in mind the kind of "desert landscape" we'd seen at my folks' in Phoenix, a gravel surface. In rebuilding the access road a few years earlier, we'd used a grey-brown, stream-rounded stone that would do the job. I called a trucking contractor Merrick recommended.

That stone had come from near Kingston, he said. He could get white gravel from a place near Mandeville, with less trucking expense. Would we mind white stone?

Mind? Wonderful! I ordered two truckloads, and before we left Mister Valney and his sons had begun wheeling it in and spreading it. The white stone, against the grey retaining wall and blue pool water, proved the perfect final touch.

On the last of our four days, the little details taken care of, we met one last time with Tony and Murray and wrote the final checks.

Before they left, I drew Murray aside to offer some advice. His wife was the detail person, I observed. It was apparent that the long letter I'd written in April on the flight home had been neglected. On each trip I'd had to remind him of the specifications – which made extra work for him, and cost him (as well as me) money. Perhaps on future jobs, I suggested, he could have his wife go over such contracts and agreements periodically, and remind him of the details.

"Oh, Mist' Don, the problem is I lost your letter." He'd read it carefully, he said, but it somehow disappeared before he began the job.

No wonder there'd been so many lapses! Why hadn't he told me, so I could send him a copy?

"I was embarrassed, mon, to have been so careless to lose your letter."

# 27

## Black River Hospital

**A** power-drill wood bit is a flat paddle on a steel stem, square except for a pointed tongue that drills a pilot hole for the wider blade to follow, reaming with its sharp edges. On the bit for a two-inch hole, the pilot-point is a narrow, ¾-inch-long triangle of very sharp steel.

The accident was my own fault. The trigger on my drill had been immobilized by sea-frost. I should have bought a new drill, but we could make the old one work by plugging it in or out of an extension cord. Mister Valney and I were taking turns working from a scaffold 14 feet off the ground, drilling holes for pipes from the new roof-top solar heater to the bathroom showers.

"Ready," said Mister Valney, atop the scaffold.

"Mind how that blade kicks when it gets crooked in the hole you've started," I cautioned, and plugged into the extension cord.

It kicked. He lost his grip, and the drill came down, still turning. It caught me in the crook of my right arm, that wicked point straight down.

I knew immediately it had hit an artery. I pulled a handkerchief from my pocket to try to staunch the flow of bright red blood, shouted to Mister Valney to come down and unplug the drill, and headed through the house to the patio where my mother and her friend May were reading.

"I have a major problem here," I said, sitting down on a chair, trying to sound calm.

●

Mom loved Hikaru. She and Dad had joined us every few years since it was built, taking enormous pleasure in being with family, and at the sea.

She had given up painting, but the changeable ocean, the flowers and the birds inspired her to take it up again. She'd make watercolor sketches in Jamaica, and take them home to use as models for more oils to grace our walls.

It was Mom who spotted a baby doctor bird one spring on a branch of the lignum vitae that shades our cactus garden. It appeared to have made its maiden flight, gotten this far, and lost heart or strength. From a people perspective, it was in plain view; we tiptoed down the patio to look at it from perhaps four feet away.

From a hawk perspective, it wasn't in plain view at all, and was well protected: A six-foot high pillar of our night-blooming cereus, a cactus with inch-long thorns, poked up into that branch. Mama had parked her fledgling on a perch that would deter a kestrel even if it spotted a prospective meal.

The baby stayed there a day and a half. Mama and papa came regularly – usually hovering like tiny helicopters, but sometimes perching, giving us a better look -- to stuff its mouth with pollen or insects, keeping it nourished until it got its courage up again. Then next morning it was gone.

This was Mom's first Jamaican visit since Dad's death the previous summer; she was 82. She'd invited May, the British widow of one of Dad's colleagues, to join us. Brad and our other guests had gone home Saturday, leaving the old ladies to keep me company as I worked with contractors to finish the solar hot-water system and pipe the new concrete tower.

Her first thought when she saw me pumping blood onto the terrazzo floor, she said later, was to wonder if she would within this year lose a son as well as a husband.

●

It took more than five minutes to staunch the blood; it seemed forever. A handkerchief tourniquet did no good. Mister Valney found a bit of rope; that didn't stop it either, even when twisted tighter with a stick. He said fishermen's lore prescribes a "triangle" with a second tourniquet on the leg opposite the arm; sounded crazy, but we tried that too. No result.

While Mom went to get an ice cube, I had Mister Valney find a washbasin to contain the blood I was spattering on the terrazzo floor –perhaps two pints by then.

The ice cube didn't help either.

It popped into my mind that I wanted to avoid a transfusion in a country whose blood supply must be marginal. Then I wondered whether I would get to a hospital.

In desperation, I grabbed the crook of my right arm with my left hand, squeezing hard into the wound with my forefinger.

The bleeding stopped, and we had time to think.

Someone had gone to Miss Olive's house. (This was in April 1992, just before she retired.) She came back with her son-in-law Martin Grant in his car, and we set off for Black River. Mom insisted on coming along. Martin wanted to drive fast like an ambulance; I persuaded him to slow down. The major danger now was that jouncing might make me lose my vise-like forefinger grip and start the wound bleeding again.

We arrived at dusk, and headed to the wooden building, as Spartan as an army barracks, that housed the emergency room; a few mismatched chairs lined the hallway waiting room. A doctor was still there, in an examining room with a patient. I opened the door a crack to holler in that I had a significant emergency.

"Be with you in a minute," came the answer – in an unmistakeably American accent!

Rodney Bell was about to graduate from the University of Wisconsin School of Medicine, and was one of the few in his class taking an extra course in Third World health care; he was three weeks into a four-week stint. The Jamaican ER nurse, Cherry Jones, was a competent 10-year veteran, as bustlingly efficient as hospital nurses anywhere in the world.

She gave me an anti-tetanus shot and a dose of penicillin. He pumped in Novocaine and probed the deep wound. The artery, he said, to his and my relief, had sealed itself in the hour of iron finger-pressure. After a protocol phone call to the home of the head doctor (with an Indian name) to give him an opportunity – declined -- to come in, Dr. Bell sewed me up. Five interior stitches pulled the flesh together, five more sealed the skin. He had Nurse Jones dress it very tightly, in part I suspected to discourage me from using that arm.

Miss Olive drove me in my rental car next morning to Black River, Southfield and finally Junction to fill the penicillin prescription he'd given me. This is not a country overstocked with medications.

I managed a little careful work in the afternoon, mostly showing Mister Valney the work that would now have to be done without me. Next morning I drove left-handed to MoBay, got Mom and May to their planes, and flew home, the arm swollen and black-and-blue, but otherwise hardly the worse for wear. My doctor in Hartford pronounced the repairs well done.

Before leaving Black River Hospital, I'd asked Dr. Bell how my arterial puncture measured up against other wounds he'd treated here.

"Piece of cake," he said. In his three weeks, hardly a day had gone by without a machete wound to treat. "Bar brawls, domestic disputes – the first thing some of these men do is grab their machetes and start swinging. The blades aren't very sharp or very clean. Ugly wounds."

●

My second hospital visit came five years later.

We'd taken to storing planks and timbers up on the second level of the tower. Wood is expensive in Jamaica, and my occasional improvement projects seem always to involve planks on which to run the wheelbarrow, or framing lumber, support timbers, scaffolding. If left on the ground, ants or dry rot would quickly consume the wood. When we finished a project, we'd hoist the used lumber to the second set of cross-pieces on the tower, 18 feet off the ground, out of harm's way.

We had a new project, and wanted the wood down. I climbed up Mister Orel's ladder, gingerly made my way to one of the four-by-four timbers and straddled it, feeling fairly secure. Then I began sliding the other timbers off the concrete cross-pieces, one at a time. As each fell end-first to the ground, Mister Valney could haul it farther away and wait for the next.

I was down to the last timber save the one on which I sat -- more precariously now -- when one of our guests came out of the house, walked around to the side to watch, and called up in astonishment, "What *are* you doing, Don?"

I hadn't heard her come out. I turned to look where the voice was coming from, and lost my balance. I remember the fall; I tried to grab at a two-by-four on the first level, but didn't succeed. Suddenly Mister Valney was there feeling my twisted left leg, joined by Doug, our curious guest's husband.

We had no car at the moment. Brad had gone out with Miss Joyce in search of a gifted young guitarist we hoped would play for us. She returned -- triumphant that she'd arranged an evening's entertainment -- to find that her husband needed transportation to the hospital.

There was no American intern this time, but a competent young Jamaican doctor took an X-ray and decided it was a complex ("spiral") fracture that would better be handled by an orthopedic surgeon.

Where could I find an orthopod? Almost all of them were in Kingston, he said, at the University of West Indies Hospital, but there was one in Montego Bay. We got his name and phone number. The young doc strapped my leg into an air splint, and Brad drove me home to join our guests for a late supper.

We called the orthopedic surgeon first thing in the morning; he said come along. Brad drove me over, two hours in the back seat with the splinted leg propped into the front seat, not entirely painless. We arrived in MoBay and – crutches having been unavailable at Black River Hospital -- I hopped carefully into his clinic, X-rays in hand. He took some more.

He could repair it, but it would probably involve a bone graft, and the after-care available here would be inferior. "Go home!" he said. He made a plaster cast, which he promptly sawed open lest swelling inside the cast become a problem; it would still immobilize the leg.

In my obstinacy and hubris, I'd assumed he would set the leg and let me spend the remaining week supervising work I'd planned. If I'd been smarter, I'd have brought my passport and toothbrush and flown home that afternoon. Instead, Brad drove me back to Hikaru. We phoned our daughter Emily, who arranged first-class passage on a flight the next day.

Brad wanted to accompany me back, but I was adamant. Not only did we have a new set of house-guests who'd arrived while I visited the orthopod; I needed her to do some of the chores I'd planned for our second week. We phoned Arnold Service -- a taxi/van driver in MoBay who had become our preferred transporter -- to come for me.

He got me to the airport and saw me to a first-class lounge. I hopped aboard the plane – I still didn't have a crutch – and flew back to Hartford. Emily and her husband Tim met me at midnight and took me to Hartford Hospital, where a team of residents and interns decided there was no dangerous swelling, and I could wait until next morning to have the leg set.

Hartford Hospital is one of the best in the country, and I was in the hands of a skilled orthopod. He avoided the bone graft, instead implanting a stainless steel rod in the broken shin and several plates and screws in the shattered ankle. I went back to work at the newspaper within a few days, got off crutches in a month or two, and recovered completely. I walk, run and jump with no impediment.

Had I been a Jamaican dependent on the services at Black River Hospital, I would surely have recovered with use of both legs, but might have had a limp, and probably more serious impairment.

When push comes to shove, nothing beats being a prosperous American.

# 28

## Jason and the fishermen

**W**hen the owners of a small inn two miles up the road from us began building a sea-wall a few years ago to enclose their beachfront patio, angry fishermen tore it down. The incident made some American newspapers, with a report that a dozen tourists at the inn had fled in fright.

We got details on our visit a month later. The owners of Golden Sands, a local couple whom we knew, wanted to enclose their property, as defined in their recorded deed, down to the high-water mark – not an especially high wall, but enough to define their seaside area and give their guests a bit more privacy.

Fishermen had for years gone down a public right-of-way next to the inn, and then cut across – on the inn's beach -- to reach their boats at Frenchman's Cove.

The wall would have denied them their best access to their boats. At high tide or in stormy weather, they'd have had to wade through the surf with their outboards and gear. Taking matters into their own hands, they tore the wall down while the mortar was still damp, pitching broken cement block onto the sand. Only a few tourists – not a dozen – had been staying at the inn, we were told, and the press (ah, the press!) had exaggerated: They hadn't really felt threatened; if any fled, they'd come back an hour later.

The fishermen had gone to court; early rulings appeared to be in their favor: Under Jamaican law (as in many American states), untrammeled public use of private land establishes a *de facto* public right-of-way.

A few days later we stopped in to visit with our favorite hotelier at Treasure Beach, Jason Henzell, to get his take on the event.

"I'm glad they're winning," he said, somewhat to our surprise. "It establishes the principle that fishermen come first here."

In much of Jamaica, he observed, what once were local fishing beaches have become tourist enclaves where fishermen are tolerated – if that – to add local color. Tourists are welcomed in the villages of Treasure Beach, but fishing remains the primary purpose, the honored occupation of most residents.

Jason wants to keep it that way.

●

A handsome blond, stocky third-generation Jamaican, Jason is the grandson of our early friends Basil and Joyce. His father wrote and directed *The Harder They Come*, the first major film to celebrate reggae music, setting the stage for the great Bob Marley. It became an international cult movie, providing the money with which Jason and his mother Sally – his father has been ill for several years – built Jake's, a restaurant and boutique hotel.

Under the wing of Chris Blackwell, who made it part of his international resort chain called Island Outposts, Jake's has become easily the best-known tourist attraction on the South Coast.

For an establishment that attracts enough film stars and starlets to be written up repeatedly in travel magazines, it's surprisingly unsophisticated. Even with recent renovations, the restaurant looks – deliberately -- like a wooden beach shack, a bit bigger but otherwise hardly distinguishable from Jamaican eateries all over the island. It has an open-sided area of rough tables in front, and an outdoor patio of tables on the seaside; a small, irregular-shaped pool; a narrow, rock-enclosed beach. Drinks come from a shack bar.

The design is Sally's handiwork, and her style – sometimes-gaudy hues, bits of colored glass imbedded in concrete – is occasionally more eye-pleasing than practical. The guest cabanas are also of rough wooden plank construction, some up on pilings, some with only outdoor showers, and most with mosquito netting over beds instead of screened windows. An older couple who stayed at Jake's a few nights before coming to Hikaru described the style as funky. Jake's appeals primarily to the younger set.

The entire design, though, makes a statement: This is a hostelry that fits comfortably in a Jamaican village, and is part of the village.

On the more-developed North Coast – where fishing is no longer the dominant way of life –accommodations range from budget motel to luxe. Most large hotels have become gated communities. The Jamaicans most tourists encounter, if they venture beyond the guarded gates, are hucksters selling tee-shirts, wooden carvings and sea-shell jewelry; the government devotes considerable energy trying to keep tourists from feeling beset and hassled.

One can buy Jamaican souvenirs from another shack on the Jake's compound, but there are also a few stands on the street. Several restaurants and bars have sprung up nearby, where sunburned tourists can hoist a glass with a fisherman who may have just come back from far sea.

Jason understands that a major charm of his place, as of ours, is its being an integral and natural part of a real Jamaican community.

That doesn't mean he wants to keep villagers backward. A few years ago, while still in his 20s, Jason created the Breds Foundation (borrowing a local patois word for "brothers") that has provided a computer lab, basketball court and other extras for the children at Sandy Bank Primary School. Part of the money has come from an international triathlon.

Who would have imagined a triathlon – swimming, running and bicycling a prescribed course – at sleepy Treasure Beach? Jason. Who would think athletes from several countries would come to participate? Jason, drawing on the upscale network Jake's and Island Outposts have created. He had to subsidize it the first year, but since then it's drawn increasing participation and has made a profit for the foundation.

He also initiated a program to have all the tourist accommodations kick in a voluntary tax for the foundation.

And he's tapped the energies of American Peace Corps volunteers. The co-op no longer needed the work that Neil and his successors put into it. Jason found other tasks – improving Sandy Bank, adding a health-education component, offering computer courses for adults as well as children -- that would keep Peace Corps volunteers coming; in recent years there have been two at Treasure Beach.

With the help of Rebecca Wiersma, a young American running a villa-booking and tour business, the computer skills of a Peace Corpsman stationed up at Malvern were tapped to create a Web site, www.treasurebeach.net.

(One pair of volunteers, a retired couple, Pete and Anne Wilson, in addition to other duties, helped one of our guests, a Midwest dentist and college professor, set up periodic dental clinics. American volunteers, mostly recent graduates, spend a week once or twice a year peering into the mouths of village folk who've never seen a dentist – filling cavities, pulling rotted teeth, and even fitting some for dental plates. It is a mission.

(Our guest Dr. Jim began with clinics in the Blue Mountains behind Kingston. He found he could lure more dentists to his mission by coming here. For several years, they spent the early morning swimming and playing tennis like any tourist, then set off in late morning for an improvised clinic in a local church or school or other borrowed quarters, putting in a busy eight hours at volunteer dentistry.)

And Jason has played a role, along with Merrick Gayle, in creating the South Coast Tourism Development Board, one of whose successes has been to have the police assign one officer to patrol tourist areas. Spread between Black River and Treasure Beach, it's too large a beat, but it's a start at keeping Treasure Beach free of the crime and the pestering hucksters that afflict the North Coast.

He's also taking the lead in trying to limit density. He helped get consultants to do a South Coast Sustainable Development Study, which found residents strongly opposed to large-scale development. Jason hopes for a zone change to allow only 10 rooms per acre instead of the present 30. He wants to make Treasure Beach, he told me, "truly the model for community tourism."

His next project, with starting help from Pete Wilson, is to develop a sewage system for the intensely-developed part of Treasure Beach. Our Hikaru septic field needs only occasional pumping. In the area near Jake's, reliance on septic systems is an environmental disaster waiting to happen. Jason is pro-active: He doesn't want to wait until catastrophe strikes.

Not bad for a young man still in his 30s. And he's not through. He and Sally have begun building a series of villas down the road from Jake's, expanding the tourist accommodations available at Treasure Beach -- and of course expanding the clientele for Jake's Restaurant.

We occasionally worry that Jason will over-extend himself. He's aware of the danger – having watched Merrick come close to burn-out -- and says he'll pace himself.

We're pleased that he occasionally finds time to join our guests, or others staying at Treasure Beach, for a tennis match on our court, and we look forward to a visit each time we're at Hikaru. He's rarely on time, but we understand.

●

We've had occasion to help defend the primacy of fishing at our end of Treasure Beach, too. A new American neighbor bought a hilltop overlooking the Billy's Bay fishing cove a few years ago, and built a villa. We thought the site a bad choice, but he didn't ask our advice.

Soon after the house was completed, he began complaining that the sound of the fishing boats setting off for far sea was an intrusion on sleep, and asked if the men couldn't tether their boats and start their engines farther from his new house -- or put silencers on the engines!

I was reminded of news stories I'd covered in Connecticut: Developers bought farmland and built homes with bucolic views of a working dairy. Once they'd moved in, the new homeowners discovered that dairy cows produce manure that's composted in the farmyard and then spread on the fields, sometimes adjoining their manicured lawns. Some invariably try to change the zoning to ban dairies. Generally, they lose, but not before making a stink that rivals the manure.

Déjà vu all over again, as Yogi Berra famously said. Our Billy's Bay newcomer had bought land next to the fishing beach, and now wanted the fishermen out of the way.

He also complained about the thatched-hut gazebo on the public beach right next to his fence. Nobody really owned it; some men had just brought a few timbers and palm fronds and built it. At one time, there were probably similar huts on every fishing beach in Jamaica, arguably built illegally on public land, but offending no one – until tourism arrived.

The hut is a shady place where men working on their boats or traps can get out of the sun to enjoy a Red Stripe or soft drink. Sometimes they bring along a boom-box, but it seemed to us the fishermen were thoughtful about their new neighbor and kept the volume down.

They also gather there on nights they go to sea, chatting quietly among themselves – and undoubtedly toking up on ganja – for an hour or so until all the crew has assembled. The newcomer found those evening gatherings offensive; perhaps he thought his guests would be fearful of village men within earshot after dark.

There was an ugly scene one morning: The newcomer came down to the hut with a Black River policeman who moonlighted for him as a security guard. A boy lounging there concluded – perhaps erroneously – that he intended to tear it down, and ran to get some of the men. There was a tense confrontation; the newcomer retreated, assuring them he had no designs on the hut.

Next he wanted to move the narrow right-of-way that provides access to the beach, right beside his property. How about moving it to the other end of the beach, 100 yards away from him? And he talked of buying the narrow plot of land between the beach and the road.

Bunny Delapenha, the man who'd found us the sea-blaster, had a tiny weekend cottage there; for years he's let the fishermen's activities spill onto his land, above high tide. When a storm threatens, every boat at Billy's Bay is parked on Bunny's land. Even in good weather, there are always a few boats drawn inland for repairs. We and our neighbors were relieved to find that Bunny wasn't interested in selling.

Arthur James came to talk about the new tensions. He was sure the fishermen could win, as they appeared to be winning at Golden Sands. He remembered when – 40 years ago -- the then-owner of that land tried to fence off the fishing beach. It had been his father who'd led the fight. Mister Arthur and Endley Parchment had joined him at the beach to protest the proposed fence – and had been driven back by a man who'd been brought along with guns.

But they knew their rights, and the Beach Control Authority sent an informal adjudicator. The turning-point came when the new landowner said the men had no long-standing claim to the beach, since they'd only recently begun using it. The corporal at the Pedro Police Station said he'd seen fishing boats on the beach when he first came five years earlier, and would swear to that in court if need be. "That man knew he would lose, and put the land up for sale," Mister Arthur said. "It was Mist' Bunny who bought it," and has happily co-existed with the fishermen ever since.

(The present right-of-way to the beach, the one the newcomer wanted moved, thus dates back at least four decades. We helped Mister Arthur persuade MP Derrick Sangster to put a light on the beach at the foot of that passage.)

"I don't need another fight, Mist' Don," Mister Arthur said. "I'm gittin' to be an old man." But he was still the dean of the village, so this fight was his. He hoped the precedents of four decades earlier and more recently at Golden Sands would hold firm. A reporter for Jamaica's public radio station came to do a story on the controversy. I gave him an interview supporting the primacy of fishing, and assured Mister Arthur I'd go say the same thing to the newcomer.

I did, but it was a strained conversation. Several of our neighbors had already told him— apparently more than once – about our help in blasting the reef, bringing flares and sails and helping after Hurricane Gilbert. He was less than pleased at the comparison.

Jason came for dinner a night or two later. He was aware of the controversy – not much at Treasure Beach escapes him – and I filled him in on details. This time I wasn't surprised: Jason would support the fishermen.

This is a fishing community that welcomes vacationers; keeping it that way is important.

# 29

## The sea

**I** wakened at 2 to the sound of an outboard leaving the fishing cove. The engines are more powerful nowadays, deep and throaty. The first boat was beyond the sound horizon by the time I was fully conscious. "They're late," was my first sleepy thought. "And they're not waiting for each other."

Another engine coughed into life. It, too, was quickly gunned to a deep pitch to maneuver through the reef opening, and headed southward out of earshot, lost in the sound of the sea.

Fully awake, I remembered: Bigger engines, shorter trips, more independence. On the first morning of this February 2002 trip, I'd walked down to the cove at dawn and counted a dozen boats tethered in the water, nine more drawn up on the beach. Every one had at least a 65-horse engine. Some had 75s, and a few had twin 65s mounted on their transoms.

Boats were under-powered when we built the house 30 years ago. With a 40-horse Evinrude/Johnson, a captain had to get under way before midnight and run flat-out all night – shortening his engine's life -- to make the Pedro Banks by dawn. With almost double the horsepower, and a boat built to handle it, he can leave two hours later, run his engine at three-quarters throttle, and still be at his pot-set by dawn. The sea is more accessible.

There's a downside to that: It's easier for dishonest men to get to sea; pot thievery has become more common. Men get to far sea only to find that someone has pulled their traps and emptied them of fish. A neighbor told me of encountering a brigand crew -- Fort Charles men, he thought -- pulling his pots. When he challenged them, one showed a handgun; he retreated.

There have been protest meetings, demanding that the puny Jamaican Coast Guard patrol more vigorously. The United States is equipping Jamaica with high-speed boats to intercept drug smugglers. Maybe they could spend some time patrolling the Pedro Cays, challenging fishermen to show that markings on each trap match the registration number painted on the boat. But I sense little confidence.

●

I padded barefoot in my pajamas to the edge of the patio to contemplate the night sea. The moon, nearing full, was almost overhead; Orion was sliding off to the west, little but his belt and sword visible in the moonswept sky. If I go around to the side of the house, sometimes I can see one of the Dippers hanging down. No chance of seeing the Southern Cross on this bright night, although I thought I could detect its brightest star a handspan above the horizon.

Although never staying long, I savor these night moments. The sea is a gift of which I never tire. It is restless, always changing. Its varied rhythms lull me to sleep and waken me.

The waves this night crested gently as they neared -- quicksilver moon-bright ribbons in the dark water -- then stumbled noisily on the reef, spilling white water toward shore. I came back to bed, replaying the scene to the sound of the waves as I fell back asleep.

Two days later, a frontal system worked eastward across the Caribbean. I saw it on the satellite photo I check each morning on the Internet, but Mister Valney was as usual ahead of me. "Don't go swimmin' today," he cautioned. "The wind be northwest."

He knew I didn't need the warning, but it's one of his duties when guests are here. At home, a northwest wind presages clearing weather. Here it is a storm wind, producing rough water, and waves – somehow, an idiosyncrasy of this ocean -- from the southwest.

The swells grew; under gray skies, the troughs deepened and widened into valleys between small mountains of water. Waves crashed heavily over the reef, combers that threw up a fog of sea-spume. On days like this, one marvels at the resilience of the aquatic life on that reef: Fragile-looking mosses and plants that grow on top, coral colonies on the walls and bottom, somehow are not torn off. I wish it were possible to snorkel out to see where the fish hide. Perhaps, like ships, they steam out to sea.

At the fishing cove, men had gathered in early morning to bring boats ashore. The spirit of cooperation is not dead: Those fiberglass boats are heavy, and it takes ten men to get them up on the beach. Later in the day, Mister Valney saw one of the boats, which hadn't been dragged back far enough, washed back into the cove. He ran down; in the nick of time its captain appeared, wading into the foam to keep it from being sucked back against the reef. Reinforcements came, and it was hauled back higher, away from the advancing waves.

I walked down next morning. Although the wind was shifting back around from the southeast, waves still washed far inland. The shingle here is usually 10 yards wide; one can stay on dry sand as each wave advances, stepping onto the firmer sand as it retreats. Today there was no dry sand: Water came up beyond the usual high-tide mark, carving a two-foot high bank, exposing bare roots of the sea-grape and the ground-hugging sea potato that grow at the margin.

●

We marvel at the way the sea sculpts the shoreline: The beach looks a little different every time we come.

Six weeks after the 1988 hurricane, there was no beach to speak of: At high tide or low, I couldn't walk down to the surfing beach without wading through surf. When the sea calmed enough that I could snorkel one morning, I found a broad river of bright sand out beyond the reef, as though swept there by a crazed King Canute.

I hardly recognized the surfing beach: Our "permanent" sand bar, which usually covers the inshore outcrops of dead coral, had been washed out. I swam among craggy coral protruding two or three feet from a rocky bottom with almost no sand.

When I came with the family two months later, the beach was almost back to its normal width, and the surfing beach was nearly restored. In even the most serene sea, each wave picks up a few handfuls of sand, and empties its pockets on the beach.

We have few hurricanes; this part of the South Coast has very rarely had a direct hit. Most tropical depressions veer northwest out of the Atlantic; venting their fury on the Leeward Islands, Puerto Rico and Haiti – the nearest of those 200 miles to our east – and then threaten the Bahamas or the American east coast. Only occasionally does a hurricane steer straight westward through the Windward Islands and into the open Caribbean, and most of those hold that course to pass south of Jamaica and strike Central America or the Yucatan Peninsula.

A decade after Gilbert, Hurricane Michelle passed uneventfully to our south, gathered strength as it neared Honduras, then became a monster that lingered at the western tip of Cuba for two days. It was nearly 400 miles from Jamaica, but its huge waves did major damage at Negril, the western tip of the island, and gave even Treasure Beach two days of heavy seas.

When it was finished, our beach had been rearranged: Where I'd been unable to walk without wading after Gilbert, there was suddenly a broad, dry beach 40 yards wide, reaching almost out to the barrier reef.

Storm surges have twice undermined our cement-block sea wall and knocked it down. We had guests there when Gilbert brushed Jamaica. As the skies cleared, they went down to the gate to admire the still-heavy seas chewing at the foot of the five-foot wall. Suddenly, they said, it went down like a massive set of dominoes.

We rebuilt it, setting the footing so deep into the sand that we were shoveling concrete into puddles of seeping seawater. Four years later, another storm surge toppled most of it again.

Rebuilding it a second time, I contrived a series of lateral concrete wings dug back into the sand inside the wall, which I hoped would hold it erect even if waves scoured the footings. For extra insurance, Mister Valney buried all the rubble just outside the new wall and cemented it into an apron. Hurricane Ivan in 2004 ripped away that protective barrier, the wall and ten yards behind it, leaving the shallows strewn with bits of concrete, and the usually-sandy beach a brier-patch of exposed coral, flat but sharp.

I hired men to pick the concrete out of the water and off the beach, and had a new rock wall built, farther inland and we hope impervious to storm surges. Repairing the beach itself we could only leave to natural processes.

The onshore breeze is the sea's ally in sculpting the shingle: Before long the foot of the wall is again covered by sand, and in another month or so the bottom-most concrete step outside the sea-gate is buried in sand.

Proteus was the Greek sea-god, son of Poseidon, who knew the past, present and future but changed his shape to avoid prophesying.

Wind and waves make our shoreline protean, restless and mutable; they carve it into new shapes. Mister Valney can prophesy when change is imminent, but even he can't predict what the seascape will look like from one month to the next.

●

A day after threatening boats in the harbor, the sea abated. Three days later, it was as calm as a lake; the waves lapped gently, almost inaudibly, over the reef. That little-understood ocean current just beyond the Pedro Banks had moved "down and in." The water was as limpid and clear as a glass of tap-water, and the sea was drawn back, exposing the reef, a tracery of dark rock embracing the shallows. The surreal low tide lasted all day.

We grab snorkel masks on such mornings, and go for a long swim. We paddle through an opening in front of the house and head westward. For the first hundred yards, there is little to see save for a few fish and the vegetation that somehow survived the storm waves. The outcrops of older, dead reef are a nondescript brown.

Then we're into what we call the Coral Gardens, an underwater fairyland. There are a few great branching formations of elkhorn coral. On top of the ancient coral, like cliffs facing out to sea, are new colonies: the pale white brain coral, wrinkles and whorls that look like a textbook picture of the human brain, and a green coral that spreads over the rock in abstract patterns, as though a pailful of thick paint had been splashed there.

And fire coral, thin, fragile-looking, light-colored leaves overlapping one another to make cups, each no bigger than one's palm. It takes little imagination to see a colony of fire coral as consuming its host reef in flames.

The smallest fish hide in the fire coral. The blue chromis, hardly the size of one's thumb, has astonishingly luminous blue spots on its dark body. The blue-headed wraisse, hardly bigger, has a diagonal band of black and blue stripes behind its gills, like the bow stripes on a U.S. Coast Guard ship.

This morning, the sea is teeming with sergeant-majors, bright yellow fish with black chevrons. The tiniest of them, fingernail-size, hide in the fire coral; the grand-daddies, the size of my hand, swim by proudly on parade.

My favorite, the most common on our reef, is the ocean surgeon, or sea-doctor. As flat as a pancake skillet and sometimes almost as big, it has a dark stripe defining its gills and a bright nick near the tail that one might imagine to be a scalpel in its pocket. It is bluish-grey, but when it turns and catches the filtered sunlight, it turns an iridescent purple. I've encountered a school of more than 100; if I lie still in the water, they eddy past me unafraid, shimmering like a cloud of violet-tinged mirrors as they turn with the currents.

On the bottom is the sea fan, a soft, light-colored coral that starts out smaller than a geisha's ceremonial fan and grows into a great branching web. Its thick mesh waves back and forth as the waves ebb and flow. When we first came, we would dive down repeatedly to wrench one from its stubborn hold on the rock bottom, and bring it home. After a while the bookcase was festooned with sea fans, and we learned – more ecologically aware -- to leave them alone.

Also down there is another soft coral, the sea-whip. Its thick fingers are more than a foot tall, a cluster of elongated cat-tails that wave in the briny breeze.

Another hundred yards of less spectacular reef brings us to the surfing beach. We wait for a following wave – not much, on these still mornings – and body-surf ashore, watching the sea-bottom come closer through the snorkel plate.

Ten yards from the beach, the morning sun is caught in the lapping waves. It casts quavering bright ripples of light, as intense as though caught in a magnifying glass, onto the sandy bottom that is now inches below our masks, a kaleidoscopic pattern of ragged octagons and pentagons and diamonds etched momentarily into the sand.

We stand and wade the last few steps ashore, remarking on the fairyland we've wandered through, and walk back up the beach. A pelican hovers beyond the reef, then tucks its wings and dives for breakfast. We startle a pair of sandpipers, picking at the reef; they fly in a flash of barred wings to land a dozen yards farther from us. A tern swoops for fish just outside the reef, as acrobatic as a barn swallow.

I cannot imagine a better way to work up an appetite for breakfast.

●

I asked Mister Valney one morning, while we shared coffee as he pumped water to the tower, what it meant to him to live by this sea.

He mistook my meaning at first. "I used to live by the sea, Mist' Don," he said. "It was hard sometimes, but it was a good living. Now I work for you."

Then he caught my meaning. "I listen to the sea at night, to hear if it be calm or hard. I catch sea-breezes in my yard, and it isn't so hot like farther in.

"I love the sea."

"It be music to me, Mist' Don," Mister Arthur once said, echoing his neighbor. "I love the sea.

"It can be hard, and sometimes men die at sea, but it is how we live. Not just the fish we take from it. As the pastor says, it nourishes our bodies but our souls too."

And so it does. As Shakespeare had Antony say admiringly of Cleopatra, age cannot wither this seascape, nor custom stale its infinite variety.

We come to get away from chores at home, to relax, to visit with friends, to soak up tropical sunshine – but most of all, perhaps, to nourish our souls in the sea that washes this Jamaican shore.

-30-